An introduction to
Menander

By T. B. L. Webster

Studies in later Greek comedy
An anthology of Greek verse
   (with E. S. Forster)

T. B. L. Webster

An introduction to

Menander

Manchester University Press
Barnes & Noble Books · New York

© 1974 T. B. L. Webster

Published by
the University of Manchester
at the University Press
Oxford Road, Manchester M13 9PL

UK ISBN 0 7190 0590 6

USA

Harper & Row Publishers Inc
Barnes & Noble Import Division

US ISBN 0 06 497504 5

Printed in Great Britain by
Western Printing Services Ltd, Bristol

Contents

Preface

Studies in Menander grew out of a series of lectures which I was asked to give at the John Rylands Library immediately after the war, and the second edition had an appendix on recent finds, including particularly the *Dyskolos*. When a reprinting was suggested it seemed to me impossible to include all the new finds without rewriting the whole book, and I compromised on rewriting the Menander chapter in *Studies in Later Greek Comedy*, of which the second edition was published in 1970.

Since then, largely as the result of a seminar here in 1971, I have worked through all the material again and it seems to me that there is a case for trying to evaluate afresh all that we have left of Menander. The addition of more complete or partly complete plays— *Dyskolos, Sikyonios, Misoumenos, Aspis*, the rest of the *Samia*—has added immensely to our knowledge, and besides these major gains we have had a considerable number of other minor gains. We can see much more clearly now how Menander works, and this illumines first of all the plays which survive only in fragments and secondly the Latin adaptations: both the complete plays of Plautus and Terence and the fragments of the other Roman adapters. There is a further point: a considerable number of papyri, which is continually increasing, has come down to us without any clue to the author. It is now clear, first, that a papyrus of comedy written in the Christian era is much more likely to be by Menander than by anyone else, and secondly that the later a papyrus is, the more restricted the number of Menander plays from which it is likely to come. We can therefore apply our increased knowledge of Menander also to the task of identifying unattributed papyri.

I have separated off the reconstruction of Menander's plays and the discussion of unattributed papyri from the body of the

book. The first appendix contains summary reconstructions of
all the plays of which anything useful can be said; they are in
alphabetical order and include references to ancient sources,
arguments for the reconstruction, and as much bibliography as
is necessary. The second appendix is a list of papyri in alpha-
betic order of their publication, with brief description and
possible attributions. The body of the book is a discussion of the
plays under various headings. I found the terminology of armature and codes which Claude Lévi-Strauss uses for American
Indian myths a useful means of organising the material. The
armature is the underlying theme of union through obstacles,
which is common to all the plays (ch. II). The codes are the
various kinds of clues in the plays which the original audience
and all subsequent audiences and readers interpret according to
their lights. Some clues lead to historical events or to the age of
the author (ch. I), some to the social position of the characters and
to social criticism (ch. III), some to contemporary philosophy and
to an ethical standpoint (ch. IV), some to tragedy and the reali-
sation that Menander has some particular purpose in recalling
tragedy (ch. V). Finally, Menander is a professional dramatist,
and his organisation of the play, his methods of production, his
masks, costumes, names, and language, are all clues causing
audience and readers to make predictions which may prove right
or wrong (ch. VI).

T. B. L. W.
Stanford, 1973

I

Chronology of the plays

Menander first produced when he was still an ephebe, the *Orge*, probably in 322/1 and probably a Lenaian victory. He produced the *Dyskolos* in 317/6 at the Lenaia, and won his first city victory in 316/5. He was fifth in the city Dionysia in 313/2 with the *Heniochos* and in 312/1 with the *Paidion*. In 302/1 he was prevented by the political situation from producing the *Imbrians*.[1]

This is all the external dating that we possess. For the rest we are dependent on allusions to persons, places, and events and to one possible metrical criterion. The metrical criterion is the presence or absence of scenes in trochaic tetrameters catalectic. I do not think that the rare occurrence of other metres has chronological significance: the hexameter hymn to Kybele in the *Theophoroumene* and the anapaestic address by the priestess in the *Leukadia* are called forth by the situation and might have been written at any time. But scenes in trochaic tetrameters (and the final scene of iambic tetrameters in the *Dyskolos*) are part of the tradition of Attic comedy. It is surprising, therefore, to find no trace of a trochaic scene in the *Epitrepontes* or the *Misoumenos*; enough survives of both plays to make it unlikely that this impression is misleading. As both seem to be late plays, Menander may have given up the variation between iambic and trochaic scenes in the latter part of his career. We can only use this criterion in this way: plays with surviving trochaic tetrameters are probably earlier than *Misoumenos* and *Epitrepontes*. They are *Adelphoi A*, *Aspis*, *Dyskolos*, *Epangellomenos*, *Georgos*, *Halieus*, *Heniochos*, *Hiereia* (?), *Hydria*, *Hypobolimaios*, *Naukleros*, *Olynthia*, *Orge*, *Pallake*, *Perikeiromene*, *Phasma*, *Plokion*,

[1] References are conveniently found in Körte and Thierfelder, II, 5 f., Testimonia. For *Paidion* cf. Pickard-Cambridge, *Festivals*[2], 109–10.

Rhapizomene, Samia, Sikyonios, Synaristosai (?), *Thesauros, Thrasyleon, Thyroros,* and of the papyri which may be Menander P. Milan 8, P.S.I. 1176 (possibly *Demiourgos*), and P. Vienna 29811 (possibly *Paidion*). The range in date is from *Orge*, 322/1, to *Heniochos*, 313/2 or possibly a year later if the identification of P. Vienna with *Paidion* is valid. We shall have to consider how far the metrical evidence agrees or conflicts with other kinds of evidence.[2]

The poets of New Comedy, except on very rare and special occasions which do not concern Menander, abandoned the comic poet's licence to attack the prominent politician year by year, but the situations which they produced had to make sense to the audience of the festivals at which they were produced. To take the obvious case of a young man going abroad to fight, in a play written in the early 1940's he might go to North Africa, in the early 1950's to Korea, and in the 1960's to Vietnam; and in the play written in the 1960's the young man's father might reminisce about his fighting in World War II. This is the kind of actuality that we have to look for in Menander, and it is worth suggesting that the plays with a considerable historical perspective—*Sikyonios, Eunuch, Andria, Kolax* and particularly *Heautontimoroumenos*—were not written until he had himself a considerable historical memory to draw on.[3]

In fact he mentions only two events which he cannot have remembered himself. Olynthos was destroyed in 348, six years before he was born. This discreditable memory survives in the title of the *Olynthia*, which, as we shall see, was produced about 314. The Olynthian woman cannot be less than thirty-four years old, so that she is presumably the mother or the supposed mother of the heroine, and her nationality makes her a sympathetic character. Perinthos was destroyed by Philip in 340, when Menander was two years old. If the plot of the *Perinthia* had the same lines as the *Andria*, an Athenian girl was deposited in

---

[2] In the list of plays with trochaic scenes *Hiereia* and *Synaristosai* are queried. *Hiereia* depends on a possibly trochaic-sounding phrase in the Summary, P. Oxy. 1235, 93. *Synaristosai* 389 K–T can equally well be divided to give iambics.

[3] See *L.G.C.* 100 ff. for a general account of the political background. Here I am concerned only with persons, places and events which were news in Athens and which Menander mentioned immediately or later or both in his comedies.

Perinthos, brought back by a Perinthian woman, and recognised twelve years later. The Perinthian woman presumably came to Athens to escape the siege; this would give a latest production date of 328, which is impossible, since Menander first produced in 322/1. I think, then, we have to suppose that the Perinthian woman, like the Olynthian woman, was the mother or the supposed mother of the heroine (rather than the supposed sister, as in the *Andria*) and that the child was not born until after she got to Athens: on this calculation the corresponding date for the play is 306, but it may have been considerably earlier.[4]

Alexander's Eastern campaigns covered Menander's boyhood. The overrunning of Pamphylia in 334/3 was famous for its speed, and is taken by a clever slave in an unknown play (751 K–T) as a model for his own success. The soldier of the *Kolax* (fr. 2) had a drinking capacity greater than Alexander. These are both obvious memories of a very famous man, which do not help in dating. The only character who is likely to have served with Alexander is the sixty-year-old Menedemus of the late *Heautontimoroumenos* (111).

Menander grew up in the tradition of Middle Comedy and took over in his early plays a number of stock jokes about figures, some contemporary and some earlier. The *Orge*, his first play, probably 322/1, gives a useful lead: jokes about the parasite Chairephon, the thin man Philippides and the spendthrift Ktesippos are all legacies from Middle Comedy. But such jokes did not go on very long: they do not occur in the *Dyskolos* of 317/6 or the *Perikeiromene* of 314 (see below). Chairephon is the target again in the *Androgynos*, *Kekryphalos*, *Methe* and *Samia*, so that one would expect these plays to belong to Menander's first five years, and for all of them we have other evidence. Nannion, a *hetaira* known to comedy since soon after 350, is a past triumph of an old soldier (?) in the *Pseudherakles*, which must then be very early.[5]

These years were bad years for Athens. After the death of Alexander the Athenians formed a league of Greek cities, including the island of Leukas and Sikyon, against the

---

[4] The supposed stylistic difference of *Perinthia* from *Andria* need not have chronological significance. The title may have been particularly acceptable after the democratic restoration of 307.

[5] On these names cf. C.Q., 2, 1952, 21 f.

Macedonians, but after preliminary successes, including the battle
of Lamia in 323, were generally defeated in 322. Antipater
imposed an oligarchic constitution and a garrison in the Peiraeus
and forced the Athenians to evacuate Samos. Antipater's death
sparked a revolution in Athens in 319 but it was put down next
year by Antipater's son, Cassander, who in 317 installed the
Peripatetic Demetrios of Phaleron as dictator.

Most of this was too painful to be remembered in comedy.
But someone in the *Androgynos*, perhaps a Cretan soldier, ran
away from the battle of Lamia. The *Methe*, which also mentions
Chairephon and is tied by its title—Drunkenness instead of
Anger as prologue figure—to *Orge*, names Kallimedon as a
possible fellow banqueter: Kallimedon was a pro-Macedonian
who escaped with Demetrios of Phaleron to the Peiraieus in 322
and was condemned to death in absence in 318. Since Leukas
joined the Hellenic league, it is worth remembering that Menander called a play *Leukadia* and set it in Leukas: such a memory
and the similar memories of Sikyon in the *Sikyonios* and *Synaristosai* would perhaps not be evoked until after Demetrios of
Phaleron was removed in 307. These war years are the war in
Athens which Chremes' brother is escaping when he deposits
Chremes' infant daughter in Andros and goes on to seek his
brother in Asia (*Andria* 935).

The evacuation of Athenians from Samos in 322 evidently
made a great impression on Menander. Chrysis in the *Samia* need
not have been long in Athens when she met Demeas, and
Moschion implies that Demeas had not installed her for long
before he went abroad. The play jokes at Chairephon, as we have
said, and Androkles, who may be the Androkles known 350/40.
The two old men have come back from Byzantion. Probably they
brought grain, but Athens was in such continual need of grain
during this period that the allusion does not help any more than
does the other allusion to Byzantion in the *Arrhephoros*.
Moschion threatens to go to Bactria and Caria. At least Eastern
campaigning must be possible at this time—and on the evidence
of the evacuation of Samos and the proper names I suppose the
limits are 320–18. About this time Chremes in the *Andria*, as
we have said, went to fight in Asia. This same memory that
Caria (and Mylasa in particular) was a good place to go may
account for the references to Mylasa in the *Katapseudomenos*

(with which, unfortunately, we can do nothing) and in the *Sikyonios*: in the *Sikyonios* the supposed father of the hero buys in the *agora* at Mylasa a four-year-old Athenian girl, who had been kidnapped by pirates from Halai on the south-east coast of Attica. If this means that kidnapping was a memory of 320–318, the kidnapping of the Athenian girl from Sounion in the *Eunuch* (107 ff) may belong to the same time.

The *Eunuch* brings us back to Samos. Thais (Menander's Chrysis) had a Samian mother who was living at Rhodes when a merchant gave her a little girl, said to have been stolen by pirates from Sounion; she was brought up as Thais' sister. Again, it looks as if Thais' mother left Samos in 322, probably when Thais was quite small, and received the Athenian child in Rhodes about 318. The other play which mentions Samos is the *Dis Exapaton (Bacchides)*. The twin *hetairai* (probably both called Chrysis in Menander) came from Samos. One has found her way to Athens and is established there. The other has been in Ephesos, where she captivated Mnesilochus (Sostratos); Mnesilochus has been in Ephesos two years. The girl has arrived in Athens before him and is being pursued by a soldier, who had probably brought her back with him. The two years brings the date down at least to 320. The only other indication is the slave's remark (910) that Mnesilochus shall be more abused than ever Clinias was by Demetrius: this sounds like the sort of joke that is made against Chairephon and Kallimedon, and I think it is more likely to belong to the years before Demetrios of Phaleron was installed as tyrant of Athens than afterwards. This would give 320–317 as the limits for this play. Menander is certainly interested in Ephesos at this time, but this is not enough to fix the *Kitharistes*, which also contains a voyage from Ephesos, at the same date.

The remaining play with an allusion to Chairephon is the *Kekryphalos*. It also alludes to the *gynaikonomoi* established by a new law. Here they are concerned with the number of diners at banquets. In the *Aulularia (Apistos)* Euclio, after hearing Megadorus' strictures on women's extravagance, says that he ought to be made prefect of women (503), the Latin translation of *Gynaikonomos*. They are mentioned again in plays of Timokles, Philemon and Diphilos. The *Kekryphalos* certainly, and probably the other plays, were written soon after their institution. They are commonly associated with Demetrios of Phaleron but it has recently been suggested that they were part of the oligarchic constitution imposed by Antipater in 322.[6] The evidence seems to me better for the traditional date and I should be inclined to date these plays near the beginning of Demetrios of Phaleron's rule, possibly even city Dionysia 318/17 and certainly Lenaia and city Dionysia 317/6. But it was Antipater who gave enlarged authority to the Areiopagos: the respect accorded to Kleainetos in the *Fabula Incerta* (11), perhaps *Arrhephoros*, would suit any date between 322 and the restoration of the democracy in 307.

Demetrios of Phaleron ruled Athens for ten years, 317–307. Some allusions can be generally dated to this period; some can be fixed more precisely within it. The *Didymai* has an allusion to Krates, the Cynic philosopher, and his wife (104 K–T, the further extension about Krates' daughters has been rightly removed from Menander); he was apparently forty in 328 and was associated with Zeno in 314 and with Demetrios of Phaleron in 307. His pupil Monimos was quoted in the *Hippokomos* (215 K–T). Both these allusions belong essentially to the Chairephon type, and the plays should be earlier rather than later. In the *Stichus* (first *Adelphoi*) the parasite is refused his dinner because a state delegacy from Ambracia is to be entertained (491): this apparently must be earlier than 312, unless, of course, the name is due to Plautus. The *Encheiridion* mentions both Egyptians and Sarapis (P.S.I. 99; 139 K–T): the context is unclear, perhaps an Egyptian rival in a love affair, but Egypt is more likely to have been in the Athenian mind when Athens was under the friendly rule of Demetrios of Phaleron than later.

In Eratosthenes' Olympic victor list Astyanax of Miletos is entered under 316–12 as *periodonikes* for the sixth time unopposed: this is the end of a brilliant athletic career. Gnathon in the *Kolax* (P. Oxy 2655) says that even the strong man like Astyanax can be upset if taken unawares. This is one of a number of allusions in the *Kolax* which are difficult to fit together chronologically. The soldier (1) had drunk more than Alexander in Cappadocia (fr. 2), (2) had served under a king who had Indian elephants: presumably Seleukos after 306 (*Eun.* 401 ff.), (3) had

[6] The *Gynaikonomoi*: L.G.C., 103. Dating to Antipater, D. del Corno, *Dioniso*, 32, 1962, 136 ff.; to Demetrios of Phaleron, W. S. Ferguson, *Hellenistic Athens*, 45.

the *hetairai* Chrysis, Korone, Antikrya, Ischas, and Nannarion in her heyday (fr. 4), (4) made a joke at the expense of a Cypriote (fr. 3; 8. Terence changed the Cypriote to a Rhodian to suit the plot of the *Eunuch*, 498), (5) commanded his troops from behind like Pyrrhus (*Eun.* 783). Pyrrhus was born in 319, and according to Plutarch was very successful from 302 onwards, so that perhaps 301 is the earliest possible date for this completely untrue description of him. I do not know of any instance of Terence putting in a historical allusion for the benefit of his Roman audience so that I should prefer to keep this as Menander if possible. Cyprus, as we shall see, seems to have been in the Athenian news about 306. The names of the soldier's *hetairai* cause some difficulty. Plutarch (*Life of Demetrius*, 24) names Chrysis and Antikyra as two of the *hetairai* used by Demetrios Poliorketes in Athens in 304, but Ischas is named also in Axionikos' *Tyrrhenos*, with a parasite of Phryne, which should put her back to well before 320. But the soldier is not a young soldier, and his flatterer reminds him of his whole history in love and war. Astyanax, who according to the ancient commentator was mentioned by many comic poets, was sufficiently famous for his memory to last fifteen years or so. But if we accept this late date for the *Kolax* we have also to accept a late flaring of personal allusion in the Middle Comedy manner. I am not sure that this is out of keeping with the Athens of the period immediately after the defeat of Demetrios Poliorketes at Ipsos in 301, but it must be admitted that we have no parallel for it in Menander, though even if we reject the reference to Pyrrhus we have in any case to come down to something like 305, which separates the allusions by more than ten years from the early group.[7]

Menander reflects a number of events which occurred in the middle years of Demetrios of Phaleron's tyranny. The *Perikeiromene* refers to 'a universal crop of misery in Greece' (283), to 'increasing Corinthian evils' (5), and more specifically to a manager of armies stabbed by mercenaries (90). The last probably alludes to the murder of Alexander, son of Polyperchon, at Sikyon in 314, which naturally would distress the Athenians, since Polyperchon himself had tried to give them back the island of Samos.[8] This would mean that the universal crop of misery is

[7] The *hetairai*: cf. C.Q., 2, 1952, 21. Pyrrhus: Plutarch, *Life of Pyrrhus*, v. Personal abuse: L.G.C., 106.   [8] E. Schwartz, *Hermes*, 64, 1929, 3.

the war of the First Coalition against Antigonos the One-eyed in
315. Each of these three events is referred to in another play. The
prayer for peace in P. Hibeh 6, 22 has reasonably been thought
contemporary with 'the universal crop of misery'. In the *Heautontimoroumenos* (96, 629) Chremes' daughter was given to a
poor Corinthian woman, who had recently arrived, to expose.
This was some sixteen years before the date of the play; if Menander was recalling the same Corinthian troubles as the cause of
the old woman's migration, the play was produced about 298.
The murder of Alexander is alluded to again in an unplaced
fragment of the *Aspis* (68 K–T): garrison commanders and rulers
of cities always have the suspicion that they are easy targets for
assassination. This dates the *Aspis* soon after 314; the young
hero has been fighting in Lycia, which is not mentioned elsewhere in Menander, but his booty is brought home via Rhodes.

In 314 also Lemnos and Imbros were encouraged by Antigonos
to free themselves from Athens. Aided by the Carian satrap
Asander, Demetrios sent an expedition under Aristoteles, which
after initial success suffered complete disaster at the hands of
Antigonos. In the *Olynthia* (297 K–T) someone gets four obols
a day with Aristoteles. This may be what he hopes to do rather
than what he is doing. Menander would hardly refer to the
expedition after the disaster. It looks as if the play was produced
at the Lenaia 314/3, and as we have said, the Olynthian woman
was the mother or the supposed mother of the heroine. Lemnos
was certainly in the news but the plays in which characters
travelled to Lemnos must have waited for the more cheerful news
of its return to Athens in 307/6.

In 310/9 Ophellas of Cyrene, who married an Athenian aristo-
crat, persuaded many to escape these miseries in Greece and join
his expedition against Carthage. It seems likely that the *Karchedonios* owed its title to this enthusiasm.[9]

In 308 Ptolemy freed Andros, Corinth and Sikyon. In 307
Demetrios Poliorketes, the son of Antigonos, captured Athens
and expelled the tyrant Demetrios of Phaleron, and Lemnos and
Imbros returned to Athens. We can probably see reflections of
much of this in Menander. The *Imbrians*, we know, was written
a little later for the city festival of 302/1. In the *Andria* Chrysis
has been in Athens three years (69). If the reckoning is inclusive,

9 On Ophellas, *cf. L.G.C.*, 104.

the play was probably produced in 306, and for the past history when the little Athenian girl was shipwrecked in Andros with her uncle, who was taking her from war in Athens to join her father in Asia (923), Menander remembers, as we have seen, the troubled times of the beginning of his stage career.

To those troubled times also belonged the kidnapping of Athenian children from Attic coastal demes: these girls have now reached the marriageable age of sixteen or so, and the *Sikyonios* and the *Eunuch* were accordingly produced soon after 308 (the *Eunuch* must in any case have been produced before 301, when ephebes ceased to serve outside Athens: Chaerea is doing duty at the Peiraeus (290)). Another link between the two plays is Caria: in the *Sikyonios* Stratophanes, like his father twelve years before, has been serving in Caria: in the *Eunuch* (126) the soldier who had fallen in love with Thais in Athens (she had come there from Rhodes—perhaps about 314, *cf.* above—with an Athenian who died and left her his money) went a year or so before the date of the play to serve in Caria and on his way back bought the Athenian girl from Thais' uncle after the death of Thais' mother. Thus Menander draws on the same memories for both plays.

The freeing of Sikyon is perhaps enough reason for the title *Sikyonios*. The hero is, however, recognised as an Athenian; he was given as a child to a Sikyonian woman who wanted a son. This must have been about the time of the Lamian war, and Menander would remember that Sikyon sided with Athens then. The *Synaristosai* combines Sikyon and Lemnos. The setting is Sikyon and the hero is a Sikyonian. The heroine is the product of a visit by a Lemnian seventeen years before (*Cist.* 755), which again goes back to about the time of the Lamian war. After raping the Sikyonian girl he went back to Lemnos, married a Lemnian, who bore him a daughter and died, and fairly recently returned to Sikyon, married the woman he had raped and started a search for the daughter who had been exposed. So the whole story suits a production a year or two after the freeing of Sikyon and the return of Lemnos to the Athenians. Lemnos is mentioned again in the *Heros* (46): Laches has gone abroad for three months on private business to Lemnos. The choice of Lemnos suggests a date when Lemnos was in the news, soon after 307 rather than before 314.

For these plays which were produced near the date of the restoration of democracy in 307 Menander draws on his past memories to give them a background, and sometimes seems to allude to the hopeful moment of the Hellenic league when he was young. In 306 Demetrios Poliorketes won Cyprus from Ptolemy in a successful naval battle. This, I think, is the background of the *Misoumenos*. The soldier Thrasonides was very successful under one of the kings (presumably Demetrios Poliorketes) in Cyprus. After the battle he bought a captive, Krateia, who was the daughter of Demeas, an Athenian living in Cyprus, who was probably absent at the time. The play is set in a place where one expects to ransom captives, and Demeas makes his headquarters with another Athenian, Kleinias, who lives there. I owe to my colleague, Lionel Pearson, the suggestion that the most likely place is Rhodes. This makes it very likely that we should date the *Misoumenos* between the capture of Cyprus and the siege of Rhodes; probably, therefore, 305. There are two other mentions of Cyprus in Menander: the soldier in the *Kolax* is reminded by his flatterer that he made a joke at the expense of a Cypriote; he may also have served in the campaign of 306— the date fits perfectly well into his train of memories. In the *Adelphi* (229 ff.) the brothel-keeper has a cargo of girls which he is in a hurry to ship to Cyprus: the moment when the news of the successful battle arrived in Athens would be auspicious for such an undertaking, so that the *Adelphoi* B should also be dated 305.

The stories of Dionysios of Herakleia must have been known in Athens long before his death in 305. Menander made exiles from Herakleia quote them in the *Halieus* (fr. 21–3 K–T). But 'he was too luxurious to live long' does not imply that he was already dead, and the play need not be dated later than 308.

Finally, in the *Heautontimorumenos* (118) Clinia comes back from his three months' service under one of the kings to find Athens safe (194), which is a reasonable description of the government of the Moderates between 301 and 295. A date in 298 fits with the memories of Corinthian troubles in 314 which brought the old woman to Athens to take over the exposed Antiphila and with Menedemus' youthful service in the campaigns of Alexander.

Two of the plays with scenes in trochaic tetrameters have now been dated later than the *Paidion*, 312/11. A date in or soon after 308 would suit the *Sikyonios* and the *Halieus*. The *Misoumenos*, the only dated play with no trochaic scene, was probably produced in 305. All we can say, then, is that the plays with trochaic scenes are likely to be earlier than 305. Among them is the *Thesauros*, which refers to a Rhodian war less than ten years before, possibly the war of 312.[10]

The following table puts together these results:

322/1	Orge
321–19	Pseudherakles, Androgynos, Methe, Samia, ? Katapseudomenos, Arrhephoros (perhaps Fabula Incerta). Dis Exapaton, ? Kitharistes, ? Ephesios.
318/7	Kekryphalos, Apistos (Aulularia)
317/6	Dyskolos
316/5	First city victory.
314/3	Olynthia, Perikeiromene, Aspis; P. Hibeh 6
313/2	Heniochos
Before 312	Adelphoi A
312/1	Paidion
310/9	Karchedonios
308–306	Halieus, Sikyonios, Synaristosai, Eunuch, Heros, Andria, ? Perinthia, Leukadia
317–07	Didymai, Encheiridion, Hippokomos
Before 306	(trochaic scenes) Epangellomenos, Georgos, ? Hiereia, Hydria, Hypobolimaios, Naukleros, Pallake, Phasma, Plokion, Rhapizomene, Thesauros, Thrasyleon, Thyroros; P.S.I. 1176 (perhaps Demiourgos); P. Milan 8
305	Misoumenos, Adelphoi B
302/1	Imbrians offered but not produced. Kolax
299/8	Heautontimoroumenos
Before 292	(absence of trochaic scenes) Epitrepontes

Such a list is, of course, speculative, but it shows something of how Menander reacted to the contemporary scene and what events so impressed him that he felt he and his audience would remember them much later. It is unfortunate that it gives us no

---

[10] Körte, *ad loc.*, rejects the suggestion that the 'Rhodian war' which according to the old man caused him to bury his treasure was the war of 312 between Cassander and Antigonos, when Antigonos had the aid of ten Rhodian ships, but it is difficult to see what else it can have been.

help in placing some plays of which we know a good deal, notably the *Daktylios*, *Koneiazomenai* and *Theophoroumene*. The result is that we cannot proceed chronologically; it will be more useful to group plays of the same type together. But the table may show where the types started.

II

Typology of the plays

Comedy was produced in Athens at the Lenaia and city Dionysia, both festivals held in honour of Dionysos. The Lenaia was held in January–February and the city Dionysia in March–April. Both were intended to secure the fertility of men, animals and vegetation. Comedy had a place because it grew out of earlier masked and costumed dances which traditionally promoted fertility. One song that was certainly sung by the early dancers and was later repeated as the theme of satyr play and comedy was the return of Hephaistos: Hephaistos had bound his mother, the earth goddess Hera, by invisible bonds to her throne. He refused to return and unbind her until finally Dionysos made him drunk and brought him back on a mule. He then released Hera, and in return he was given Aphrodite in marriage and Dionysos was admitted to heaven. The story is obviously suitable for a late winter and early spring festival, but is also the mythical model for the kind of comedy in which man and woman achieve union after surmounting a series of obstacles. Old Comedy often ends in marriage, or at least union with a *hetaira*, but Old Comedy has a number of other traditional concerns, political and cultural. In Middle Comedy the type becomes clearer, particularly after the middle of the fourth century.[1] All Menander's comedies of which we know anything conform to this basic type.

Menander wrote, according to ancient sources, 108 plays, of which some ninety-six titles survive (excluding alternative titles for the same play).[2] Of sixty plays we can say that they conform to the basic type described; of the rest we can say only that nothing in their titles or fragments precludes it. His production was very large. He must have written more than three plays a year, and this agrees roughly with the number between seventy

[1] *Cf. L.G.C.* 74 ff. [2] K–T, II, 1, Testimonia 1 and 2.

and eighty attached to the *Imbrians*,[3] which he wrote for production in the twenty-first year of his stage career. The maximum that he could have produced under his own name at the
Lenaia and city Dionysia is sixty-two, supposing that he survived
to produce at both the Lenaia and the city festival in 292/1;
and we know that he won only eight victories at the two festivals
together. For the remainder of his plays there are three possibilities: he may (like Aristophanes) have given them to someone
else to produce at the Lenaia or city festival; he may have produced at Attic deme theatres; he may have produced outside
Attica. All we can say is that we have no evidence. It is conceivable that the *Perikeiromene*, which is set in Corinth, the *Synari-
stosia*, which is set in Sikyon, and the *Misoumenos*, which seems
to have been set in Rhodes, were written for production in those
cities, but it is wise to remember that such an argument is completely invalid for Attic tragedy and that the *Dyskolos*, which is
set in the Attic deme of Phyle, was certainly written for the
Lenaia in Athens.

The sixty plays of which we know or can guess the story-line
fall into a number of sub-types. The union of lovers which is
achieved after surmounting obstacles may be union with a
hetaira, or reunion of a divided married pair, or marriage. I take
them in this order because the plays ending in marriage are by
far the most numerous and need further subdivision. Here I give
little more than the titles, because the evidence can easily be
found in the appendices.[4]

The one clear case of union with a *hetaira* is the *Dis Exapaton (Bacchides)*, dated above 320–17. However much Plautus has
altered, there is no sign of either of the young men contemplating
marriage, and the twin *hetairai* not only conquer them but also
their fathers: the female principle triumphs completely. In the
Thesauros the young man has run through his father's money
and has even sold the land with his father's tomb. He presumably
wins the arbitration against the buyer and gets the treasure found
in the tomb. It seems more likely that he spends it on a *hetaira*
than on marrying a wife. The *Thais* and the *Hymnis* certainly
took their names from *hetairai*, and the fragments show no sign
of the young men marrying. The *Parakatatheke* probably also

[3] P. Oxy. 1235, 107 (K–T, I, 149).
[4] See below, p. 111, plays of Menander; p. 194, papyri, mostly unattributed.

belongs here. In other plays, notably the *Eunuch*, *Heautontimor-oumenos* and *Adelphoi* B, love for a *hetaira* is a sub-plot, in the first successful, but it is a sub-plot and not the main story, so that they are not to be reckoned *hetaira* plays.

Three, but possibly five, plays are concerned with reunion. In *Adelphoi* A, probably produced before 312, the two husbands have gone abroad to recoup their fortunes and their father-in-law tries to persuade their wives to remarry. Apparently neither of the pairs has children. The husbands return and the marriages continue. This play seems to be a unique experiment. It is not clear what happens in the *Misogynes*, which is undated. The husband is certainly living away from the wife, possibly with a *hetaira*, Glykera, and is threatened with a suit for desertion (or ejection? Cf. fr. 679). He may go back to her in the end. In the probably late *Epitrepontes* and the undated *Daktylios* the husband has raped the wife before marriage and she has borne a child just before the play begins and exposed it. In the end the truth comes out and the marriage is restored. In all these plays the father of the wife or wives tries to break up the marriage. The title of the *Progamon*[5] may place it also here.

The plays which end in marriage are numerous. The young man may or may not have had intercourse with the girl before the play. If he has, the child may have been born before the play or may be born during the play or there may be no mention of a child. It must be made clear here at the beginning that for the fragmentary plays our information is very incomplete: a child may have been born or a girl may have been raped without any fragment surviving to tell us.

The early *Samia* is unique in that the child is born before the play begins. Of course, Menander may have used this scene in other plays (P. Oxy 1825 is a possibility, and P. Hibeh 6 may belong here rather than in the next section). He may, however, have thought it more suitable for plays of the type of the *Epitrepontes*.

In a number of plays the child is born during the course of the play. In chronological order they are *Pseudherakles*, *Androgynos*, *Arrhephoros* (perhaps the *Fabula Incerta*), *Apistos* (*Aulularia*), *Andria*, *Heros*, *Perinthia*, *Georgos*, *Plokion*, *Adelphoi* B,

---

[5] Cf. K–T, II, p. 128. Knemon in the *Dyskolos* finally goes back to his wife, but that is a sub-plot.

Imbrians. Anepsioi Rhapizomene and *Titthe* are undated. P.
Hibeh 6, Milan 8, Ant. 55 and Ghoran II also belong, but may
not be by Menander. In both the *Heros* and *Georgos* the mother
of the girl has herself been raped in youth and deserted.

In the next group there is no mention of a child, but the youth
and the girl have had intercourse before the play begins or during
the play (*Eunuch*). This is not stated in the *Perikeiromene*, but is
surely implied in the phrase 'I treated her as my wife' (239), and
by the similar phrase in the *Heautontimoroumenos* (98), implied
also by the mention of an adulterer in the *Orge* (fr. 306) and by
the title of the *Methe* (drunkenness), where Menander may well
have had Euripides' *Auge* in mind. We can also make a distinction between cases where the girl's parentage is known and cases
where the girl's parentage is unknown and she has to be recognised as a citizen before a marriage can be arranged. As far as we
know, the early *Orge* and *Methe* belong to the former class;
Kitharistes, Epikleros and *Heautontimoroumenos* certainly do,
and probably *Koneiazomenai* and *Kanephoros*. Recognition is
necessary for the girls of the *Perikeiromene*, 314/3, *Eunuch* and
Synaristosai, 308–6 (perhaps also in the *Phanion*). The *Synaristosai* is like the *Heros* and *Georgos* in that the mother of the girl
was herself raped in youth and deserted. P. Oxy 2826 also
belongs in this group: at the beginning of the play a youth
comes out into the night in great distress and in his speech occurs
the phrase 'I treated her as my wife'; but we cannot say whether
she is a poor citizen or has still to be recognised.

In the final group of plays the heroes of the *Sikyonios* and
Misoumenos are said not to have touched the girls whom they
ultimately marry, and this is surely also true of the young man
in the *Dyskolos, Aspis, Paidion* (cf. fr. v), *Hiereia* and *Phasma*.
For the rest of the plays it seems probable but there is no clear
evidence. Here too a distinction can be made between the plays
were the girl's parentage is already known and the plays where
she must be recognised as a citizen before she can be married. To
the former belong in chronological order *Dyskolos, Aspis,
Paidion, Karchedonios* (but here perhaps the youth has to be
recognised as an Athenian), *Hiereia, Phasma*—in these last two,
as in the *Heros, Georgos* and *Synaristosai*, the mothers were raped
and deserted in youth so that the girl is fatherless. The plays
where the girl has to be recognised are the *Kekryphalos, Olyn-*

thia, Encheiridion, Sikyonios (here the youth also has to be recognised), *Leukadia, Demiourgos, Hydria, Naukleros, Thrasyleon, Misoumenos, Kolax* and undated *Empimpramene, Hypobolimaios* (with perhaps a double recognition), *Karine, Messenia, Parakatatheke, Theophoroumene* and, if it is by Menander, P. Hibeh 181.

The most popular types run through the whole of Menander's career. The plays that end in marriage but with a child already born start with the *Pseudherakles* and *Androgynos* and run through to the *Imbrians*. The plays that end in marriage after earlier intercourse but with no mention of a child run from the *Orge* of 322/1 to the *Heautontimoroumenos* in 299/8. I do not think that we can argue from the 314/3 date of the *Perikeiromene* that the sub-type where the girl has to be recognised is a later development. Similarly I do not think we can argue that there were no plays where the girl was both a virgin and a citizen before the *Dyskolos*, 317/6, or after the *Phasma* (before 306). Here too we must take the longer range of the other sub-type (where the virgin heroine has also to be recognised) from the *Kekryphalos*, 318/7, to the *Kolax*, 302/1.

The rarer types of play may have a more restricted time range. I should like to think that the plays where a young husband has raped his wife before marriage are late, and it is true that the *Epitrepontes* has no trochaic scene and the *Daktylios* is unconventional in having recognition tokens in the prologue. The case for thinking that the *hetaira* plays are early is rather stronger. These plays are in the tradition of Middle Comedy, and the *Dis Exapaton* (*Bacchides*) is dated early.

But the grasping *hetaira* does not die out. She survives in the sub-plots of the *Heautontimoroumenos, Paidion* and *Karine*. And she has an interesting variant. In an ancient summary of a play by Menander which has been plausibly identified with the *Demiourgos*[6] the *hetaira* is described as 'bold but not wicked', which presumably means that she has other concerns than the ruin of young men in the pursuit of her trade. The description would fit the *hetairai* of the *Andria* and the *Eunuch*, both of whom have taken a great deal of trouble to help a supposed younger sister. Their motives are, of course, mixed, because identification of the younger sister will produce goodwill and greater security. But in spite of this the concern that the younger

[6] Borgogno, *Aegyptus*, 49, 1969, 82.

sister should have her rights is genuine, just as Habrotonon's
concern in the *Epitrepontes* that the baby should have its rights
is genuine as well as self-interested. Luckily we need not limit this
sympathy for an unsympathetic class to Menander's later plays
because we have the Chrysis of the early *Samia*, who is prepared
to risk her security to protect the baby.

Another unsympathetic and traditional character is the soldier
accompanied by his flatterer; we can trace this pair in Menander from the early *Pseudherakles* to the late *Kolax*. But again
Menander breaks the traditional mould in the *Perikeiromene*,
Sikyonios and *Misoumenos*, where the soldier is the hero. These
run from 314 to 305, and we do not know that Menander wrote
any more. In these plays the soldier, though some of his characteristics are traditional, does not have the traditional flatterer.
The nearest approach to the flatterer is Theron in the *Sikyonios*,
who is a parasite. He does not, as far as we can see, act as a flatterer; he is a helpful friend like Gnathon and not like Strouthias
in the later *Kolax*. The parasite also is a traditional figure: in two
early plays, *Dyskolos* and *Adelphoi* A, he is useless or rejected; in
the later *Sikyonios* and *Kolax* (and possibly in the *Thrasyleon*,
fr. 207) he has a part to play in helping the hero, and from the
little we can see is portrayed more sympathetically.[7]

I should like to argue that as he grew older Menander viewed
old men more sympathetically. There are two obvious objections:
we sympathise with Demeas in the early *Samia* and we have little
sympathy with Smikrines in the late *Epitrepontes*. It is fair to
remember that, as far as he knows, Smikrines has a very good
case indeed: his son-in-law has deserted his daughter for a *hetaira*
and in the course of the play accepts her child as his; nevertheless
what makes him unsympathetic is his overriding concern for the
financial aspects of the situation. It is also fair to remember that
the audience of the *Samia* knew before they set eyes on Demeas
that the baby was the child of Moschion and Plangon, and therefore Demeas' mistakes must have struck them primarily as
funny. The case for sympathy in the late plays would have to be
made rather on *Adelphoi* B and *Heautontimoroumenos*, where
even the less sympathetic in each pair of old men, Demeas and
Chremes, have strong principles which command some respect.
In some early plays, however, the chief obstacle is a twisted old

[7] On traditional *hetairai*, soldiers and parasites, *cf. L.G.C.* 63 f.

man who is represented sympathetically only for the moment when he is got out of his fixation. We can see this happen to Knemon in the *Dyskolos*, and I think we have to suppose that at some definite moment in the past he renounced the world. Later Menander would probably have told us about this as he has given the past history in the *Perikeiromene*, *Phasma*, *Heros*, *Synaristosai* and later plays. In the *Apistos* (*Aulularia*) we are told the effect the discovery of the pot of gold had on Euclio, and enough remains to show the change in him at the end. In the *Androgynos* the father lost his wife in childbirth and for that reason denied his daughter all male society; possibly the safe birth of a grandchild restored his balance.

Knemon is not a miser but behaves like one, particularly in his dealings with Getas and Sikon. Euclio is a miser. We cannot tell whether the old man in the *Methe* belonged to the Knemon type or the Euclio type, but he evidently behaved in the same way (fr. 267). Probably the last man we know of this type who forms the major—in fact the sole—obstacle in the play is Smikrines in the *Aspis*, and he is pure miser. Different but allied extensions of the Knemon type are found in Kleainetos of the *Georgos* and Menedemus of the *Heautontimoroumenos*. In both cases their hard and lonely life seems to be self-punishment, and in both they are charmed out of it.

The discussion of types of union in Menander's plays has led on into a discussion of certain kinds of character, and that in its turn has shown up one of the obstacles which have to be surmounted to achieve union, the twisted or miserly old man, father of the girl in *Methe*, *Dyskolos*, *Apistos* (*Aulularia*) or, in the *Aspis*, her senior uncle. But this is only one kind of obstacle, although in the early plays that we have mentioned it is the chief obstacle. On the boy's side a very common obstacle is marriage with another girl arranged by his father or, exceptionally, his mother (*Plokion*). The list is *Andria*, *Demiourgos*, *Epikleros*, *Georgos*, *Kanephoros*, *Paidion*, *Perinthia*, *Phasma*, *Plokion*, *Synaristosai*; probably also *Arrhephoros*, *Heros*, *Kitharistes*, *Koneiazomenai*, *Naukleros*, and P. Oxy 1825. In some of these plays a further obstacle is that the girl whom the youth loves is either fatherless or has to be recognised as a citizen: *Andria*, *Georgos*, *Demiourgos*, *Phasma*, *Synaristosai*, *Heros*. A further obstacle in the *Georgos* is that a marriage is also proposed for the girl, and this is the chief obstacle in the *Apistos* (*Aulularia*) and perhaps in P. Ghoran II. The *Adelphoi* A is a special case: the father is proposing remarriage for the two wives whose husbands have gone abroad to recoup their fortunes.

The status of the girl is a very common obstacle: she rates low socially if she is fatherless, and she is debarred from marriage legally if she is not a citizen. I need not repeat the titles, as this obstacle (which is very effective dramatically because it leads to a recognition scene), is usually used in conjunction with other obstacles; one such combination is noted in the last paragraph, and more will be mentioned below. Fatherlessness is evidently a major obstacle in the *Hiereia*, and the mistaken tactics of the father delay the solution. In the *Sikyonios* the youth has to be recognised as a citizen as well as the girl.

In these recognition plays a further obstacle may be a rival who tries to get possession of the girl: *Sikyonios, Perikeiromene, Leukadia, Kolax,* probably *Encheiridion, Misoumenos, Thrasyleon,* and perhaps *Hypobolimaios* (but the details of the plot there are very unclear).

Sometimes the main marriage might be achieved fairly easily, even if it needs to be clinched by recognition, but is complicated by the sub-plot, which deals with the affair of a brother, cousin or friend with a *hetaira*: *Adelphoi* B, *Anepsioi, Eunuch, Heautontimoroumenos, Imbrians.*

A final group of obstacles is formed by the misunderstandings of the characters themselves. The simplest case is the *Dis Exapaton*, where the old slave has failed to distinguish one twin *hetaira* from the other and this throws the whole story askew. In the *Samia* Demeas is told that he is the father and Chrysis the mother of the baby; when he learns that Moschion is the father he never considers the possibility of Chrysis not being the mother, and Moschion is too frightened of him and Nikeratos to tell the truth. In the *Misoumenos* the girl Krateia rejects Thrasonides because she thinks that he has killed her brother and the obstacle only gets greater when her father appears and discovers that Thrasonides has the brother's sword; her discovery of her father in this play only makes things more difficult. It is not quite clear whether at the beginning Thrasonides knows why she hates him. He cannot know that he is innocent until the brother turns up and claims the sword. The mistaken recognition token is here a major obstacle, like the shield of Kleostratos in the *Aspis*.

In these plays what Aristotle calls *Agnoia*, misunderstanding, is the major obstacle, and in the *Perikeiromene* Menander gives the prologue speech to personified Agnoia: Polemon misunderstands that she had kissed not her lover but her brother. His treatment of her (and probably the titles—*Orge* (anger), *Empimpramene* (the girl who is set on fire), *Rhapizomene* (the girl who gets her jaw slapped) allow us to suppose similar mistreatment of the girl in those plays), cutting off her hair, arouses furious resentment, which is mollified only by his repentance when her identity is established; here recognition aids the solution as normally. A misunderstanding of the same kind is the major obstacle in the *Epitrepontes* (and probably in the *Daktylios*): Charisios discovers that his wife has had a baby after they have been married five months; he assumes that another man is responsible and completely forgets that he himself had raped an unknown girl at the Tauropolia nine months before. This emphasis on misunderstanding shows Menander's essentially Aristotelian view of human behaviour.

The obstacles are overcome with the assistance of slaves, parasites and friends, and a considerable amount of what we should call luck. Menander calls it *Tyche*, the way things happen, and he gives Tyche the prologue speech in the *Aspis*: she describes herself as 'empowered to arbitrate and manage all these events' (147) and she calls herself a god (98). I do not see any clear distinction between Tyche here, Agnoia in the *Perikeiromene* and Pan in the *Dyskolos*, who claims that he has rewarded the girl's piety by making Sostratos fall in love with her (36 ff.). Whether the prologue speech is given to a personification (Agnoia), a personification with a cult (Tyche), or a god (Pan) depends partly on the type of story and partly on the setting: Knemon lives in Phyle, and Phyle had a famous cave of Pan and the Nymphs. The obstacles have to be overcome because this is comedy; therefore the prologue figures must be beneficent. They tell us nothing about Menander's religious beliefs.

We can consider the sixty plays rather as the anthropologist[8]

[8] I hope I have interpreted correctly C. Lévi-Strauss, *Le Cru et le cuit*, 207 ff. (English translation, 199 ff.). I find his theory of the armature and the codes, so adapted, useful to explain to myself Menander's procedure.

considers a group of myths related to meet a common need. They all have a common armature, union of youth and girl in spite of obstacles. But the common armature is clothed in sixty different ways to produce sixty different plays, and this process of differentiation has to be discussed further. The demands of the winter or spring festival are met by the armature, union in spite of difficulties. All beyond this is irrelevant to the festival but relevant to Menander. We have in fact already seen a number of differentiations or, as the anthropologist would call them, codes. I think that we might distinguish a professional code, a historical code, a biographical code, a social code and an ethical code.

By professional code[9] I mean what immediately shows Menander as a comic dramatist by profession. He must have frequented the theatre from his earliest years, and it may well be true that the great poet of Middle Comedy, Alexis, was his uncle. So he naturally continues the tradition of *hetaira* plays, and besides the grasping *hetaira* introduces other traditional figures and situations into his plays—the braggart soldier and his flatterer, the miserly old man, the parasite, the garrulous cook, the running slave, the intriguing slave, etc. We have seen a little how he occasionally—particularly in later plays—transmutes traditional figures, but under the heading of professional code we have to examine further his whole dramatic technique, including the relation of what the audience can actually see to what Menander wants them to imagine.

Use of traditional figures and situations creates an expectation in the audience which the dramatist may fulfil or may intentionally disappoint. Middle Comedy had also its traditional masks and traditional names for characters. These are two other elements which cause the audience to make predictions, and again we shall have to see how Menander uses them: Bias (Violent) in the *Kolax* is the traditional braggart soldier, Polemon (Warlike) is not; they are not distinguished by their names and there is no reason to suppose that they were distinguished by their masks. Menander wants to startle the audience into accepting his Polemon.

The characters are placed in a story, and their characteristics are the major forces which drive the story along. The story is

9 *Cf.* below, ch. vi.

divided into five acts, each of which has its own function in forming a shape rising to a climax in the fourth and winding down in the fifth. Here Menander shows very clearly how strongly he was influenced by Aristotelian theory.

Aristotelian theory was formed on tragedy, and Menander transferred it to comedy. But tragedy itself must also be reckoned as a code. A classical tragedy, Euripides or Sophocles, was played every year at the city Dionysia, and classical tragedy was probably frequently revived at the deme festivals. Aristotle used classical tragedy for examples to illustrate his lectures on rhetoric and ethics. Menander and his audience knew tragedy. So a situation taken from tragedy, and remodelled, a quotation from tragedy correct or garbled, an approximation to tragic language or tragic metre was a message which the audience could interpret to understand the particular moment presented to them.[10]

The historical and biographical codes have been discussed, already fairly fully. New Comedy does not react violently and immediately to historical events like Old Comedy. But we have seen from Menander's earliest years (and a little earlier where he relied on the memory of those older than himself) down to the beginning of the third century certain events that impressed him and turn up in contemporary plays as allusions or more than allusions—the Corinthian evils give the setting of the *Perikeiromene* and the war in Cyprus the setting of the *Misoumenos*—and recur in later plays as memories which he expects his audience to share. We have seen also that Menander, from his mid-thirties, gives his characters a much more precise back-history because his own memory is now longer and that possibly he is now more kindly disposed to elderly characters than he was in his early twenties.

The union of youth and girl is enough for the festival, but Menander encodes into the story and the obstacles a social message too. A marriage arranged by the two fathers is always an obstacle and, I think, never comes off. In the marriages with which the play ends the youth and the girl are always in love. This kind of marriage is superior to the arranged marriage, and the obstacles of status (the girl has no father or is a foreigner) are overcome by recognition: Menander says clearly that status does not matter. This kind of marriage is also superior to union

10 Cf. below, ch. v.

with a *hetaira*, which is reduced often to a sub-plot, and generally the youth ends up marrying a girl of his choice. But this is only one aspect of Menander's sociology, and his social world needs further investigation.[11]

Menander was a pupil of Theophrastos, and there is no reason why he should not have read Aristotle in his youth. The refusal to accept the obvious social rating in marriage, the sympathy with the traditionally unsympathetic character—hetaira, soldier, even the tiresome old men to the extent of explaining the twist that makes them tiresome—and above all the emphasis on misunderstanding as an obstacle in the development of human relationships recall Aristotle, and particularly the *Nicomachean Ethics*, which is the reason for calling these aspects of Menander his ethical code.[12] But Agnoia's analysis of Polemon in the prologue speech of the *Perikeiromene* also reminds us of the discussion of the tragic hero in Aristotle's *Poetics*,[13] where the *hamartia* (error rather than flaw) has its position on a scale of actions ranging from misfortune (externally caused) to premeditated crime. The *Poetics* as well as the *Ethics* is part of Menander's equipment. We can show (as noted already) that he took over both the Aristotelian conception of probability in the sense that the incidents of the plot procede from the particular make-up of the characters[14] and the Aristotelian complication and denouement, which he formalises into the five-act play.[15] For the audience Aristotle's influence is recognisable both in Menander's ethics and in his dramatic technique: Aristotle belongs both to the social code and to the professional code.

[11] Cf. below, ch. III.   [12] Cf. below, ch. IV.
[13] Ch. 13, as glossed by N.E., 1135 b 11.
[14] Poetics, ch. 9 .   [15] Poetics, ch. 18.

III

The social code

Menander tells his audience where his characters belong in society, but the clues are not as clear to us as they would be to them. Nor does he necessarily mention the whole of the family; he gives only as much as is needed for the play. One guide to wealth is the dowries given to the girls, usually when the formal betrothal is made at the end of the play. We can list these and then consider what we know about the givers and the receivers.

Ten talents: Chremes in *Andria*. (The heiress mother's dowry in *Plokion*.)

Six talents: Chremes in the alternative ending of the *Andria*, the dowry for his other daughter who is marrying Charinus (*Perinthia*).

Four talents (Smikrines in the *Epitrepontes* had given this to Pamphile when she married Charisios).

Three talents: Pataikos to Glykera in *Perikeiromene*. Kallippides to his daughter in *Dyskolos*.

Two talents: Demeas to Krateia in *Misoumenos*. Chairestratos to his neice in *Aspis*. Chremes to Antiphila in *Heautontimoroumenos*. Kleainetos to his daughter, P. Oxy. 2533 (?*Arrhephoros*).

One talent: Knemon to his daughter in *Dyskolos*. Perhaps the four-pound jar of gold (*Aul.* 821) in *Apistos* is worth about the same.[1]

No dowry: Nikeratos to Plangon in *Samia*. Sostrata to her daughter in *Adelphoi* B. Laches in P. Oxy. 1824.

It is sometimes said that these dowries are exaggerated, but we

---

[1] Plautus may equate the Roman libra with the Greek mna, and gold is worth ten times the amount of silver, so that this is forty mnai or two-thirds of a talent.

know in fact of a ten-talent dowry in the fifth century, and
of a three-talent dowry in the fourth century, and the worth of
money had gone down by the late fourth century.[2] What Menander is saying is that, down at any rate to the two-talent level,
these fathers are very rich, probably among the top 300 richest
men in Athens.[3]

Chremes in the *Andria* seems excessive, especially as he has
two daughters to provide for. We know that he had gone to
make his fortune in Asia when his elder daughter was lost. He
presumably did well, came back and married and had another
daughter but no son; this may be the reason why he can give
so large a dowry. Krobyle in *Plokion* is expressly stated to be an
heiress. This may also be the reason for the high dowry of
Pamphile in the *Epitrepontes*; no mention is made of a brother,
and Smikrines does not give the impression of being very rich;
he apparently lives alone with his daughter's old nurse, like
Euclio in the *Apistos*.[4]

Krobyle married a man less well off than herself; they have a
son and a daughter and presumably slaves, but, as we have only
fragments, we hear only of the lady's maid with whom the husband is supposed to be in love; they have a house in Athens and
estates in the country. For this we can quote many parallels.[5] We
have most detail about Kallippides in the *Dyskolos*, who gives
his daughter a three-talent dowry. He farms land worth 'many
talents'. In the earlier fourth century estates worth from three
to twenty talents can be quoted, and Menedemus in the *Heautontimoroumenos* has put all his money into an estate worth fifteen
talents. Kallippides probably also has a town house, as his son is
described as used to city life. He has a wife who spends a good
deal of money making elaborate sacrifices, a son and a daughter,
three and perhaps four male slaves, and at least two female
slaves.[6]

[2] Cf. W. K. Lacey, *The Family in Classical Greece*, 109 f., 283 n. 24.

[3] Cf. A. H. M. Jones, *Athenian Democracy*, 85.

[4] *Andria* 951, his earlier life 923 ff. *Plokion*, fr. 333. *Epitrepontes* 8.

[5] Property in town and country: *Adelphoi* B (Micio), *Georgos* (the boy's
father: Kleainetos only has country land), *Heros* (Pheidias' father; probably
also Laches), *Hypobolimaios*, *Kitharistes* (Moschion's father), *Paidion*, *Perikeiromene* (Philinos), *Samia* (Demeas), *Synaristosai* (Alcesimarchus' father).

[6] *Dyskolos*; Kallippides' land, his son's city life, 40 f; his wife 261; slaves,
Pyrrhias, Getas, Donax, Syros (960); females, 950. I am not sure whether
Plangon (430) is his daughter or a poor dependent or another musician (cf.

Let us look for a moment at other instances and some variants of the standard rich family. Chremes in the *Heautontimoroumenos* gives a two-talent dowry to his newly discovered daughter. Evidently sixteen years before he had been much less well off and had given orders for his daughter to be exposed, but had gratefully accepted a son when one was born. What these rich men want is a son who will inherit. Two sons, however, are comparatively rare.[7] Simo in the *Eunuch* has two sons (he also has a town house and a country estate); the rich father in the *Demiourgos* has two sons; and perhaps Kleinias and Lysias in the *Theophoroumene* are brothers. But in *Adelphoi* B the hard-working Demea, who apparently lives in the country, had his elder son adopted by his brother, and Smikrines in the *Sikyonios*, who was probably not so well off when his first son was born, gave the baby to the Sikyonian woman. The rich father needs one son, and if his wife fails to produce one she is in danger of divorce: so she gets hold of a male baby somehow. In the *Perikeiromene* Philinos and Myrrhine are well off, with a town house in Corinth and a country estate; they have a daughter, but the son, Moschion, was smuggled in as a baby. The same is true of the elder son of the priestess's neighbour in the *Hiereia* and of the son of the rich family in the *Hypobolimaios*, but in both those cases the mother produced a son of her own afterwards. Demeas in the *Samia* and Micio in *Adelphoi* B, both bachelors, get themselves an heir by adoption.

These rich men do not depend only on farming. Kallippides perhaps may; Kleainetos in the *Georgos* and Menedemus in the *Heautontimoroumenos* are rather special cases. They seem to have retired to the solitude of a large farm. Many of them, however, have interests overseas. In the *Dis Exapaton* (*Bacchides* 229) the son has been sent to Ephesos to recover a debt of two talents, which has been piling up interest. In the *Georgos* the son has been sent to Corinth on business. Probably Moschion in the *Kitharistes* has been in Ephesos on his father's business. In the *Heros* the old man Laches has gone to Lemnos on private business. In all these cases business is in addition to property-holding. On

below, ch. VI, section 5, on names). Fourth-century estates: Jones, *op. cit.*, 86 ff. Menedemus, *Heautont.* 145.

[7] Chremes: dowry 940, exposing 626. Two sons: *cf.* also *Imbrians, Phasma* (household A). Commonest of all is a single son *or* a single daughter.

the other hand, the father in the *Arrhephoros* (perhaps the Laches of the *Fabula Incerta*) has gone abroad on a public embassy (1), and I suspect that this may have been what took that very unequal pair, the rich bachelor Demeas and the poor father Nikeratos of the *Samia*, to Byzantion. A similar explanation may account for the seemingly unequal pair in P.S.I. 1176 (probably *Demiourgos*), where Laches sends his friend home ahead to propose his daughter in marriage to Laches' son, who rejects her.

The three brothers of the *Aspis* are interesting. Chairestratos is younger than Smikrines. We are not told whether Kleostratos' father was the eldest brother or came between the other two. Presumably the estate of their father did not cut up into three very large portions. Kleostratos' father did not leave enough to support his son and daughter, and Kleostratos had to go East as a soldier to make money. Smikrines was a miser and lived alone with an old woman to look after him; he was presumably building up his share. But Chairestratos was very rich; Daos rates him at sixty talents. This does not include his wife's dowry, because Smikrines could not hope to succeed to that. The characterisation of him as 'melancholic' rules out military success.[8] If Menander thought about it, he must have supposed that he made a fortune in trade. He married a widow with a son, Chaireas; she bore him a daughter, and he has taken in his niece. The dowry of two talents which he proposes for her is a free gift, and she was marrying his stepson. We do not know what dowry he gave to his daughter when he engaged her to Kleostratos— presumably much more.

Pataikos gives a dowry of three talents to his newly found daughter in the *Perikeiromene*. His wife died when his son and daughter were born. The day before, he heard that the ship which was the source of his wealth had sunk; he therefore decided to expose the children. We have a parallel for the ship in the *Naukleros*, where Straton welcomes the news of the return of his ship from across the Aegean with his son on board. Straton seems to be a normally rich father with a son in love, against his wishes, with a girl who is subsequently recognised.[9] The audience could make an estimate of the wealth of the young Pataikos, who had evidently counted on bringing up his son and

[8] *Aspis*; the family, 114–36; sixty talents, 350; melancholic, 338.
[9] Fr. 286.

daughter. The cargo would probably be worth between one and two talents on each voyage, and the profit was sufficient to offset the 22 ½ per cent charged on shipping loans.[10]

We have lost the beginning of the prologue speech, in which Agnoia must have told the audience how Pataikos recouped his fortunes, but we have an obvious hint in the fact that he is a friend of Polemon; surely he did what most impoverished young men did and went to the wars. This gave him a salary and foreign booty. The three-talent dowry to Glykera and the fact that he is going to have to support Moschion puts him in roughly the same class as Kallippides in the Dyskolos. The only figure that we have for Eastern booty is Daos' estimate of four talents in the Aspis (351), which is made up of a talent of gold, two-thirds of a talent in silver cups, and the rest in textiles, male and female slaves, and baggage animals. The ingredients are much the same in the booty that the two brothers bring back from Asia in Adelphoi A (Stichus 374 ff.) but they had been away for over two years.

What is clear from plays like the Kolax, the Eunuch, or the Dis Exapaton is that the successful soldier can always outbid the sons of rich fathers, however indulgent their fathers or ingenious their slaves.[11] And when soldiers marry the daughters of the rich, they are thereby recognised as belonging to the same class as their fathers-in-law. The three soldier households that we know differ slightly from each other. Polemon, as a Corinthian citizen, has bought his house; the other two, Stratophanes in the Sikyonios and Thrasonides in the Misoumenos, presumably rent houses, as they are not citizens. Polemon treats Glykera as his wife (like Clinia in the Heautontimoroumenos); he feeds, houses, clothes her and gives her jewellery; but she has no known male relative to make the marriage legal. He has other slaves (176) besides Sosias and Doris, whom he has presumably given to Glykera. Thrasonides has received Krateia as a captive with an old woman slave; the phrase 'she was captured and came to us' (235) suggests that he bought them rather than captured them himself. We do not hear of his having any slaves except Getas.

---

[10] Perikeiromene: dowry, 437; wife and ship, 373 ff. Loans: cf. Demosthenes XXXII, XXXIV, XXXV.
[11] Cf. probably also Androgynos, Karine, Leukadia, Parakatatheke, Pseud-herakles, Xenologos.

Stratophanes (if I interpret *Sikyonios* fr. 1=371 K–T right)
bought Philoumene and Dromon out of his supposed father's
estate and had them sent to him in Athens, knowing that she
was an Athenian citizen; he was living there with a *hetaira*,
Malthake, and at least provided board for the parasite Theron.
He had two named slaves, Pyrrhias and Donax, and in addition
barbarian slaves, donkey drivers and donkeys, and textiles (385–
395)—the proceeds of his last campaign (unless the textiles belong to Malthake).

Civilian parallels for this kind of household are found in the
Samia and *Synaristosai*. The elderly and rich Demeas, who has
town and country property and a son adopted in infancy, lives
with a *hetaira*, Chrysis, and has a male slave and a number of
female slaves (221). Presumably security and probably the hope
of a legacy persuaded Chrysis to give up the ten drachmai (392)
or more that she had been earning per night on her own.
Alcesimarchus in the *Synaristosai* is the son of a rich man and
has rented a house in town (*Cist.* 319) where he can live with the
girl he loves; the father presumably allows and pays for this. The
girl is held by the promise of marriage.

Alcesimarchus is an extreme case, but Laches in the *Kitharistes*
is quite happy that his son should spend the time in town drinking: in his own youth he had himself been a noted wealth-
reducer (60). Micio in *Adelphoi* B is prepared to spend on his
adopted son's dining, drinking and visiting *hetairai* until the
money runs short; then he may disown him (119). Simo in the
Andria does not mind money going on horses, dogs, philosophers
and parties but draws the line at his son treating a poor girl as if
she were his wife (55). We naturally hear more of the sons'
love affairs and parties, whether held with friends or in the house
of a *hetaira* or at an inn,[12] than we do of their serious pursuits.
I have quoted the cases where a son is sent on business by his
father, but we have also Moschion's description of his youth in
the *Samia* (13); he was *choregos*, he bred dogs and horses, he
commanded a section of cavalry. The first and last, particularly,
put him very clearly among the wealthiest.

The two-talent dowries still mark the fathers as very rich.

---

[12] Parties with friends: *Andria* 61, *Eun.* 540, *Kolax*, fr. 1, P. Lund 4. With
a *hetaira*: *Dis Exapaton*. At an inn; *Theophoroumene*, *Encheiridion*, perhaps
also *Perikeiromene*, *Misoumenos*.

Below that, Knemon in the *Dyskolos* is a special case. He orders
Gorgias to sell off half his farm to provide a talent for his
daughter's dowry. The proportion is absurd by the standards of
all the other fathers but characteristic of him. His two-talent
farm is, of course, small compared with the fifteen-talent farm
of Menedemus, but it is evidently more than twice the size of
the plot which supports Gorgias and his mother. In Demosthenes'
time[13] it would have put Knemon among the 1,200 richest men
in Athens, and still at this time he must be very comfortably
off, and Menander wants the audience to realise that he insists
on living poor.

Below him come the really poor. Euclio in the *Apistos* can give
his daughter the pot of gold as a dowry, but that is a windfall.
Nikeratos in the *Samia*, partly—but, I think, only partly—out
of cussedness, will not give Moschion a dowry while he is alive;
Sostrata, the widowed mother of *Adelphoi* B, cannot provide a
dowry, nor can Hegio (her brother in Menander). With Euclio
we should probably class Kichesias in the *Sikyonios* and other
old men like Kraton in the *Theophoroumene*.[14] With Sostrata
belong the women who have been deserted by their husbands or
lovers: Myrrhine in the *Dyskolos* and *Georgos* and the priestess
in the *Hiereia*. Myrrhine in the *Dyskolos* has the plot and her
son and a slave to work it. Myrrhine in the *Georgos* has a town
house, her daughter and a female slave. The priestess has given
(or sold?) her son to the neighbour; she presumably has her
dowry and supports herself and her daughter from her cures.

Like the priestess, the old woman who found Pataikos' twins
in the *Perikeiromene* gave (or sold?) the boy to the rich Myrrhine
and kept the girl; but when the war made her situation worse
she gave (or hired?) the girl to Polemon, pretending she was her
own daughter. The other Corinthian old woman, in the *Heautontimoroumenos*, took Chremes' infant daughter to expose it but
kept it for herself. She had also two female slaves (275 ff.), and
they supported themselves by weaving, presumably like Myrrhine
in the *Georgos* and like the poor girl from Andros until she began
to take lovers (*Andria* 70 ff.). In the *Heautontimoroumenos* the
old woman gives (or hires) the girl to Clinia, and he fears that she
will have become a *hetaira* (232). Menander sees three alternatives

[13] Cf. A. H. M. Jones, loc. cit., n. 6.
[14] Cf. *Halieus, Anepsioi, Epikleros, Hypobolimaios, Plokion, Parakatatheke.*

for the poor woman and her daughter or supposed daughter: weaving, a long-term liaison, and being a *hetaira*. In all the cases that we know, the supposed mother who permits a long-term liaison knows that the girl's real parents belong to the city in which she is living; so that the chance of recognition and formal marriage is real. In the *Synaristosai* Melainis knows this and her supposed daughter is recognised, but her friend the *lena* hires out her daughter as a *hetaira*.

The *hetaira* is wealthier than these women. But she depends entirely on her beauty, and her old age is insecure; the old women of the *Synaristosai* had themselves been *hetairai* (38). While they can, *hetairai* make a lot in money and gifts.[15] The ten-drachma rate which Demeas throws in Chrysis' teeth (*Samia* 392) is probably low, but the 2,000 and 1,000 drachmai which are extracted from reluctant fathers in the *Dis Exapaton* (879) and *Heautontimoroumenos* (835) to get rid of rival soldiers are probably for a long-term hiring. Thais in the *Eunuch* (120) was left all she had by the Rhodian or Athenian with whom she came to Athens, but she has to go on and she evidently feels a new security at the end, when she achieves Simon as her patron in return for committing herself entirely to Phaedria. Essentially it is what Chrysis achieved in the *Samia*, but here the father is the patron and the son the lover.

The great *hetairai* were foreigners (many of them Samian) with metic status in Athens. But many of the young heroines are slaves owned by a *leno* or *pornoboskos*. This was a profitable trade; Habrotonon in the *Epitrepontes* (10) gets twelve drachmai a day, but her owner presumably provides upkeep, clothes, and her musical instrument.[16] The *pornoboskos* in the *Kolax* (117) claims that Philotis gets 300 drachmai a day from the rich soldier, which seems enormous. Sannio in the *Adelphoi B* (223, 242) asks 2,000 drachmai for one of his girls and is prepared to accept 1,000. The trade has its risks: a girl might be recognised as a citizen and so lost, or might be stolen on the road or at a party or from the *pornoboskos's* house.

We have mentioned already the flatterers of the rich soldiers

[15] Cf., besides the plays mentioned below, *Demiourgos, Karine, Paidion, Parakatatheke, Thais.*

[16] With Habrotonon cf. *Eun.* 132, the girl sold at a profit because she is a good musician. Other plays with *pornoboskos: Imbrians, Messenia, Thrasyleon.*

and the parasites, who could be the helpful friends of the young heroes;[17] they certainly are to be reckoned among the poorer citizens. Another figure of traditional comedy is the cook, who is both butcher and cook at the sacrifices and dinners of the rich.[18] The two names Karion (*Epitrepontes*) and Sikon (*Dyskolos*) are slave names, and this probably means that the cook is a freedman. He is a pompous and garrulous person, who talks his own jargon. He brings with him his waiter and sometimes another slave. He brings his own favourite pots and borrows from the neighbours if he has not enough. In the *Aspis* (223) he hopes for three drachmai for cooking the marriage feast, and this is the first engagement he has had for ten days. His status is roughly parallel to that of the miller, general salesman and cheese-seller, which are the professions considered by Daos in the *Perikeiromene* (93) when he thinks that Moschion is going to free him.

The two old women in the *Synaristosai* were probably the slaves of a *pornoboskos* before they were freed and became *hetairai*. The old woman who had been Moschion's nurse in the *Samia* was freed by Demeas and stayed on in the house (237). We cannot tell whether most of the nurses of whom we hear are still slaves or have been freed. The professional nurses who come from outside and the midwives are probably freedwomen.[19]

In the country most of the outside work is done by slaves. The charcoal-burner in the *Epitrepontes* is a slave living outside with his wife (204). The shepherd Daos is certainly not the slave of Chairestratos, but he may be the slave of a neighbouring landowner. On the other hand Tibeios in the *Heros* is described as a young house slave of Laches when he took over or found the twins (21); but sixteen or so years later when he was a shepherd he borrowed money from Laches: this surely means that Laches had freed him and set him up as a shepherd. His supposed son Gorgias works as a free labourer with Laches to pay off the debt.

In society there were many graduations of wealth between the rich landowner or industrialist or soldier and the poor citizen,

---

[17] Cf. II.

[18] Cf., besides the plays mentioned, *Apistos* (*Aulularia*), *Arrhephoros*, *Demiourgos*, *Kolax*, *Messenia*, *Misoumenos*. *Perikeiromene*. *Phasma*. *Pseudherakles*, *Rhapizomene*, *Samia*, *Trophonios*, P. Cairo 65445 (? *Paidion*).

[19] Nurses and midwives: *Adelphoi B*, *Andria*, *Arrhephoros*, *Heros*, *Georgos* (?), *Perinthia*, *Plokion*, *Pseudherakles*, *Rhapizomene*, *Titthe*.

resident alien, or freedman. But Menander, like the orators, historians and philosophers, sees them as two classes, rich and poor, with a gulf between them across which they often face each other as enemies, though in special circumstances they may become friends.

The marriage between the rich youth and the poor girl is always a love match on his side and also, where we hear her opinion, on hers (e.g. *Cistellaria* 58 ff; *Heautontimoroumenos* 230, 404), but the girl's relatives regard the earlier stages at least as exploitation of the poor by the rich. This is certainly an element in Nikeratos' rage in the *Samia* (585, 599). It is very clear in Hegio's discussion of Aeschinus' conduct in *Adelphoi* B (605) and in Gorgias' very similar phrasing when he first attacks Sostratos in the *Dyskolos* (270 ff., particularly 298). In the same terms also Thais in the *Eunuch* (865) regards Chaerea's rape of her supposed sister as 'violence 'unworthy of his standards as a freeborn Athenian.[20] In the *Synaristosai* the *lena* regards poor *hetairai* as a closed society always on the defensive against rich mothers (21), and Melaenis naturally sees the treachery of the rich in the news that Alcesimarchus is to marry his Lemnian relation (492).

In every case the opposition, as far as we can see, comes from the father and not from the son. The father thinks only in terms of an undesirable liaison with a *hetaira*. The father in the *Eunuch* has long hated Thais as a typical *hetaira* (1000), and his slave prides himself on having taught his young charges what *hetairai* are like so that 'they may hate them always' (929). Simo in the *Andria* views everything that happens in Glycerium's house, including the claim that the girl is a citizen, as an attempt to capture Pamphilus (475, 492, 834, 919). Alcesimarchus' father is perfectly prepared to make love to Alcesimarchus' girl himself (306).

Legal action can be threatened or taken by poor and rich. Suits against adulterers are mentioned in several plays.[21] This is probably the charge that would be brought on behalf of the poor girl in the *Plokion* (XVI, XVII), and may be the content of the

---

[20] Cf. *Kanephoros*, fr. 218; *Georgos* 129 and frs. 1–3. So also Euclio's attitude in *Aul.* 220 ff.

[21] *Andria* 780; *Chalkis*, fr. 445; P. Oxy. 11, 17 (? *Paidion*); P. Oxy. 429 (? *Arrhephoros*).

challenge in P. Ant. 55. Chremes in the *Andria* (810) is afraid
that if he claims his inheritance someone will sue him on behalf
of the poor girl. The poor have the reputation of being too quick
in going to law, and this is what Kleainetos warns Gorgias in
the *Georgos* (132): 'the man in poor clothes is immediately called
a sycophant, even if he has in fact been wronged'. It is because
Euclio has avoided this reputation that the rich Megadorus is
prepared to marry his daughter (*Apistos–Aulularia* 215).

The poor man who is politically active appears very clearly in
the *Sikyonios* (150 ff.) The account of the meeting at Eleusis at
which the deme assembly foiled Moschion's attempt to get hold
of the girl and accepted Stratophanes' suggestion that she should
be lodged with the priestess, until her parents are found, is a
tremendous set piece, and carries the story forward to the recognition first of Stratophanes and then of the girl. What interests
us here is not obviously relevant to the story. Menander seems
to expect the audience to approve the political activity of the
small man and to be thereby prejudiced against Moschion and
his father. The narrator characterises himself as a militant jury-
man in the tradition of Aristophanes' *Wasps*, and he promptly
joins the assembly. This political colour is carried over from the
dialogue before the account of the assembly. There Smikrines,
the rich father of Moschion (and, as it later ironically turns out,
of Stratophanes), protests against the decision as typical lower-
class yielding to emotional appeals. The narrator then calls him
a stuck-up oligarch, a rich exploiter, who is no better than a
common thief. After the narration Moschion rushes in and
demands the arrest of the slavers (Stratophanes and his party)
and is apparently told by the narrator to go and get his facts
straight from the priestess. The contest is between the rich soldier
Stratophanes and the rich youth Moschion, but Menander has
drawn the poor politicians of the deme assembly into the picture
and, in the person of the narrator, on to the stage, so that the
decision for Stratophanes becomes a popular decision against a
rich conservative. Menander could equally well, as far as the
story is concerned, have shaped the decision as an arbitration
between Stratophanes and Moschion by Smikrines: this also
would have been ironical—the irony of Smikrines deciding for
his unknown son against his known son. Or he could have made
Kichesias the unknown father of the girl the arbitrator. If the

Sikyonios is rightly dated to the time of the democratic restoration, this democratic shaping of the story would appeal to the
audience. The climate has changed since the rich Megadorus
praised Euclio under the tyranny of Demetrios of Phaleron as a
poor man devoid of malice.

We have been considering so far mainly relations between the
household and those outside it. We can now turn to consider the
relations between husbands and wives, parents and children,
masters and slaves. This could be termed family code as distinct
from social code, but it hardly seems necessary to make a separate
category.

The misery of the husband in a marriage of convenience is an
old comic theme which goes back at least as far as Aristophanes'
Clouds. The complaint against the rich wife is that she exercises
all the power in the house. This we hear in the *Plokion, Hypobolimaios, Kybernetai*, and it is probably the reason for the
arbitration between husband and wife in the *Epikleros*. Megadorus inveighs against the power of the dowry in *Apistos–
Aulularia* (498). Then there is the extravagant wife who wastes
her husband's money, particularly on sacrifices, in the *Misogynes*
and *Orge*; Kallippides in the *Dyskolos* is rich enough to bear this,
and he makes no complaint of his wife's extravagant sacrifice to
Pan. In the *Hiereia* the objection is that the wife gossips, in particular that she gossips with an undesirable neighbour, the priestess. Probably talkativeness was what made Knemon's marriage
intolerable to him (*Dyskolos* 14). Chremes in the *Heautontimoroumenos* (632, 1009) regards his wife as a fool. What was
the cause of misery in Demea's marriage (*Adelphi* 867) we are
not told. In the *Samia* we have lost the essential early scenes
which might clarify Nikeratos' relations with his wife, and
Demeas' remark (200) 'It will be difficult for him to persuade
his wife' remains a mystery. The three scenes—but they are only
partially preserved—where there is no trace of misunderstanding
between husband and wife are the three scenes where the past
is being revealed, past seductions in the *Heros* and *Phasma* and
the recognition of Stratophanes in the *Sikyonios* (280).

The elderly pairs are not a very good advertisement for the
arranged marriage. Of course, an arranged marriage can turn
into a love marriage, and in the two young marriages where the
husband had seduced the wife before marriage Menander empha-

sises that he does fall in love with his wife: the whole conduct of Charisios through the *Epitrepontes* shows this, and Kratinos in the *Daktylios* states it in his opening speech. For the other young men whose marriage is arranged at the end of the play passage after passage can be quoted to show the violence and reality of their passion. Stratophanes in the *Sikyonios* burst into rivers of tears to support his claim in the asembly (219). Thrasonides in the *Misoumenos* threatens suicide if Krateia leaves him (309, 321). Polemon in the *Perikeiromene* becomes almost incoherent when he thinks that Glykera has left him (256 ff.). We can add the violence of Alcesimarchus in the *Synaristosai* (*Cistellaria* 639, 650) and the boy in the *Phasma* (P. Oxy. 2825, fr. B) and the transports of joy of Clinia in the *Heautontimoroumenos* (679 ff.) and Chaerea in the *Eunuch* (1031 f., with *Andria* 959 f.). Some, however, describe their love more quietly and not less effectively, like Chaireas in the *Aspis* (286 ff.) or Moschion in the *Samia* (623 ff.). The youth in the *Georgos* (14 f.) says it would be impious to desert and wrong his dearest Hedeia. Pamphilus in the *Andria* has decided to rear the child, which Daos regards as madness (401). Sostratos in the *Dyskolos* is prepared to abandon his city context to win Knemon's daughter (302–92).

Very often this love causes a direct clash with the father, particularly when he has already planned a conventional marriage. In many plays we know this happened, but we have not got the texts to show the details of the relationship between father and son. We can see this relationship best in the *Samia*, *Andria*, *Heautontimoroumenos* and *Adelphoi* B, although only the *Andria* provides the direct clash over marriage. But there, although Pamphilus necessarily falls foul of his father's conventional view of *hetairai*, 'respect for my father, who has till now so generously allowed me to do whatever I liked' (262 f.) is a real factor in his character and at the end the idea of deceiving his father is repugnant to him (896–902).[22] In the *Samia* Moschion is the adopted son of Demeas. The trouble between them is entirely due to misunderstanding. Moschion followed a conventional rich youth's career and helped Demeas, who was a bachelor, to install the *hetaira* Chrysis as his mistress. He has been very careful to avoid getting entangled with her himself, particularly in the absence of Demeas. Then he falls in love with

[22] *Cf.* also the young man and his father in the *Epikleros* IV, V, VII.

Plangon, and when the baby is born Chrysis takes it over until the marriage can be safely arranged with the return of the two fathers. The first meeting of Moschion and Demeas is not entirely clear, but certainly Moschion has no time to confess because he has to prevent Demeas from turning out the child, which he thinks is his own; probably Demeas mistakes Moschion's ready acceptance of the marriage proposal as an admission of interest in Chrysis and a desire to escape. When he learns that Moschion is the father and still believes that Chrysis is the mother, he holds on to his belief in Moschion's essential decency and at whatever cost to himself blames Chrysis (270 ff. 328 ff.). The long fourth act continues the misunderstanding until the momentary absence of Nikeratos gives Moschion a chance of confessing. Then in the fifth act Moschion is furious at Demeas' suspicions and pretends to be going off to the wars. The two are reconciled when Demeas claims forgiveness for his single mistake (709).

This is a very special relationship, but I do not think that Menander points any moral. It is true that Moschion deceives both fathers by the pretence that the baby is the child of Chrysis and Demeas, and that from this initial deceit all the subesquent misunderstandings arise, but there is no suggestion that given the circumstances the deceit was wrong. Demeas and Moschion are a decent pair who can understand one another, just as Kallippides and Sostratos are in the less complicated circumstances of the *Dyskolos* (784 ff.). In the *Heautontimoroumenos* and *Adelphoi* B Menander comes much nearer to saying how father and son (or adopted son) ought to behave. Chremes in the *Heautontimoroumenos* is officious and he is insincere. He criticises Menedemus for insincerity (154), but his son Clitipho knows that his sermons are inconsistent with his youthful escapades (200 f., 220 f.). Later Chremes himself preaches insincerity both to Menedemus and to Clitipho (478, 575). The lightweight Clitipho is the son he deserves. Menedemus' criticism of his son is irrelevant because Antiphila is not a *hetaira*, and his self-punishment, when his son obeys him and goes to Asia, is excessive, but his son, in spite of his love for Antiphila, does obey him, and when he comes back puts loyalty to his friend above his own convenience (694 f.). Menander contrasts the pairs and shows which he approves.

In the *Adelphoi* B the two old men, who are brothers, have lived different lives, one the hard life of the country, the other

the soft life of the town, and have developed two different
theories of education which one applies to his son and the other
to his adopted son. Demea educates his son by fear (75) and by
precepts (415). Ctesipho as a result is neither stable (274) nor
candid. Micio claims that it is possible to distinguish between
those who can do something safely and those who cannot (821
f.); the two boys are sensitive and intelligent and show all the
signs of a 'liberal' character; therefore they can be guided by
their sense of honour and 'liberality' rather than by fear (57),
and their excesses will be over in their youth, when they do not
greatly matter (108). Aeschinus at least, except for his long
hesitation in telling his father about Pamphila (683), justifies this
confidence. At the end Menander slightly redresses the balance
by Demeas' criticism of Micio (986), but though the truth lies
somewhere between the views of the two old men, it is pretty
clear that he thought Micio was more nearly right than Demea.

Mothers appear seldom. In the *Perikeiromene*, having given
Glykera asylum, Myrrhine is perfectly firm in keeping Moschion
out of the way (we have lost any scene there may have been with
Myrrhine after Moschion learns that he was only brought into
the house as a baby). In other plays it is the mother that the boy
goes to when he is in trouble—to appeal for leniency when his
father has disinherited him in the *Heautontimoroumenos* (1024
ff.), to confess that he has seduced a girl in the *Kitharistes* and
Aulularia (682) and to appeal for help in a love affair in the
Hiereia and *Phasma*. The two poor sons, Gorgias in the *Dyskolos*
and in the *Georgos*, work to support their mothers and keep a
jealous eye on their sisters.

Fathers are not greatly concerned with their daughters except
to marry them off as well as possible and to remarry them if
the marriage goes wrong, and they sometimes show an extra-
ordinary ignorance of their daughter's condition.[23] The only
daughters who stand up to their fathers and make their own
decisions about marriage (even though in fact this may coincide
with their father's wishes) are the very special cases of Glykera
in the *Perikeiromene* and Krateia in the *Misoumenos*. But the
women—mothers, daughters, slaves and sometimes neighbours
—stand together to defend their interests against the men. This
is most obvious when mother and servant or servant alone rally

---

[23] E.g. *Androgynos, Apistos (Aulularia), Rhapizomene.*

to help the pregnant girl in the plays where the baby is born in
the course of the action[24] or before it, as in the *Samia*, where
Nikeratos truthfully complains that Chrysis and his wife are
conspiring against him (556 f.). There must also have been an
agreement between the two wives of the *Phasma* to get the
party wall pierced and disguised as a shrine so that the wife of
house A could see her illegitimate daughter, who was working
in house B, without the knowledge of either of the husbands
(20 ff.). And as noted already, Myrrhine in the *Perikeiromene*
gives Glykera asylum regardless of the trouble which it will
certainly cause with Moschion and may cause with her husband
(174).

What Menander tells us about slaves rings, on the whole, true
to life. I have noted already the outside slaves like Syros in the
Epitrepontes, the rather special case of the slaves of the *pornoboskos*, the nurses and the other female slaves in the household,
who are loyal to their old or young mistress. Knemon. Euclio,
and Smikrines in the *Epitrepontes* each have an old female slave
whom they treat or threaten to treat abominably; Smikrines in
the *Aspis* is unlikely to have been a good master. The old nurse,
when the children grow up, may stay on (*Epitrepontes*) or may
go with the daughter (perhaps *Daktylios, Misoumenos*) or may
keep house for the son: the last seems to account for the presence
of an old female slave with the apparently rich and young or
at least youngish men, Chremes in the *Eunuch* and Kleinias in
the *Misoumenos*. The reverse, a male slave in a female household,
is found in the *Dyskolos* and *Adelphoi* B: Daos and Geta were
slaves of the dead husband and have stayed on with the widow
(Myrrhine in the *Dyskolos* reverted to her former status when
she left Knemon). Geta supports the whole household (480, cf.
Sikyonios 237).

The intriguing slave of the rich household is a traditional
figure of comedy. The *Aspis* shows some detail of how Menander
treated a rather special case. Daos opens the play with his lament
for his young master, whom he believes dead: 'I hoped that you
would become a general or a politician and give away your sister
to a worthy husband and that I should have some cessation in
old age from my long labours.' This is the hope of manumission,

---

[24] E.g. *Apistos* (*Aulularia*), *Georgos, Adelphoi B, Andria*. (A male slave plays
this part for the old widower in the *Plokion*.)

which is often expressed and sometimes attained.[25] When Smikrines shows signs of exercising his right as next of kin and marrying the girl to secure the booty, Daos immediately sets on foot an elaborate intrigue against him. But before that there are two remarkable references to slave nationality. Daos refuses to comment on Smikrines' plans, saying that he is a Phrygian and many Greek ideals seem to him extremely strange (206). A little later the cook remarks on Daos' honesty: 'A Phrygian. Nothing much to that. A coward. We Thracians are the only real men' (242). Daos is not only honest and loyal, he is extremely ingenious and, to judge from his quotations of Greek tragedy, well educated (399 ff.). It is perhaps worth noting that the other learned slave, Syros in the *Epitrepontes*, also has a name which suggests the Middle East, and two other slave intriguers, in the *Dis Exapaton* and *Perinthia*, are called Syros and Daos respectively.[26] But the slaves called Daos in the *Dyskolos*, *Eunuch* and *Perikeiromene* show no signs of coming into the same class.

Of the slaves from Thrace, Getas in the *Dyskolos* has the reputation of being 'red-hot' (183) but the only use to which he puts his intelligence is to devise the ragging of Knemon at the end of the play. It is easier to see Getas in the *Misoumenos* as a brave Thracian: he tries nobly to stand up for the interests of a difficult master, and to defend his interests against Kleinias and Demeas, although he does not always appreciate the situation correctly.

Many slaves in Menander trim their sails to the prevailing wind, most obviously Onesimos in the *Epitrepontes*, Parmenon in the *Samia* and Daos (Parmeno) in the *Eunuch*. In the household with father and son the slave is the slave of the father but allotted to the son; the son may punish him, but there is also the bigger stick of the father to fear. Most of these slaves, probably, have been the *paidagogos* or educator of the son. Very few —Lydos in the *Dis Exapaton* is the obvious example—strive openly against the son's wishes and side wholly with the father.[27] Daos in the *Aspis* remains entirely loyal to his young master,

[25] Adelphoi B 960–81; Epitrepontes 362; Perikeiromene 404; P. Oxy. 677 Cf. Andria 35 f.

[26] Cf. also P. Oxy. 11 (perhaps Paidion). We do not know the name of the intriguing slave in Menander's Andria: Terence may have adopted the name Davos from the Perinthia.

[27] Cf. also Thrasyleon, Phasma.

but the position there is peculiar: Smikrines hesitates to exert his rights, he is intensely aware of his reputation of greed, and Daos has the momentary protection of the younger brother, Chaire-stratos. In the more normal cases when the son gets into diffi-culties the slave has to decide whether to help him, usually at the expense of robbing the father. The soliloquy in which he makes his decision is a set piece, of which five examples probably by Menander survive; in only one does does the slave apparently decide against the young master.[28] The slave who decides for the young master has to accept the anger and possibly the punish-ment of the old master, but because it is comedy it will turn out all right in the end.

Menander gives a convincing picture of rich society, and of poor society in so far as it impinges on rich society. Rich and poor are more sharply divided than they would be in real life. In the end the poor are not exploited because the story has to end happily. A number of the figures are traditional figures of comedy and for that reason arouse certain expectancies in the audience: this is part of what we shall have to examine as Menander's professional code. Sometimes we seem to see Menan-der making a judgement; love matches are better than arranged matches; conduct has nothing to do with status; permissiveness is better than fear in education but may have its own dangers. This is part of the ethical code, which can best be examined now.

---

[28] *Andria* 209; *Kekryphalos*, fr. 951; P. Antinoopolis 55 a, d; P. Oxy. 11 (perhaps *Paidion*), P.S.I. 1176 (perhaps *Demiourgos*). In P. Oxy. 10 the slave seems to be abandoning his young master.

IV

The ethical code

From the time of Aristophanes' *Clouds* at any rate philosophy and philosophers are quoted, sometimes kindly, and more often unkindly, by the Greek comic poets.[1] The tradition continued through Middle Comedy, but the anthologists evidently did not find Middle Comedy anything like such a fruitful source of philosophic sentiments as New Comedy, and we have to suppose that both the audience and the poets, particularly Menander, had in the late fourth century a new interest in philosophical language and sentiments.

According to Diogenes Laertius, Menander was the pupil of Theophrastos and the friend of Demetrios of Phaleron.[2] Menander was born in 342, the same year as Epikouros, with whom he therefore served as an ephebe. But Epikouros did not found his school until 306, and Zeno founded the Stoic school five years later. Epicureanism and Stoicism could therefore be reflected only in the latest plays of Menander, and, as far as I know, no reliable reflection has been found.[3]

Demetrios of Phaleron, who was also a pupil of Theophrastos —and this may account for the suggestion that he was a friend of Menander—has his own importance because he ruled Athens from 317 to 307, and certainly his sumptuary laws showed that his principles derived from Plato: Menander's references to them are not friendly. He wrote a treatise on *Tyche* (fortune) and a few trivial coincidences between it and Menander have been noted, but there is nothing special or individual about them.[4]

Theophrastos himself, who was born about 372, was in Athens

[1] Cf. L.G.C., 34 ff., 37, 50 ff., 110 ff.
[2] Diogenes Laertius v, 36; 79 (K–T, Testimonia, Nos. 7 and 8).
[3] Cf. L.G.C., 111, 113.
[4] Cf. above ch. 1, on *gynaikonomoi*, etc. Demetrios of Phaleron *ap.* Polybius, XXIX, 21; *cf.* Menander, frs. 295, 424, K–T; Kitharistes, fr. 8; *Dyskolos* 797 ff.

before Plato died, and succeeded Aristotle as head of the Peripatetic school in 322; he did not die until about five years after
Menander. The main foundation of Peripatetic teaching under
Theophrastos, particularly in the early years, must have been
the works of Aristotle, although he gradually modified and re-
fined certain aspects in his own way. For the most part Aristotle's
Nicomachean Ethics and *Rhetoric* provide the parallels needed
for Menander, and it is a reasonable assumption that the main
views in them were known to the better educated members of his
audience.

Three of Theophrastos' own works must be mentioned because
they have been connected with Menander: *Characters*, *On Piety*,
and *On Marriage*. If the *Characters* is rightly dated to 319, it
antedates most of Menander's plays. According to Körte[5] 'the
comic poet took from his teacher not only a lively interest in
human characters, but also the method of presenting them by
a mosaic-like addition of numerous small characteristics, and it
is certainly not chance that four of his comedies are called after
characters which were treated in Theophrastos' book: *Agroikos*,
Apistos, *Deisidaimon*, *Kolax*.' This overstresses Menander's de-
pendence. The title of Theophrastos' book means something like
'Marks of quality', i.e. by what behaviour can a flatterer, for
example, be recognised. He has an underlying scheme of headings
such as personal appearance, religion, life at home, visiting and
entertaining friends, life in the market place, and public life, so
that it is in fact possible to compare the characters under these
headings.[6] Menander shows his characters in the limited number
of situations prescribed by the story, and very few of them can
be adequately described by a single Theophrastan adjective. If
we take Körte's four titles, Menander's *Agroikos* was apparently
a boy brought up on his father's farm and not a middle-aged
boor. Euclio in the *Apistos–Aulularia* certainly 'assumes that
everyone intends to wrong him 'but the only behaviour which
he shares with Theophrastos' Apistos is his refusal to lend (90 ff.).
This is also a trait of Theophrastos' Mikrologos (thrifty) and of
Menander's Knemon, the churlish man. We have not enough of
Menander's *Deisidaimon* to compare, but if he regarded breaking
his shoelace as an act of God (97 K–T), Menander did not borrow

[5] *Hermes* 64, 1929, 78.
[6] Cf. *Art and Literature in Fourth-century Athens*, 128 ff.

that instance from Theophrastos. On the other hand Strouthias in the *Kolax* (*cf.* fr. 3), like Theophrastos' Kolax, 'laughs at flat jokes' and 'cannot contain his laughter'. Outside these four plays, Smikrines in the *Sikyonios* is called oligarchic (156), and his mistrust of popular assemblies is characteristic of Theophrastos' oligarchic man (26, 3): 'We ought to get together by ourselves and plan these things, and be rid of the *agora* and the rabble'. The officiousness of Chremes in the *Heautontimoroumenos* has been compared with Theophrastos' Periergos,[7] but he has an essential element of incompetence which is lacking in Chremes.

To use behaviour to show what sort of person he is representing is part of the stock-in-trade of the comic poet, and Menander did not have to learn this from Theophrastos. If Theophrastos was working on the *Characters* when Menander was his pupil, Menander would obviously have been interested and may have given as much as he took. Once published, the book could be (and later was) used by writers of law-court speeches, ethical philosophers and educationists. So in the *Adelphoi* both Micio (821) and Demea (415) base their divergent theories of education on visible examples and signs of behaviour.[8]

Theophrastos' *On Piety*[9] says that God loves the simple sacrifice and regards the character of the giver rather than the magnitude of the gift; and he recommends the sacrifice of herbs, flowers and cakes rather than the sacrifice of animals. Three passages in Menander are related to this. In the *Dyskolos* (447 ff.) Knemon, who has seen the arrival of Kallippides' wife and the complicated arrangements for her sacrifice to Pan, rails against the use of wine and meat, of which the gods get only the uneatable parts: 'incense and cake are pious; the gods get it all when it is put on the fire'. In the *Apistos–Aulularia* (371) Euclio, who had been to market for his daughter's wedding feast, found fish and meat dear, and bought incense and flowers. In the *Methe*

---

[7] *Character* 13; 'the sort of man who promises what he will be unable to carry out', but this is not carried through in all the instances.

[8] On the use of the *Characters*, *cf. Art and Literature in Fourth-century Athens*, 132 f. The idea of 'signs' from which character can be judged is Aristotelian; *cf. Rhet.* 1383 b 31. *Cf.* also Cicero, *De amicitia*, 52, which has been claimed as Theophrastan (Regenbogen, R.E., 1486).

[9] Porphyry, *De abstinentia*, II, 14; W. Pötscher. *Theophrastos peri Eusebeias*, 1964, fr. 7.

(264 K–T) the contrast is between the ten drachmai spent on the sheep and the six thousand spent on the rest of the meal and the entertainment; 'if I were God, I would not have allowed the meat bones to be put on the altar without the eel as well'. The speaker may be a parasite or a disapproving *paidagogos*: the latter is perhaps more likely, and the passage is meant to raise a laugh. The other two passages are closer to Theophrastos: his doctrine is put forward by Knemon, who behaves like a miser, and Euclio, who is a miser.

Theophrastos [10] seems also to have been in the tradition, which we know best from Plato's *Republic*, of deploring any rite which tried to influence the gods to benefit those who paid for the rites regardless of the morality. Here again there are related Menander fragments. Two are without context: in the *Heniochos* (178 K–T) 'I have no liking for a god who walks outside with an old woman or comes into a house on a board'—a criticism of a Metragyrtes or begging priestess, and the *Thettale* presented women bringing down the moon, probably as a love charm. But in the *Hiereia* (210 K–T) it is probably the neighbour who objects to the priestess summoning, and therefore constraining, the god by cymbals, and in the *Misogynes* the disgruntled husband complains that 'we used to sacrifice five times a day, and seven servants in a ring beat their cymbals' (277 K–T). In the *Phasma* (52) it is a slave who advises the boy to let himself be purified by the women, a bogus cure for a bogus sickness. Where we can see the context, the character who takes the Theophrastan standpoint is an unsympathetic character, or at least unsympathetic in this context. Similarly Chremes is unsympathetic when he abuses his wife for her long prayers of thanksgiving for the recovery of her daughter (*Heautontimoroumenos* 879), but Menander surely approves of the simple piety of the girls at the beginning of the *Dyskolos* (36, 51) and *Apistos–Aulularia* (23), and Demeas is highly sympathetic when in his moment of agony he prays to Apollo to force him to go through with the marriage of Moschion in silence (444).

In his tract on marriage[11] Theophrastos asks whether the wise man should marry. The answer consists of all the complaints which characters in Menander raise against the wives in con-

[10] Theophrastus, fr. 146; Plato, *Rep.* 364 b ff.
[11] Known from Hieronymus, *Adv. Jovinianum*, 313 c.

ventional marriage:[12] extravagance, loquacity, tyranny. The advantages—children, care in illness, help in misfortune—which are raised in Menander against the wife-hater (276 K–T), are, according to Theophrastos, better met in other ways. Theophrastos does allow the wise man to marry if he is healthy and rich and if she is beautiful and has a good character and respectable parents, but all these requirements are seldom fulfilled in any one marriage. The criteria for choosing a wife can be found in Menander: they are the criteria of the father in the *Kitharistes* (81), the parasite Chaireas in the *Dyskolos* (65), the mother in the *Plokion* (345, perhaps also 612 K–T), Megadorus in the *Apistos–Aulularia* (239). Here Menander is not so much saying that they are wrong as that they are irrelevant; the young men concerned have all fallen in love without considering them.

These works of Theophrastos were probably all popular rather than professional, and it is extremely likely that Theophrastos himself was drawing on Menander and earlier comedy in composing them. The audience would probably recognise the sentiments, when they heard them in Menander's plays, as Theophrastan or at least philosophical. They would feel that the old men or slaves who voiced them were making some pretence to education thereby, just as they did when they quoted tragedy. How funny they seemed would depend largely on the amount of sympathy one felt for the particular character at the particular moment. When Onesimos is making fun of Smikrines at the end of the *Epitrepontes* (726)[13] he starts from Euripides' *Melanippe* and proceeds through garbled Plato, and this is obviously meant to be funny; he is using his education to good purpose, just as Daos uses his knowledge of tragedy to convince Smikrines in the *Aspis* (401). The old man in the *Hypobolimaios* (416 K–T), probably the old man who turns out to be the father of the supposititious son, elaborates the common sentiment of Greeks in misery—the shorter life is the better—with reminiscences of Aristotle's Protrepticus and so parades his education. In a similar situation Kraton in the *Theophoroumene* (fr. 1) makes a philosophical comparison between the life of men and animals.

---

[12] Cf. above, p. 36. Cf. also fr. 581 K–T, spoken by a father.
[13] Euripides, fr. 506; Plato, *Rep.* 619 c 4; 620 d; 379 c. Cf. also fr. 714 K–T, probably also a slave.

Knemon's apology for his life (*Dyskolos* 742) imagines a world
not unlike the state of mankind after the flood according to
Plato, and some of the audience will have known their *Laws*
(679):[14] whether it is played for laughs or as a sympathetic bit
of unpractical idealism would depend very much on the actor.
My point here is that all these philosophical quotations and
reminiscences are Menander's way of shaping a particular situation so that the audience can interpret it; they tell us nothing
about Menander's own views.

There are some places, however, where Menander does seem
to be expressing a serious view, and it is reasonable to ask there
whether it is also a Peripatetic view. I have argued that he preferred the love match to the arranged marriage. The clearest
statements about marriage are in the *Andria* and the *Dyskolos*.
In the *Andria* (560) the father hopes that his son will easily
extricate himself from what he thinks of as love of a *hetaira* if
he is bound by custom and marriage with a citizen.[15] He hopes,
although he does not so express it, that the right arranged
marriage may grow into a love marriage, and the marriages of
the *Epitrepontes* and *Daktylios* show that Menander knew it
could happen. In the *Dyskolos* (764) Gorgias accepts the single-
minded devotion with which Sostratos is prepared to dig all
day like a labourer as evidence that he will be able to endure all
the chances of fortune. Aristotle saw marriage as a species of
friendship (N.E. 1162 a 20): 'Men do not only live together for
the production of children but for the general purposes of life . . .
There seems to be both use and pleasure in this friendship. There
would be excellence if they were equitable people.' Sostratos has
shown himself equitable in the *Dyskolos*, and Simo hopes that
two liberal-minded people growing accustomed to one another,
will produce this kind of friendship. Pamphile in the *Epitrepontes*

[14] On fr. 416 see appendix II, below, p. 152. Add Megadorus' ideal of
marriage between rich and poor in *Aulularia* 162, which echoes Aristotle,
Pol. 1266 b 2. The contrast in *Theophoroumene* (fr. 1) between right standards
in dealing with criminals and wrong standards in human affairs appears again
in Theophrastos, *On Marriage*, 313 f.

[15] Custom: cf. *Samia* 625 (in a love match). Marriage with a citizen is what
the father means by *liberali matrimonio*, but the adjective also means 'liberal'
(cf. below), and the Greek equivalent is used of his wife by the young man
in P. Ant. 15 (*Daktylios*), with which compare *Dyskolos* 764, and by Sostratos
of his beloved in *Dyskolos* 201, 387.

(600) said that she had come to share Charisios' life and ought not to run away from his chance misfortune.[16]

In the love matches the young (unlike some of their elders in similar situations) accept their responsibility and in spite of the obstacles go through with it. This humanity Aristotle associates particularly with the young: 'they choose to do what is honourable in preference to what is expedient. They are guided by character rather than by calculation. The expedient results from calculation but the honourable from virtue' (*Rhet.* 1389 a 34). The obstacles also are phrased in an Aristotelian way; Menander, as has frequently been pointed out, remembers the Aristotelian scale of damages (N.E. 1135 b 11)—misfortunes, where the doer is not responsible; errors, where the doer is ignorant of some essential fact; misdemeanours, where the doer is motivated by anger and other emotions; premeditated crime. Sometimes he personifies words from this passage as prologue speakers, sometimes he uses the terminology or similar terminology in key passages.

Ignorance (or misunderstanding) is the prologue figure of the *Perikeiromene*; ignorance that Moschion was Glykera's brother made Polemon fly into a rage and cut off Glykera's hair; the rage makes the act a misdemeanour on the scale, but it was not premeditated, as Pataikos points out to Glykera (316).[17] Orge (anger) spoke the prologue in Menander's first play, and Methe (drunkenness; which Aristotle would certainly classify among 'other emotions') in another early play, so that here again a misdemeanour was committed.[18] The prologue figure of the *Daktylios* was almost certainly Bia (violence, in the sense of rape);[19] the misdemeanour was the man's rape of his wife before marriage. The verb for 'misdemeanour' is actually used in a line of New Comedy, possibly by Menander—'how noble a wife I wrong, the wretch'; from here it has been restored, but mistakenly I think, of Charisios in the *Epitrepontes* (571);[20] what Charisios says, rather disingenuously, is 'What a noble wife I married and am

16 Cf. also *Adelphoi* A? (P. Didot A and *Stichus* 133); fr. 572 K–T.
17 Cf. M. Tierney, P.R.I.A., 43, 1936, 248. Cf. fr. 359, *Rhapizomene*.
18 Cf. *Apistos, Aulularia* 792; *Epitrepontes* 296; *Samia* 339 (Demeas' account of Moschion).
19 Cf. *Epitrepontes* 277 (Onesimos' account of Charisios).
20 Kock, C.A.F., adesp. 221, cf. K–T, II, p. 280. It might, of course, fit the *Daktylios*.

now unfortunate.' But he rightly uses 'misfortune' of Pamphile herself (594). Who was the prologue figure of the *Epitrepontes* is unknown.

The switching of shields which causes Daos to bring back the false report of Kleostratos' death in the *Aspis* is completely out of Daos' control, so that as far as he is concerned it may be thought of as a misfortune, and Fortune (Tyche) is the natural figure to explain it in the prologue.[21] We do not know whether it was Tyche who explained the similar switching of swords between Krateia's brother and the man killed by Thrasonides. The word 'misfortune' occurs once in a very badly preserved monologue of Thrasonides (*Misoumenos* 370), and it may refer to the supposed killing of the brother; it is not clear whether it is Thrasonides' word or whether he is quoting Krateia.

Ignorance in the *Perikeiromene* not only explains the obstacle but also represents herself as the cause of its removal. Two other personifications, Boetheia (help to an injured innocent)[22] and Elenchos (examination) get their names only from the process of removing the obstacles. Boetheia speaks the prologue in the *Synaristosai*, where the girl who was exposed as a baby is finally restored to her parents. Elenchos (717 K–T) may, I suspect have been the prologue speaker of the *Sikyonios*: examination of credentials bulks large in that play; when he gets his credentials Stratophanes can claim to be an Athenian citizen and marry the girl, when she also has established her identity and found her father.

In three plays we know that a god spoke the prologue. Pan in the *Dyskolos* makes Sostratos fall in love with Knemon's daughter to reward her for her piety. Lar (in Greek probably

---

[21] Ross, *Aristotle*, 78, defines *Tyche* in Aristotle as 'the unforeseen meeting of two chains of rigorous causation'; cf. *Perik.* 372; *Eun.* 134. This is more often *automaton* in Menander: *Sam.* 55, 163; *Dysk.* 545; 241, 395 K–T. Theophrastos probably allowed more scope to *Tyche* (Walzer, *N. Phil. Unters.*, VII, 1929, 222 f.), and this would fit her role in *Aspis*, cf. also *Koneiazomenai* 13 f., *Eunuch* 1046, 417 K–T.

[22] The verb is used of Syros' defence of the baby's rights to its trinkets in *Epitrepontes* 180. Aristotle, N.E. 1126 b 5, approves, as a mean between the mild man and the angry man, being angry where it is right to be angry. This covers Syros and such other disinterested actions as Lyconides' unconditional restitution of the pot of gold to Euclio (*Apistos–Aulularia*, Argument II), and Gorgias' disinterested action in rescuing Knemon although Knemon had never 'helped' him (*Dyskolos* 723 ff.).

Hestia) in the *Apistos–Aulularia* has made Euclio discover the pot of gold so that ultimately his pious daughter will have a dowry. It is a safe conjecture that the Hero, who speaks the prologue speech of the *Heros*, was somehow responsible for Pheidias falling in love with the poor girl Plangon. This use of the gods is also Aristotelian, since he says in the *Rhetoric* (1386 b 15) that we ascribe righteous indignation to the gods.

The prologue figures have to convey information, and because this is comedy they are optimistic. It is interesting that Menander uses Aristotelian concepts like Ignorance in this capacity. Another clue to his thought is his use of the term 'Greek'. If an Athenian says that something is Greek, it is likely to be something of which he approves. The word is used three times. In the *Perikeiromene* (428) Pataikos says to Glykera, 'I like your "Now[23] I will be reconciled"; to accept amends when you are successful is the sign of a Greek character.' Glykera has found her father, and therefore has no further need of Polemon, but at that point she forgives him. Charisios in the *Epitrepontes* (578) calls his refusal to forgive his wife 'barbarian (i.e. unGreek) and pitiless'. The linking of 'pity' and 'Greek' comes in the second passage (*Misoumenos* 315): Getas says, 'I would not have ransomed her. It is Greek and happens everywhere. But it is only right to pity those who pity you in return!' Ransom here is a Greek custom based on pity, and Thrasonides has consented to the ransom of Krateia. The third passage has no context: 'Greeks are men of judgement and do nothing without deliberation' (762 K–T).

This ideal of rational action with an inclination to mercy is what Aristotle calls equity (*epieikeia*. Errors are part of human nature according to both Menander[24] and Aristotle (N.E. 1111 b 1), and the equitable man may therefore forgive them (*Rhet.* 1374 b 10; N.E. 1143 a 21). 'He does not demand everything that is due to him but is prepared to accept less' (N.E. 1137 b 2, 1138 a 1). His conduct is therefore rationally determined, with an inclination towards mercy. In the Aristotelian scheme (1126

---

[23] I owe this reading to E. W. Handley, Cf. now O.C.T.

[24] E.g. *Epitrepontes* 588 ff.; 680 K–T; *Adelphi* 471. So Micio forgives Aeschinus' 'wild oats', *Adelphi* 115 ff. But the boundary is narrow between this and the excessive forgiving of the mild man (N.E. 1126 a 1), cf. *Adelphi* 986. Cf. also with 'equity' 231 K–T.

b 11) the equitable man is a mean between the churlish man on the one side and the obsequious man and the flatterer on the other. Menander named one play *Dyskolos* (churlish) and another *Kolax* (flatterer).

Pataikos himself shows the discrimination of the equitable man when he points out to Polemon that Glykera was not his legal wife and therefore he has no rights over her and cannot exercise summary justice on Moschion as an adulterer (*Perikeiromene* 236). Stratophanes in the *Sikyonios* (236) not only gives up his claim to be legally responsible for the girl but voluntarily gives her the slave Dromon to support her, although Dromon was legally his property.[25]

Aristotle's equitable man does not consider 'of what sort a man is now but of what sort a man was always or for the most part' (*Rhet.* 1374 b 15). This is exactly how Demeas in the *Samia* (272, 343)[26] defends Moschion when he thinks that he has been seduced by Chrysis and how Sostratos in the *Dis Exapaton* (100) defends Moschos when he thinks that he has been seduced by Bacchis. It is amusing that both of them equitably forgive the young man (who is in fact innocent) by accusing the *hetaira* (who is also innocent). They use, although they both ought to know better, the conventional stereotype of the *hetaira's* behaviour, in just the same way as the old fathers who oppose a love match.

Menander himself applies the standard of permanent character also to such unpopular figures as the rich *hetaira* and the soldier, and so produces the sympathetic figures of Chrysis in the *Samia*, Thais in the *Eunuch*, and the soldier heroes of the *Perikeiromene*, *Sikyonios* and *Misoumenos*. The text is in a fragment (475 K–T),[27] which probably comes from the *Heautontimoroumenos* (77): 'I count no one alien if he is good. The nature of all is the same, but the affinity is made by character.' If the ascription is right, in the mouth of Chremes it is a supererogatory platitude

---

[25] His action is near the disinterested actions quoted in n. 22.

[26] Cf. also 709 f.; *Heautontimoroumenos* 282 ff. Agnoia in *Perikeiromene* 43–4 notes Polemon's swing away from his normal character: cf. Euclio in *Apistos–Aulularia*, Menedemus in *Heautontimoroumenos*, Phaedria in *Eunuch* 225. (Cf. below, n. 30.)

[27] Cf. 611, 612 K–T, the latter probably from *Plokion*. Cf. also Daos in the *Aspis* as an abnormal intriguing slave: K. Gaiser, *Das Schild*, 18; D. B. Lombard, *Acta classica*, 14, 1971, 143.

to cover officiousness. But it is a good Greek sentiment which goes back to the fifth century, and comes very near to a sentence of Aristotle (N.E. 1155 a 21): 'a man could see in his wanderings the affinity and friendship of all humanity'. The idea of affinity is extended from the inner circle of the family, where Gorgias in the *Dyskolos* (239) recognises its power, to embrace the whole of mankind (N.E. 1165 a 30).[28]

'The truly good and sensible man bears decorously all that fortune sends and pursues the most honourable course that is open to his resources' (N.E. 1101 a 1). The word 'decorous' is used in exactly the same context in a fragment of Menander (634 K–T). It is the classical exhortation to *sophrosyne*, which turns up in many forms. In the *Georgos* (fr. 2) Kleainetos tells Gorgias that excessive anger when you are wronged is merely a demonstration to everybody of smallness of soul. The phrase can be explained by Aristotle's description of the great-souled man as not being excessively grieved by misfortunes (N.E. 1124 a 15).[29] And it is evidently in the same sense that Thrasonides has been accused of smallness of soul in the *Misoumenos* (356), presumably by Getas. The correlative of the excessive anger of the poor man is the *hybris* of the rich man, which is what Gorgias in the *Dyskolos* (272–98) sees in Sostratos' approach to the girl (cf. *Rhet.* 1390 b 33). The rich man is in a dangerous position, and his riches may be upset by a swift change of fortune (*Georgos*, fr. 1), which is the argument that Sostratos uses against his father to persuade him to use his wealth on the double marriage in the *Dyskolos* (797).[30]

The Aristotelian self-indulgent man (*akolastos*) seems to be alluded to in two rather different contexts. He suffers more than he should when he does not gain his pleasures (N.E. 1118 b 30); so a slave tells his love-sick master that as his misfortune is moderate he should bear his suffering with appropriate moderation (740 K–T, very like *Phasma* 50 f.). In describing the *akolastos* Aristotle makes a distinction between 'natural' or 'general' and 'superadded' desires. Menander has this distinction in a fragment

[28] Extended by Theophrastos to include the animals. Porphyry, *De abstinentia* II, 3, 85.

[29] Cf. 519 K–T and *Rhet.* 1389 a 9.

[30] Newly acquired riches are particularly dangerous, *Rhet.* 1391 a 15; Menander 616 K–T. Cf. also Euclio and the soldiers; but Stratophanes (like Polemon and Thrasonides) escaped the danger (*Sikyonios*, fr. 3).

(620 K–T), perhaps from the old man's philosophy in the *Hypo-bolimaios*: animals have only the evils that nature gives them; our competitive desires are all 'evils superadded to nature'.[31]

Aristotle passes from self-indulgence to liberality in the sense of the proper conduct of a free man, which is a key-word of *Adelphoi* B. Liberality is a mean between prodigality (*asotia*) and illiberality or meanness. Meanness is incurable: it is the result of old age and other weaknesses (N.E. 1121 b 12). This is the text for the various mean old men in Menander—Smikrines in the *Aspis*, Demea in *Adelphoi* B, etc. In the *Rhetoric* (1389 b 22) Aristotle adds, as characteristic of the old, unwillingness to trust anybody (Euclio in the *Apistos–Aulularia*), calculation of the expedient (Smikrines in the *Epitrepontes*), absence of sense of shame (perhaps the old men in love may be included here: *Dis Exapaton, Synaristosai*, and *Adelphoi* A).

The prodigals are divided into two kinds (1121 a 19–b 10). They may be checked by growing up or by training and so reach the mean of liberality. But if they are unchecked, then they become self-indulgent and are incurable: this is what Demea thinks has happened to Micio in *Adelphoi* B (986). The first kind of prodigal is the basis of Micio's theory of education, as we have seen. He thinks that Aeschinus can be given his head and can be guided by sense of shame and liberality (57).[32] Demea, on the other hand, (411) based education on fear and example.[33] The distinction between sense of shame (which is particularly characteristic of the young) and fear as factors in education is also found in Aristotle (N.E. 1179 b 7): the many as distinct from the liberal 'do not listen to a sense of shame but only to fear, and do not keep from vice because it is disgraceful but because of the penalties; they live by passion and pursue this sort of pleasure and the means to it ... they have no notion of honour or true pleasure'—which is very like Daos' description of Smikrines in the *Aspis* (326) and Chremes' description of the old Corinthian woman in the *Heautontimoroumenos* (642). But Micio is concerned only with the education of the liberal and so he can

---

[31] Cf. 144, 251 K–T; *Epitrepontes* 588 f.

[32] Cf. 598 K; *Andria* 262; *Bacchides* 416; *Anepsioi* I. The mild father: 608 K–T; *Adelphi* 707; *Andria* 262; *Eunuch* 1048; *Synepheboi* I; cf. Aristotle, N.E. 1180 b 3–15.

[33] Cf. 521 K–T; *Andria* 54; *Heautontimoroumenos* 210; *Bacchides* 424.

trust to Aeschinus' sense of shame. Demea has treated his son as if he did not belong to this class, and so he gets the result that he deserves.

Again and again in reading Menander we are reminded of Aristotle's *Ethics* and *Rhetoric*, particularly in the passages like Micio's theory of education or Demeas' defence of Moschion in the *Samia*, where he seems to be saying something serious, or as serious as comedy permits. Aristotle's brief and epigrammatic description of the equitable man—his discrimination, his willingness to forgive, his attachment to real values, his humanity and his determination to defend the rights of humanity—gave a formula and a terminology, which the audience would be able to recognise and interpret; Menander embodies the formula in real situations peopled by individuals.

V

The tragic code

The fifth-century tragic poets, Aeschylus, Sophocles and Euripides, occupied a special position in Menander's lifetime which overshadowed their contemporaries and successors. From 386 one of their plays was revived every year at the city Dionysia, and for the only three years for which we have information, 341, 340, 339, the play revived was by Euripides. In Menander's childhood the special position of the three classical tragic poets was still further emphasised: as part of his programme to restore morale after the defeat of Chaeronea in 338, Lykourgos rebuilt the theatre of Dionysos in stone, set up in it bronze statues of the three poets and caused an official text to be made of their plays. Aristotle had already focused attention on Sophocles and Euripides in the first draft of the *Poetics*, which he wrote before he left Athens in 347. Aristotle returned in 335 and, as far as we know, lectured on poetic theory till the time of his death.

Menander and his audience could see classical tragedy every year at the city Dionysia and almost certainly also at the rural Dionysia in the demes. Classical tragedy had not only become a classic but was also linked firmly with Aristotle. Aristotle both wrote the theory of classical tragedy in the *Poetics* and used examples from classical tragedy to illustrate his points, particularly in the *Ethics* and the *Rhetoric*, the two books to which, as we have seen, Menander could appeal and expect to be understood. At the same time Menander was composing in the comic tradition, which had itself been reacting to tragedy since its inception. Probably we cannot hope to disentangle these three strands—tragedy seen on the stage, tragedy seen through Aristotelian spectacles, tragedy taken over second-hand from earlier comedy—and it would be unrealistic and not particularly profitable to try. And, as far as comedy is concerned, two new factors have to be considered. The first is the new respect for clasical tragedy; criticism in the Aristophanic sense is unlikely. The second is the new decent costume of comedy; when comic characters look like ordinary Athenians, parody in the Aristophanic sense is much less likely than when their costume was padded and obscene.

A number of the armature situations of New Comedy were first put on the stage in classical tragedy: rape at a festival (Euripides, *Auge*),[1] birth of a child in the course of the play (Euripides, *Skyrioi*), supposititious children (Euripides, *Melanippe Desmotis*), recognition of exposed child (Euripides, *Melanippe Sophe*), of brother and sister (the Elektra plays), or of parent and children (Sophocles, *Tyro*; Euripides, *Antiope, Alkmaion in Corinth*)— and the recognition may occur early in the play (Euripides, *Electra*) or at the climax of the play (Sophocles, *Electra*) or more perfunctorily at the end (Euripides, *Ion*). It is obvious that rape, birth before marriage could be formally arranged, and the provision of a male heir by taking in an unwanted male baby were common fourth-century events for which no tragic parallel was needed. But on three occasions at least Menander invited the audience to observe the parallel with tragedy. In the *Heros* (83) Myrrhine, according to Körte's certain interpretation, asked whether her raper did not respect the shrine of the hero, replies, 'Did Herakles respect Athena Alea?'—the scene of his rape of Auge. Secondly, in the *Androgynos*, in which a child is born in the course of the play, the youth had passed the guard of the father by dressing up as a girl, which was what in fact Achilles had done in the *Skyrioi*. Thirdly, in the *Epitrepontes* the name scene in which Smikrines arbitrates between two shepherds as to

---

[1] Rape was common but in Menander it often takes place at a festival or, exceptionally, before a festival: (1) Adonis: *Samia, Phasma*; (2) Artemis: *Epitrepontes, Kitharistes*; (3) Athena: *Hypobolimaios, Arrhephoros*; (4) Demeter: *Apistos–Aulularia, Titthe*; (5) Dionysos: *Perinthia, Synaristosai*. I suspect that the festival is chosen to be nine months before the birth of the child, which was assumed to take place either shortly before (*Epitrepontes, Samia*) or during (*Apistos–Aulularia*) or well after (*Synaristosai*) the Lenaia if the play was first produced at the Lenaia, or the city Dionysia if the play was first produced at the city Dionysia. Possibilities are:

Lenaia: *Samia* (Adonia), *Epitrepontes* (if Tauropolia, like Brauronia, was in the spring), *Perinthia* (city Dionysia).
City Dionysia: *Apistos, Titthe* (both Skirophoria), *Arrephoros* (Arrhetophoria), *Hypobolimaios* (Little Panathenaia was *after* the rape).

whether the child, not yet recognised as his grandson, shall have its recognition tokens or not, is taken over from Euripides' *Alope*. The scene is completely modernised and no reference is made to the *Alope*. It is possible that here Menander did not mean his audience to be conscious of his source. But the parallel to the story of Achilles is inescapable in the *Androgynos*, and Myrrhine herself points the parallel in the *Heros*. The audience must interpret these references as meaning that these situations in comedy are to be taken seriously, as in tragedy.

Recognition scenes are rather different. They are absolutely necessary to produce formal marriage (most plays) or reunion of estranged husband and wife (*Daktylios, Epitrepontes*) at the end of the play. Yet they cannot have happened often in everyday life. Tragedy provided the necessary models. We know that the recognition scene of Sophocles' *Tyro* was parodied in an old comedy, and it seems very likely that recognition scenes first entered comedy as parodies of tragedy: Euboulos parodies Euripides' *Auge* before 348. But we have enough evidence to show that Middle Comedy also included recognition scenes of contemporaries in its intrigue plays. But before Menander began to write Aristotle had emphasised the importance of recognition scenes in tragedy and classified the means of recognition (*Poetics*, XVI), and this may partly explain why Menander's recognition scenes often remind us of tragedy. Even if the recognition does not avert death, as in the *Ion* or *Iphigenia in Tauris*, or lead to lyrical transports of joy as in both these plays and many others, it is a serious moment because directly or indirectly it will lead to the required formal marriage, and an allusion to tragedy underlines the seriousness.

The placing of the recognition scenes early, at the climax, or late corresponds roughly to Aristotle's distinction between recognitions with 'a reversal of fortune' and recognitions for assurance. I should prefer a threefold division: (1) early, leading gradually to 'a reversal of fortune', (2) at the climax, leading swiftly to a reversal, (3) late, for assurance. In Menander the recognition in the *Daktylios* starts in the first scene; in the *Epitrepontes* Onesimos recognises Charisios' ring among the baby's trinkets in the second act, and in the *Misoumenos* Demeas recognises his son's sword in the gap between the second and third acts; in each case the recognition starts a long chain of events.

The recognition of Glykera and Moschion in the *Perikeiromene* and of Stratophanes in the *Sikyonios* both take place in the climactic fourth act, and after that developments are swift. I think that the late recognitions of Kichesias in the *Sikyonios* and in the *Eunuch*, *Andria* and *Heautontimoroumenos* can be regarded as recognitions for assurance.

Aristotle distinguishes in tragedy and epic recognitions by signs, recognitions invented by the poet, recognitions by memory, recognitions by reasoning, recognitions by false reasoning, recognitions arising from probable happenings. All these can be found in Menander, including the second if we admit that all recognitions in comedy are invented by the poet. The signs used by Menander occur in classical tragedy—the ring (*Daktylios*, *Epitrepontes*, etc.) in Euripides' *Auge*, mixed tokens, including parts of drapery (*Perikeiromene*, etc.) in the *Ion*, the sword (*Misoumenos*) in the first *Hippolytos*. Pataikos in the *Perikeiromene*, seeing Glykera's patterned robe, remembers his wife's weaving, Moschion in the same play reasons from what he has heard and what he is seeing that he must be the son of Pataikos. In the *Misoumenos* Demeas reasons falsely from the sight of his son's sword that Thrasonides has killed his son, just as Theseus in the first *Hippolytos* reasoned falsely from the fact that Phaidra was pretending to commit suicide with Hippolytos' sword that Hippolytos had raped her. Most of Menander's recognition scenes arise from probable happenings in the same sense as in the *Oedipus Tyrannus*, Aristotle's example.

Menander's recognition scenes make such a good commentary on Aristotle's chapter in the *Poetics* that the conclusion is inevitable that Menander knew the Aristotelian classification, whether from Theophrastos' lectures or in some other way. This discussion, therefore, belongs also to the chapter on Menander's dramatic technique. It is placed here because the concrete examples that Menander could see existed already in comedy and tragedy. The treatment in the *Poetics* is concerned only with tragedy, and the outside references that we can discern in Menander are to tragedy. By these references Menander must have wanted his audience to perceive that his characters were seriously affected by the situation.

One way of alerting the audience was by a quotation of tragedy that they would recognise. But where he did not want to play on their memories of a particular tragic line or even to cast the words in recognisably tragic language, Menander could also use metre to tell his audience that he had some special intention. The iambic trimeter consists of three metra, each consisting of anceps: long–short–long syllables. Comic trimeters differ from tragic trimeters in three main ways,[2] (1) tragic trimeters have a word break between either the anceps and the first long or between the short and the second long of the second metron. Sophocles occasionally divides the trimeter differently for special effects; *Philoctetes* has four instances in 1,078 trimeters, but Aristophanes' *Acharnians* has eighty-seven in 810 and Menander's *Epitrepontes* seventy-four in 542. (2) If the tragic trimeter ends with a word or word group of three syllables (or five, if the opening long is resolved) the preceding anceps must be short unless it is an independent monosyllable or (very rarely) tied in by elision; in Aristophanes' *Acharnians* this restriction is neglected 111 times, in Menander's *Epitrepontes* 110 times. (3) In tragedy the first anceps can be resolved into two shorts, with certain restrictions; the other two anceps syllables and even the short syllables are occasionally resolved to admit proper names. In comedy there are no restrictions: thus, if we leave out resolution of the first anceps as common to tragedy and comedy, in the *Acharnians* seventy anceps syllables and 181 short syllables are resolved, and in the *Epitrepontes* thirty-one anceps and ninety-three shorts are resolved, while in the late and free *Orestes* Euripides resolves anceps six times and short twelve times for proper names in a total length of 1,165 iambics against the 810 of the *Acharnians* and 542 of *Epitrepontes*. These figures show clearly that in these three characteristics Menander and Aristophanes stand together as opposed to the tragedians. The figures for the two comic poets are (1) Menander 13·6 lines per 100 without normal caesura, Aristophanes 10·7; (2) Menander 20·3 lines per 100, neglecting the restriction on long anceps before trisyllable ending, Aristophanes 13·7; (3) Menander 22·8 resolved anceps and short per 100 lines, Aristophanes 30·9. Probably the

---

[2] The statistics which follow are derived from Descroix, *Le Trimètre iambique*, Paris, 1931. Cf. for (1) caesurae, 261 ff., (2) Porson's law, 318 ff., (3) resolutions of anceps and short, 115 ff. Descroix used the Budé text of Aristophanes and the 1912 Körte text of Menander: hence the figure of 542 lines for *Epitrepontes*. To keep all figures consistent in this preliminary survey it seemed better not to recalculate the *Epitrepontes* with the 1937 Körte text.

modern ear perceives the greatly increased number of short
syllables brought in by resolved anceps and short more clearly
than absence of caesura or presence of long anceps at the beginning of the third metron, and it is this that makes Menander's
verse appear more formal than Aristophanes'.

The listener expects the freer verse of comedy. What may
alert him is the stricter verse of tragedy. But over 50 per cent of
Menander's lines in the plays where we can check conform to the
metre of tragedy: the figures are: *Samia* 57 per cent, *Dyskolos* 53
per cent, *Perikeiromene* 61 per cent, *Aspis* 61·5 per cent, *Epitrepontes* 56 per cent. The figures have no chronological significance: the high figures in the less well preserved *Aspis* and
Perikeiromene are due to the chance preservation of long 'tragic'
sequences. To appreciate the reaction of the audience one should
probably make a more rigorous definition of 'tragic'. If, for
instance, the number of 'tragic' lines containing resolved long
syllables in the *Epitrepontes* is compared with the similar figures
for Euripides' *Orestes* and Sophocles' *Philoctetes*, the percentages
are: *Epitrepontes* 36 per cent, *Philoctetes* 12 per cent, and
Orestes 39 per cent. Menander's 'tragic' lines are much freer
than Sophocles', though he does not go so far as Euripides at his
most free. But it is probably safe to say that the audience is aware
of a heightening of tone if three or more successive lines are
'tragic', particularly if there is also a reminiscence of tragic language or situation. A brief examination of the better preserved
plays will give some idea of Menander's practice and his purposes.

In the *Samia* Moschion's opening speech has one patch of
tragic metre where he describes the rape (45–51), and here he is
deadly serious. Then the dialogue where Chrysis agrees to keep
the baby is serious (76–85).[3] Demeas' two big speeches in the third
act, where he suspects that Moschion is the father of the baby
and resolves nevertheless to go through with the marriage, have
well above the average of 'tragic' lines—73 per cent compared to
57 per cent. The first (206) is mainly narrative; the simile at the
beginning is in tragic style and the description of the old nurse
may recall the *Choephoroe* (743 ff.), and the situation is tragic:

---

[3] Chrysis is serious here, and we tend to see Menander's women in serious
situations: the Pamphile–Habrotonon scene (*Epitrepontes* 532–57) has only
seven comic lines in twenty-five. Cf. perhaps also Myrrhine in the *Georgos*,
22 ff., Knemon's daughter and Simike in the *Dyskolos* (see below). (Papyrus
Didot A has only two comic lines in forty-four.)

Demeas imagines himself to be in the position of Proitos or Amyntor. In the second (325) he starts in fury with a quotation of Euripides' *Oidipous*; the argument that character is a sounder criterion of judgement than immediate behaviour is, as noted in the last chapter, Aristotelian, but comes very close to a fragment of Euripides' *Phoinix* (812 N), and his final self-admonition recalls the Herakles of the *Trachiniae* (976). The audience is meant to see clearly that Demeas believes himself to be in a tragic situation.[4] In the fourth act Nikeratos in his fury compares Moschion to Tereus, Oidipous, Thyestes and Phoinix (495), and Demeas later calms him with the story of Danae and the golden rain (589); nothing in the metre suggests tragedy—it is trochaic without the restrictions observed by tragic trochaic. The heroic examples are a form of comic exaggeration. But in the fifth act again Moschion's first speech, particularly the first twelve lines (616 ff.), shows his seriousness by tragic metre.[5]

In the *Dyskolos* the percentage of tragic lines is slightly lower than in the *Samia*, and no character gets himself into a tragic situation like Demeas. Pan's speech is in comic metre, like the speeches of Agnoia in the *Perikeiromene* and Tyche in the *Aspis* (only Agnoia heightens the tone a little towards the end, 42 f.).[6] Knemon's rather imprecise reference to Perseus and the Gorgon's head (153) is comic exaggeration. When he has gone the first three lines of Sostratos are in tragic metre (179); he is completely serious, and this seriousness runs on into the meeting with the girl (185–93).[7] The seriousness of Gorgias (271) when he attacks Sostratos is very clearly marked by metre and carries over

[4] Cf. perhaps where Alcesimarchus (like the Sophoclean Ajax) threatens suicide in the *Cistellaria*: 527 with *Aj.* 480, 639 with *Aj.* 831–2, 854; 641 with *Aj.* 815, 649 with *Aj.* 579, etc. But this is also a visual reminiscence like the angry exit, *Cist.* 528, with S. *Ant.* 766.

[5] Other instances of the serious young man (not mentioned below): *Georgos* 12–17, *Dis Exapaton* 18–22. Cf. also *Andria/Perinthia* 640 with E. *Hipp.* 1297. The serious old man (like Demeas in *Samia*): *Theophoroumene*, fr. 1; 416 K–T, with S. *O.C.* 1224, E. *Hel.* 906. And rather differently *Georgos*, fr. 1, with E. *Tro.* 1203 f.; *Adelphi* 739 with S. fr. 947 P.

[6] Cf. also *Sikyonios* 1 ff.

[7] Cf. E. W. Handley, *Entretiens Hardt*, 16, 1970, 21, with a possible allusion to Euripides' *Electra*, Electra's entrance with the hydria, a visual reminiscence, cf. n .4. The girl's 'Alas, wretched am I in my misery' is tragic and is repeated with variations by *Simike* 620; *Samia* 398, 568 (Chrysis), 245, 260 (the nurse); *Misoumenos* 247 (Krateia); *Epitrepontes* 353 (Pamphile); *Heros* 69 (Myrrhine); *Georgos* 49 (Myrrhine).

into Sostratos' answer later in the scene (382). Knemon ends his
duel with Sikon with twelve lines in tragic metre (503 ff.).
Neither language nor situation is tragic, but the regularity of the
metre would add to the comedy.[8] Similarly, when Knemon has
fallen into the well, the beginning of the act with Simike and
Sikon is in tragic metre. Sostratos has a moment of high seriousness as he describes himself and the girl standing at the top of
the well (672) and again later when he argues with his father
(809 f.). The trochaic tetrameters of Knemon's apology are comic
in metrical technique (712 ff.).[9]

In the *Perikeiromene* (276 ff.) Moschion's despairing speech
after he has been left alone in the *andron* has well below the
average of comic lines (32 per cent), and this is the seriousness
of a young man in trouble. The recognition scene[10] (338 ff.) has
only six recognisably comic lines out of 59, and four of them are
spoken by Moschion, the onlooker, whose language is prevail-
ingly prosaic, whereas Glykera and Pataikos have three reminiscences of Euripides.[11] To metre and language Menander adds the
form of tragic dialogue: for forty lines (341 ff.) no line is divided
between two speakers. Here I think Menander is saying that one
should take this scene as seriously as the recognition scene in the
Helen or the *Ion*. Certainly on the modern stage and in English
it stands out as a moving and dramatic scene because of its strict-
ness.

The *Aspis*, which shares the low overall percentage of comic
lines with the *Perikeiromene*, has three patches of 'tragedy'.
Daos begins the play with his lament for the supposedly dead
Kleostratos; the first nineteen lines are all in tragic metre and
have reminiscences of Sophocles' *Electra* and *Trachiniae*, of
Euripides' *Hercules Furens* and *Helen*.[12] This dead-serious tone is

---

[8] O.C.T. transposition in 505 spoils the run and is wrong. The reason for
'tragic' metre cannot always be seen. Why, for instance, are there only two
comic lines in *Theophoroumene* 17–30 (report of Parmenon and Lysias' plan)?

[9] The trochaics disregard the Porson–Havet law. But whether Knemon is
wheeled on or brought on the *ekkyklema*, he plays a dying tragic hero and
in the opening iambics 692 recalls E. *Hipp.* 1454 (cf. Handley *ad loc.* and 758).

[10] Cf. F. H. Sandbach, *Entretiens Hardt*, 16, 1970, 126 f.

[11] Sehrt, *De Menandro Euripidis imitatore*, 59 f. (to which I am much in-
debted for the parallels noted) compares 358 with fr. 484 N; 379 with *Tro.*
88; 380 with *H.F.* 631, 1484. In E. *Alkmaion in Corinth* son and daughter
were recognised both by their father and by each other.

[12] C. Austin *ad loc.* compares S. *El.* 1127, 872, 1149; *Trach.* 81; E. *H.F.* 1099;
Hel. 412.

what Menander wants to hit the audience at the opening. The second patch (284 ff.) is Chaireas' speech when he has discovered both that Kleostratos is dead and that he will not be able to marry his sister: this is the young man in distress again. The third patch is entirely different: it is the deception scene, when Daos adds verisimilitude to the supposed fatal illness of Chaire-stratos by quoting a number of tragic lines (399 ff.). This is comic exaggeration used for a special purpose.

The *Misoumenos*, like the *Aspis*, starts with a speech of great seriousness in tragic metre, Thrasonides addressing the Night in his misery because he will not take Krateia; fr. 3, which pro-bably comes very soon after this, has a reminiscence of Herakles in the *Trachiniae* (1058–63). Tragic metre is next clear in the meeting of Demeas and Krateia (210); Getas breaks it in 219, but it picks up again in 230 to be broken again by Getas in 235, and seems to pick up again in 247. This is on a smaller scale than the recognition scene in the *Perikeiromene*, but here too Menander underlines the seriousness.

Three passages in the *Sikyonios* have to be considered—the messenger speech and the two recognition scenes. The messenger speech is a wonderful set piece; it starts (176) with a reminiscence of Euripides' *Orestes* (866) and like the Orestes messenger speech describes a public hearing.[13] Moreover it is preceded by two lines in tragic metre and language in which the recital is announced (169 f.). The result of the hearing is of the greatest importance to Stratophanes and the girl, but it is told in comic metre from the point of view of the democratic man, and the tone only rises for the quotation of Stratophanes' speech (236–9, 241–5). It is the same technique as Menander adopts for Getas' narration of the disastrous meeting between Thrasonides and Demeas in the *Misoumenos* (284 ff.); there again the tone rises for a moment for a quotation of Thrasonides (306–9).

The recognition scene between Stratophanes and his parents (280) is badly preserved, but it looks as if metre and form are as strict as in the *Perikeiromene*. The recognition of Kichesias and Dromon develops out of the comic scene where Theron tries to bribe Kichesias to claim the girl as his daughter (313 ff.). The tone rises as Kichesias recalls his past (357). Then at the sight of

13 Cf. Sandbach, *op. cit.*, 128 ff.; *Handley*, 22 f.

Dromon Kichesias faints, like Peleus in the *Andromache* (1076).[14] The metre is tragic for ten lines (367 ff.), and the language also rises for Kichesias' recovery: 'Where in the world am I and what utterance of omen did I hear?'

Whether the audience are expected to catch the reminiscences of Euripidean situation in the *Epitrepontes* is doubtful. It does not add much to the arbitration scene to remember that a grandfather similarly arbitrated the fate of an unknown grandson in the *Alope*, but to remember Xouthos and Kreousa in the *Ion* does give an extra dimension to Charisios and Pamphile.[15] In the arbitration scene itself Syros rises to tragic metre when he describes the possible future of the baby if it is recognised (146 ff., 156 ff., 164 ff.). It does not matter that his allusions to tragedy are slightly muddled: he mixes the Sophoclean Tyro with the Euripidean Antiope (150) and has a confused idea of the Euripidean Aiolos. He is characterised as an educated and serious orator pleading in a just cause. Charisios in his monologue (588) belongs to the class of young men in distress; he has a conscious or unconscious reminiscence of the Euripidean Orestes (922) and probably a patch of tragic metre in the middle (595 ff., 599 ff.) but the text is much damaged there. The final scene between Onesimos and Smikrines (720) is rather below the average in comic lines (note particularly 725 ff., 753 ff., 764 ff.); Onesimos' muddled philosophy takes off from a reminiscence of Euripides' *Melanippe* (506 N), and he ends his mystification of Smikrines with a quotation of Euripides' *Auge*.[16] This is not essentially different from the use of tragic quotation by Daos in the *Aspis*.

Onesimos names Euripides when he quotes the *Auge*; Daos in

---

[14] *Cf.* also Antiphila seeing Clinia, *Heautontimoroumenos* 403; Melaenis suspecting the truth, *Cistellaria* 622; but we have not the Greek text to give the tragic reminiscence, if any.

[15] For Alope *cf.* my *Tragedies of Euripides*, 94. Similarly the name scene of the *Perikeiromene* recalls Sophocles' *Tyro* (fr. 659 P); the father's mistaken greeting of his son in the *Hiereia* may recall Xouthos and Ion in Euripides' *Ion* 520 (Körte, *Hermes*, 1940, 114). Add perhaps the suspicion of illegitimacy in *Heautontimoroumenos* 985 f. with S. O.T. 779 f.; the jealous wife selling the slave girl, *Plokion* 333 K–T with E. *Alkmaion in Corinth*: Geta's arrival with bad news, *Adelphi* 299 f. with E. *Ion* 808 f.; the dream of Sostratos' mother, *Dyskolos* 407, with, e.g., E. I.T.; the faked death of the *Aspis* with S. *El.* and E. *Hel.* Perhaps also when Menedemus returns home in the *Heautontimoroumenos* (125) after his son has gone to the war, the audience might remember Menelaos in a palace empty of Helen (A. Ag. 410).

[16] This is Onesimos, *not* Sophrone; *cf.* Sandbach, *op. cit.*, 134.

the *Aspis* deception names Aeschylus, Euripides and Chairemon. Syros when he makes his claim for the baby's trinkets says, 'You have seen the tragedians,' and Demeas, to impress Nikeratos, says, 'Haven't you heard the tragedians tell . . .?' A slave in another play (740 K–T), arguing with his love-sick master, has a near-quotation of Euripides' *Helen* (903) and ends, 'to speak to you in the manner of tragedy'. Tragedy is a well known repository of impressive examples, but tragedy is also, as it seemed possibly already to Solon and certainly to Gorgias and Plato, a deceit: it is in this sense that Moschion in the *Sikyonios* says that Stratophanes is getting hold of the girl 'by a baseless tragedy' (262) and that Daos in the *Aspis* (329), when he proposes the intrigue, says, 'you must compose a different sort of tragedy'. These explicit references to tragedy in fact mark the range of Menander's own practice in quoting tragedy, recalling tragedy, and using tragic form or metre, and the audience has to be ready to interpret the tragic code aright.

Much would depend on the acting. The extremes are clear. Thrasonides' first speech in the *Misoumenos*, Daos' first speech in the *Aspis*, and the recognition scene of the *Perikeiromene* must have been played as serious. Daos' deceit of Smikrines in the *Aspis*, Onesimos' insolence at the end of the *Epitrepontes*, and Nikeratos' list of tragic criminals in the *Samia* must have been played for laughs.[17] Between the extremes is an area where I do not think we can be certain how an actor would have played the part or how an audience would have reacted. I do not feel sure that Demeas' two big speeches in the *Samia* were necessarily played seriously or that Knemon's near-quotation of the dying Hippolytos could not be made humorous, nor on the other hand that the old *paidagogos* arguing with his love-sick young master[18] was necessarily funny, but these would be my personal preferences, shared, I hope, by some of Menander's actors. When

[17] Further instances: Deceit: 286 K–T with E. *Tro.* 10, and a rather special case, *Heros*, fr. 1, with E. fr. 431 N. Insolence: *Dis Exapaton* 111 K–T (*Bacchides* 816) near S. *Phil.* 415 f.; 113 K–T (*Bacchides* 820) with S. fr. 945 P. Old man's exaggeration: 88 K–T with Danaos in A. *Suppl.*; 288 K–T with E. *Phoen.*; perhaps also 178 K–T with E. *Hipp.* 106.

[18] 740 K–T., quoted above. Cf. 714 K–T with S. *El.* 916 (I am not sure if Körte is right in cutting out the first line, which is identical with E. fr. 598 N): 187 K–T identical with E. fr. 1024 N; *Kolax* 85 f. formal reminiscence of S. *Ant.* 295 f., 672 f.

Menander uses the tragic code he certainly alerts actor and audience to a new tone. Often it is clear whether this means a new seriousness or riotous comedy; sometimes the interpretation might be different in different performances.

VI

The professional code

1. *Aristotle and probability*

According to Plutarch (Mor., 347 E), a friend once said to
Menander, 'The festival is nearly here and you have not composed your comedy, have you?' and Menander answered, 'I most
certainly have. I have my treatment of the theme worked out—
I have just to set the lines to it' (tr. E. W. Handley).[1] However
the two stages may have been divided in Menander's mind, the
story inevitably recalls two passages in Aristotle's *Poetics*,[2] one
where he contrasts poetry and history and speaks of the comic
poets composing their stories of probable incidents and then
adding chance names, and the other where he instructs the tragic
poet to lay out his stories in general terms; after that the names
must be put in and the episodes added. Menander's knowledge of
the *Poetics* has been sufficiently demonstrated from his treatment
of recognition scenes, and I have wondered whether the very
general terms in which he phrases the past history of his characters in his set prologue speeches may be a sort of echo of Aristotle's instructions. Knemon is the only name in Pan's speech in
the *Dyskolos*; no name is preserved in Agnoia's speech in
the *Perikeiromene*; Kleostratos is the only name in Tyche's speech
in the *Aspis*.[3]

In our terminology Menander's first step was to choose the
type of armature—reunion of husband and wife, union with
hetaira, marriage with poor citizen or with unrecognised citizen,
achieved in spite of obstacles. The story had to be composed of
probable incidents. Probability includes both the natural course
of events (the way things happen) and incidents due to the

[1] E. W. Handley, *The Dyskolos of Menander*, 10.
[2] *Poetics* 1451 b 11; 1455 b 1.
[3] Perhaps this suggests that Hegemon is *not* a proper name in *Sikyonios* 9.

characteristics of the people involved in them. But there is a third category of probable events: what has actually happened. The tragic poet can appeal to this because, for Aristotle,[4] he is dramatising history. It is possible that Menander felt that a tragic parallel would legitimise an improbable event such as the recognition of an exposed baby or grown-up child or Polemon cutting off Glykera's hair. Pyrrhias' arrival in the *Sikyonios* with the news of the death of Stratophanes' mother with his recognition tokens possibly did not need such legitimisation, but structurally and in effect it is strangely reminiscent of the arrival of the Corinthian messenger in the *Oedipus Tyrannus* (990), the event noted by Aristotle[5] as the beginning of the reversal of fortune. Similarly one might say that Menander in the *Dyskolos* needed the presence of Sostratos' family at the Nymphaion to carry his story to a successful conclusion; they come because Sostratos' mother has had a bad dream about him which needs expiating by sacrifice to Pan. The dream (407) is not an illogical realistic jumble like Medeia's dream in Appollonios Rhodios but precisely tailored to foreshadow the actual event, like the dreams of Atossa in the *Persae* or of Iphigeneia in the *Iphigenia in Tauris*; Menander may have wanted the audience to see this.

It is hardly necessary to illustrate probability in the sense of the natural sequence of events. Onesimos (*Epitrepontes* 206), coming to the door because the cook is so slow and finding Syros examining the baby's trinkets, including Charisios' ring, is an obvious example. Or one might instance all the trains of action set off by an entirely natural misunderstanding, as the investigation which leads to the marriage of Aeschinus in *Adelphoi* B starts with Geta's misinterpretation of the story of Aeschinus' raid on the *pornoboskos* (299).[6] It is in character that the old slave should assume that the rich young man should want the *hetaira* for himself and abandon the poor girl who is bearing his child.

This brings us to the other category of probable events, those due to the characteristics of the people involved in them. To take the more obvious examples where character traits direct or impede the action, the *Aspis* is a duel between the miserly scheming

---

[4] *Poetics* 1451 b 16.   [5] *Ibid.* 1452 a 22.

[6] *Cf.* Polemon at the beginning of the *Perikeiromene* and Daos in the *Aspis*, Demeas in the *Samia* and *Misoumenos*, Lydos in the *Dis Exapaton*.

of Smikrines and the honesty and ingenuity of Daos. The
Misoumenos is a duel between the love and decency of Thrasonides and the affection of Krateia and Demeas for the lost
brother: here no solution is possible except the return of the
brother. In the *Perikeiromene* Polemon's jealousy and Glykera's
pride similarly seem to admit of no solution, but the way is in
fact provided by a characteristic action of Polemon; he is so in
love with Glykera that he insists on showing Pataikos her clothes,
and thus awakes Pataikos' memory and leads to the recognition;
Glykera, having regained her citizen status, can forget her pride.
The technique is fully developed in the earliest play we have: the
Samia is wholly concerned with the interplay between the credu-
lousness and decency of Demeas, the timidity and decency of
Moschion, the irascibility and old-fashioned morality of Nikeratos, and the quiet determination of Chrysis. This is, of course,
oversimplification. All the characters have their own make-up,
and this make-up enters into everything they do or say, and
provides the force, big or small, which pushes the action
forwards.[7]

2. The shape of the play

Having decided on this complicated web of action, Menander had
to work out what he calls the diathesis, the treatment of the
theme, or in Aristotelian terms to give it a beginning, a middle
and an end—or, more simply, a complication and a denouement.[8]
In the second formulation Aristotle defines complication as all
from the beginning of the story to the point just before the
change in the hero's fortunes; the denouement is all from the
beginning of the change to the end. The theory is not entirely
easy to apply. In the *Oedipus Tyrannus*, which Aristotle probably had in mind, one would naturally take the arrival of the
Corinthian Messenger as the last scene of the complication and
the arrival of the Theban herdsman (1110) as the first scene of the
denouement. If this is transferred to Menander's *Sikyonios*, the

---

[7] E.g. in the *Dyskolos* not only the aversion and meanness of Knemon and
the directness of Sostratos but also the high-mindedness of Gorgias and the
earthy realism of Daos.

[8] *Poetics* 1450 b 20; 1455 b 24. Cf. the excellent treatment by A. Blanchard,
R.E.G. 83, 1970, 38; I think he overstresses the cross-relationship between acts
II and IV, III and V.

arrival of Pyrrhias in act III is the last scene of the complication and the messenger scene of act IV is the first scene of the denouement. A glance at the well preserved plays suggests that the denoument always begins in act IV. In the *Samia* the turning point is Moschion's confession to Demeas (523), in the *Dyskolos* Knemon's adoption of Gorgias (731), in the *Perikeiromene* the recognition scene (338), in the *Aspis* the return of Kleostratos (491), in the *Epitrepontes* Pamphile's recognition by Habrotonon (540). The essential lines of the *Misoumenos* are lost, but the parallel with the *Aspis* suggests that the brother returned, like Kleostratos; Menander has driven both plays to a dead end—the only thing that will make Krateia yield is the discovery that Thrasonides has not killed her brother, and in the *Aspis* the only thing that can make the proposed marriage of Kleostratos' sister and Chaireas valid is the return of Kleostratos. It is, therefore, at least a probable assumption that Krateia's brother also arrived late in the fourth act.

The climax is one point in a five-act play. Now that we have the *Samia* and *Dyskolos* practically complete we need have no doubt that Menander adopted the five-act shape very early in his career, and the scenes from Menander on the Mytilene mosaics give the act number from one to five. It is at least possible that Aristotle's scheme was developed by Theophrastos into a form which combined beginning, middle and end, with complication and denouement. The new terms are *protasis* (proposal of the problem), *epitasis* (intensification), *katastrophe* (end, which corresponds to the Aristotelian denouement). The Latin commentators,[9] who have preserved these technical terms for us, explain *protasis* as the first act of the play. Then the scheme can be converted into five acts by equating *epitasis* with the second and third acts and *katastrophe* with the fourth and fifth acts. It remains to be seen how this works in practice with the well preserved plays, and in particular how far the acts denoted stages in the audience's expectations.

The total length of the plays varies from 909 lines in the *Samia* to over 1,200 in the *Epitrepontes*, and the act lengths also vary. It looks as if Menander aimed at ending the third act somewhere about two-thirds of the way through (*Samia, Dyskolos, Sikyonios*), but allowed himself great variations in the relative

9 Evanthius and Donatus in Kaibel, *C.G.F.* 67, 69. Cf. Blanchard, *op. cit.*, 42.

sizes of the first three acts and of the crucial fourth act. Accurate
figures can be given for *Samia* and *Dyskolos*:

	I	II	III	IV	V	Total
Samia	200	170	223	194	120	909
Dyskolos	232	193	194	163	185	969

He cuts, therefore, where the subject matter allows a cut and
not on any rigorous principle.

The cuts are marked in our texts by the word XOPOY, song of
the chorus, and we assume that a chorus did actually sing at
these points, but that their songs were not specially composed
for the play. Their presence is marked only at the end of the
first act: wherever the last lines of the first act are preserved,
the stage is cleared with the formula 'let us get out of the way;
some drunks are coming' (*Dyskolos, Aspis, Perikeiromene, Epitrepontes, Bacchides*). An act break is justified by the need to do
something off stage, either in the stage houses or elsewhere. Thus
in the *Dyskolos*[10] Sostratos goes home to find Getas (and Daos
goes to the field to get Gorgias) between acts I and II; Sostratos
goes to dig, and Sikon and Getas prepare the sacrifice between
acts II and III; Sostratos and Gorgias go into the sacrifice, and
Knemon falls down his own well between acts III and IV; Kallippides and Sostratos go in to eat between acts IV and V. The
convention for leaving the stage area (as distinct from entering
a house) can be formulated thus: departure and return must be
separated by an act break. So a character may go from town
house to country house, from town house or country house to
agora (to consult friends, do business, buy food or hire a cook)
or to the harbour to meet a traveller, and return; the distance
may be the fifteen miles from Phylai to Athens or the eighteen
miles from Halai Araphenides to Athens, but the audience does
not question the possibility, provided an act break separates departure and return.[11]

The principle is important because it is the chief method of
establishing act breaks in badly preserved plays and in the
Roman adaptations, which were meant to be played continuously.

[10] The analysis in the appendix will, I think, make clear what happens
during the act breaks in other plays preserved in papyrus, and the grounds
for establishing act breaks in the Roman adaptations.

[11] Cf. *Rylands Bulletin*, 45, 1962, 237 ff.

A few apparent exceptions can, I think, be accounted for. In the *Aspis* (184), still in the first act, Smikrines says that he has taken the advice of his friends about marrying the heiress, when he had only learnt that she was an heiress from Daos at the beginning of the play: I am inclined to think that the audience would accept Tyche's speech as the equivalent of an act break.[12] In the *Samia*, again in the first act, Moschion goes off at the end of his opening speech and shortly returns with Parmenon, who has already told him that Demeas has arrived at the harbour. Unfortunately about twenty-six lines of text are lost here: Moschion is still speaking at l. 57; then after the gap Chrysis says, 'I shall wait and listen to what they say,' and Moschion then says, 'You saw my father yourself, Parmenon?' Moschion must finish his opening narrative and say that he is going to the harbour to meet Parmenon, and Chrysis must account for her presence. (Does she conceivably come out with the baby like Habrotonon in the *Epitrepontes?*) I think the audience naturally assume that Moschion had gone a very little way down the road when he met Parmenon returning with the news.[13] There is a possible parallel in the *Epitrepontes*: Smikrines goes to town immediately after the arbitration in act II (194); towards the end of act III (407) he returns, apparently with the knowledge that the baby is the child of Charisios. Syros, who learnt this probability from Onesimos, had left in 286, saying, 'I will go to the city to find out what to do about this.' I think that Menander meant the audience to see that he met Smikrines on the road and naturally told him the story because Smikrines had helped him in the arbitration.

The first act sets the problem.[14] Menander used two main shapes, of which complete examples are preserved in the *Dyskolos* and the *Aspis*. The Dyskolos starts with Pan's explanatory speech; the *Aspis* starts with the return of Daos with Kleostratos' shield, captives and booty, and after his narration of the military action in Lycia and Smikrines' comment the explanatory speech is made by Tyche. We can list a good many certain examples of both types. Like the *Dyskolos*, the *Apistos–Aulularia* starts

[12] Cf. also *Perinthia* (see appendix).
[13] In *Dyskolos* 557 Sostratos goes to invite Gorgias and Daos to the sacrifice and returns with them within the act at 611, but Gorgias' property is just behind his house. In the *Georgos* Daos had been sent to the country for supplies before the play began.   [14] Cf. D. del Corno, *Acme*, 23 1970, 99.

with the speech of a god—as I think, Hestia—and there is no reason to suppose that Plautus changed the beginning. The fragmentary prologue speech of the *Sikyonios* (given by Elenchos?) has the same formula demanding the audience's attention as the *Dyskolos*, and is, therefore, also likely to have opened the play. The *Samia* substitutes the speech of Moschion for the speech of a god or abstraction, since he knows all the facts that the audience need to know. Similarly the necessary past history is known to the father in the *Hiereia* and to youth A in the *Phasma*, so that these plays probably began like the *Samia* with a speech by a character.[15]

Where Menander needs an explanatory prologue speech to inform the audience of essential past history and to hint at the future, he introduces a god or a personification either at the beginning or after an opening scene, as in the *Aspis*. The *Aspis* shape is preserved in the *Heros*, *Perikeiromene* and *Synaristosai*, and we can assume it where we know both that the play started with a scene between characters and also that it must have had an explanatory speech: this is the case in *Andria*, *Daktylios*, *Eunuch*, *Heautontimoroumenos*, *Misoumenos*, *Perinthia*. Probably *Epitrepontes*, *Titthe* and *Adelphoi* B had this shape, but we cannot prove it. The opening scene tends to be a startling one which makes the audience ask questions to be answered in part by the explanatory speech, and often gives the play its title: the slave's return with his supposedly dead master's shield (*Aspis*), the deserted young husband shown his wife's sealing (*Daktylios*), the self-punishment of the father who has driven his son to the wars (*Heautontimoroumenos*) the soldier out alone in the night because his girl hates him (*Misoumenos*), the soldier cutting off his girl's hair (*Perikeiromene*).[16]

---

[15] Possibly *Adelphoi* A (*Stichus*) needed a 'divine' prologue at the beginning. *Xenologos* 294 K–T, *Pseudherakles* 453 K–T, narration of god or abstraction, but unknown where placed. *Dis Exapaton*, *Imbrians*, *Misogynes* (280 K–T) seem to have started with dialogue: presumably one of the two characters gave the exposition to the other. *Epikleros* (152 K–T), *Plokion* (VI, VII) are probably parallel to *Samia* 20. *Thais* (185 K–T): opening serenade by lover?

[16] Other striking first scenes which gave the play its title: *Synaristosai*, *Andria*, *Perinthia*, *Leukadia*, *Messenia*, *Titthe*. The finding of the treasure was recounted in the first act of the *Thesauros*, which probably followed the *Samia* type. In the *Samia* Chrysis, who gives the play its name, makes her appearance in the first act, and takes responsibility for the plan that the baby shall be called hers and Demeas' until the marriage is safely arranged.

The rest of the first act carries the story on to a convenient break and generally ends with a scene pointing across the break. The measure here is what Menander wants to get in. The long first act of the *Dyskolos* builds up through Chaireas and Pyrrhias to the magnificent entry of Knemon and then prepares for the well story with the scene between the daughter and Sostratos, and ends with Daos' departure to fetch Gorgias. The problems are posed: Knemon has a problem with his well, Sostratos has a major problem with Knemon and a minor problem with Gorgias. Daos' commentary is an earthy misinterpretation of the romantic scene between Sostratos and the girl. This change of tone in a link scene at the end of the first act can be seen elsewhere. It looks as if Daos' realistic appreciation of the situation when he goes to fetch Moschion at the end of the first act of the *Perikeiromene* (72) was very similar. In the *Samia* the arrival of Demeas and Nikeratos is also a comedy scene, and the audience knows the problems that await them in their respective houses. The cook scene at the end of the first act of the *Aspis* is certainly a comedy break after Smikrines' intention to marry the heiress has been stated; the audience, unexpectedly seeing the cook, may think, 'Chairestratos must have gone to market before the play began and sent the cook home early; therefore he will return soon himself', and the fact that the cook is sent back into the house by Daos is an augury that all will come right in the end.

The second act, the beginning of the intensification, often brings an important new character (or characters) on to the stage. Gorgias returns with Daos in the *Dyskolos*, Moschion returns with Daos in the *Perikeiromene*, Chairestratos and Chaireas return with Smikrines in the *Aspis*, Demeas arrives unexpectedly in the *Misoumenos*, Syros arrives unexpectedly in the *Epitrepontes* (the important new character here is, of course, the baby).[17] This is the natural place for the plan of intrigue to be made, and the making of the plan points forward to execution, with successful or unsuccessful results, in the third and fourth acts.[18] This is clear in the *Dyskolos* (the final result is Knemon's

[17] Cf. the arrival of Ctesipho in *Adelphoi B*, Pamphilus in *Andria*, Megadorus in *Apistos–Aulularia*, Syros in *Dis Exapaton*, Chairea in *Eunuch*, Alcesimarchus in *Synaristosai*.

[18] Cf. *Andria*, *Dis Exapaton*, *Eunuch*, *Heautontimoroumenos*. First-act plans: *Samia*, *Theophoroumene*, probably *Heros*.

acceptance of Sostratos as a tanned farmer (754), and in the
Aspis. In the *Epitrepontes* the title scene of the arbitration is so
important and takes so much room that the last scene, when
Onesimos finds Syros with the ring, only makes the situation for
an intrigue, which is delayed till the third act.[19] In the *Perikeiromene* there were evidently two plans: Pataikos went ahead to
negotiate (and this plan was ultimately carried through), but
Sosias persuaded Polemon to try a siege, and this plan was called
off at the beginning of the third act. In the *Sikyonios* and
Misoumenos the second-act plan seems to have been a plan
against the soldier hero, which miscarried in the fourth act when
Stratophanes established his citizenship and Krateia found her
brother. The *Samia* has no plan (except the deception about the
parentage of the baby), but the second act brings trouble between
Demeas and Chrysis which prevents Moschion from telling his
father the truth, and the link forward is given by the departure
of Parmenon and Nikeratos for market. The *Dyskolos* has a new
thread to bring in, Sostratos' family, and they are preceded by
the comic entry of Sikon and Getas at the end of the second act.

The third act pushes the intensification further. It is perhaps
worth noting but should not be overstressed that Menander
seems to like a bipartite element here.[20] In the *Dyskolos* Knemon
first battles with Getas and then battles with Sikon; then the
tone alters for Sostratos' account of his troubles and again for
Simike's report of the second well disaster, which prepares for
the next act. In the *Samia* the audience expects both Parmenon
and Nikeratos to return from market; Parmenon's return with
the cook punctuates Demeas' account of his disastrous discovery,
and Nikeratos' entry with his sheep is a comic scene following
Demeas' expulsion of Chrysis. The beginning of the act in the
Aspis divides into Daos' tragic announcement of Chairestratos'
illness and the scene with the doctor. The division is very clear
in the *Epitrepontes* and *Perikeiromene*: in the former, first the
formation of the plan and then the arrival of Smikrines with new
information, which is confirmed and elaborated by the cook and
Chairestratos, and in the latter first the siege preparations and

[19] Similarly the very long sequence leading into the title scene of *Theophoroumene* has pushed the planning back into the first act. In the *Kolax*
the plan was apparently made in the third act.

[20] Cf. in *Apistos–Aulularia* (a) Euclio and cook, (b) Euclio and Megadorus;
in *Hiereia* the father's encounter with first one boy, then the other.

the return of Pataikos and then the frustration of Moschion and presumably the arrival of his father. In the *Misoumenos* the scene between Getas and the women is followed by the scene between Demeas and Krateia, which leads to the summoning of Thrasonides to go in and see them; all this time the audience has been expecting Kleinias to return from market and at the very end he comes with his cook and goes into his house, expecting to find Demeas and Krateia; the audience knows that he will not find them and perhaps takes the cook as a hopeful sign for a happy ending. In the *Sikyonios* the third act is divided between (a) the girl, Dromon, and Moschion going off to establish her citizenship, and (b) Stratophanes receiving information that he is himself an Athenian and therefore following them, so that here both parts point directly forward to the report of the assembly in the fourth act.[21]

The fourth act has, as noted above, the transition from complication to denouement.[22] Sometimes Menander introduces a great set piece here:[23] Knemon's apologia (unexpectedly in trochaic tetrameters), the 'tragic' double recognition scene in the *Perikeiromene*, the messenger speech in the *Sikyonios*, and well before the transition the wonderful recital by Getas in the *Misoumenos* of the meeting between Thrasonides, Demeas and Krateia, which is punctuated by Kleinias' unnoticed comments. The whole structure is clear in the *Dyskolos*: first the double entry of Simike to announce that Knemon has fallen down the well and of Sikon to demand silence for the libation in the Nymphaion, then Sikon's speech of rejoicing as he overhears the lamentations of the girl, balanced by Sostratos' messenger speech, then Knemon's entry and the summoning of Myrrhine to hear

21 In *Adelphoi* B, *Andria*, *Heros* the child is born in the third act; in *Apistos–Aulularia* in the fourth.

22 Only *Adelphoi* A (*Stichus*) seems to be without climax. I should mark the transitions as follows: *Adelphoi* B, 610, Aeschinus' return; *Andria* 796, arrival of Crito; *Apistos–Aulularia* 682, Lyconides' confession; *Dis Exapaton* (*Bacchides* 561), reconciliation of Sostratos and Moschos; *Eunuch* 805, defeat of the soldier; *Heautontimoroumenos* 679, prepared by the recognition of the ring in 614; *Kolax*, the recognition following the siege scene in act IV = *Eun.* 805; *Synaristosai*, *Cist.* 631, return of Melaenis with Selenium. *Daktylios*, *Heros*, *Phasma*: the crucial recognition scenes are probably in the fourth act. *Encheiridion*: act IV, the scene in which each old man has a dagger, presumably provides the solution.

23 Perhaps cf. *Andria* 721, tableau; *Eunuch* 549, Chaireas' monologue; *Kolax*, siege scene, *Eunuch* 771.

his dispositions; the arrival of Kallippides at the very end of the act is a preparation for the next. The balanced monologues of Sikon and Sostratos have a parallel in the *Epitrepontes*: there the fourth act starts with Smikrines' great appeal to Pamphile to leave Charisios. I think that Menander may have shown Charisios overhearing from Chairestratos' door, but he must have gone in before Smikrines left and before Habrotonon came out with the baby. Then the recognition scene between Pamphile and Habrotonon, then the parallel monologues of Onesimos describing Charisios' behaviour and Charisios describing his own reactions, and finally Habrotonon tells him that the baby is his and Pamphile's. The long fourth act of the *Samia* is much less elaborate because for the first part Demeas, Moschion and Nikeratos generate enough misunderstanding to drive it along. When Moschion has at last told the truth to Demeas and withdrawn, the action erupts into violence when Nikeratos sees his daughter suckling the child, and Chrysis escapes with the child into Demeas' house only with great difficulty; finally Demeas pacifies Nikeratos. There is a nice parallel with the third act here: Demeas thinks his suspicions are confirmed when he sees Chrysis suckling the child and he turns them out; here Nikeratos sees his daughter suckling the child and Chrysis returns to Demeas. Would the audience think that Chrysis was responsible for both incidents? Before, she wanted Demeas to go on thinking that she was the mother (she did not know that the old woman had talked about Moschion as the father); now she thinks that the only way to force the marriage on is to make Nikeratos see that his daughter is the mother.

Old Comedy ends in boisterous joy. The formal proposal of marriage which is the goal of most of Menander's comedy cannot be boisterous, and if the audience demands rollicking fun they must be given it some other way. A possible substitute is the more or less good-natured punishment of the chief obstacle. In the *Dyskolos*, after the double marriage has been arranged the play ends with the ragging of Knemon by Getas and Sikon. In the *Aspis* the betrothals are reported at the beginning of the fifth act and just enough remains to suggest that Smikrines, who is unaware of the return of Kleostratos, is ragged by Daos and the cook. In the *Epitrepontes*, after arrangements have been made for the freeing of Habrotonon, Smikrines arrives and is ragged by Onesimos. Perhaps we should regard the fifth act of the *Samia* as a variant: Moschion tries ineffectively but amusingly to punish Demeas.[24] Much is lost at the end of the *Perikeiromene* and *Misoumenos*, but perhaps the trepidation of the two heroes when their slaves announce that they are probably going to achieve marriage may be counted as a comedy element, and the formal proposal is the end, or very nearly the end, of the play. In the *Sikyonios* the recognition of Kichesias[25] has been shelved till the fifth act because Stratophanes has no chance to send Theron to find him until the girl is safely lodged with the priestess. Then after hurried arrangements Stratophanes goes after Kichesias to find the girl. Formal betrothal is impossible. Moschion in his depression has to be disposed of. If the play ends with the removal of Malthake and her belongings and the marriage arrangements of Theron and Malthake, that will be boisterous enough.[26]

In general we can speak of a five-act shape, and the lables—*protasis, epitasis* I, *epitasis* II, *katastrophe* I, *katastrophe* II—serve well enough to describe the function of the acts. But Menander allows himself great freedom, and he varies the length of the acts so as to get the breaks at the natural places and give the greatest emphasis to the most important scenes—particularly the scene, if there is one, that gives the play its title, and often also a key scene in the fourth act.

3. Production and imagination

We have inevitably gone beyond the strict limits of diathesis and mentioned scenes which demanded production to make their effect. The next question is, therefore, what could Menander realise before the eyes of his audience and how much had he to rely on their imagination, prompted by his words? The theatre of Dionysos had been rebuilt by Lykourgos less than ten years

[24] Perhaps cf. the Clitipho scenes at the end of *Heautontimoroumenos*, preceded by the mocking of Chremes 874.

[25] Cf. the very late recognition by Chremes of his daughter, *Andria* 904.

[26] Boisterous elements at or near the end in other plays: *Adelphoi* A, the slave *symposion*; *Adelphoi* B, the conversion of Demea and the mocking of Micio; *Apistos–Aulularia* 731, the misunderstandings of Euclio and Lyconides; *Dis Exapaton* (*Bacchides*) 1117, the luring of the two old men; *Eunuch* 941, 1002, ludification of Parmenon; *Kolax*, ? final discomfiture of the soldier; *Messenia*, struggle between youth and two slaves (mosaic).

before Menander started to produce.[27] What the audience saw
was a façade between wings divided by columns into eleven
spaces; the third, sixth and ninth spaces were pierced by doors;
the central space was wider than the other two and was the only
door used for tragedy. The other intercolumniations could carry
wooden panels representing either rocks and foliage for a comedy
set in the country or symposium decoration for a comedy set in
town. The side entrances, whether up the *parodoi* or through
the wings, would naturally be interpreted in Athens as leading
to or from the country if the left entrance was used and as
leading to or from the *agora* or harbour if the right was used.

The panels told the audience whether the play was set in the
city of Athens (or Corinth for the *Perikeiromene* or Sikyon for
the *Synaristosai* or, as I think, Rhodes for the *Misoumenos*) or
in the countryside of an Attic deme or elsewhere (the only
case we know is the sea coast and temple of the *Leukadia*). Deme
settings are certain for the *Dyskolos* (Phyle), the *Heros* (Pteleai,
on the slopes of Aigaleos), the *Heautontimoroumenos* (Halai,
perhaps Aixonides rather than Araphenides, as being nearer to
Athens), the *Epitrepontes* (probably Halai Araphenides, as that
was the site of the Tauropolia). Other references to demes do
not necessarily mean that the play was set there.[28] The panels
say only that the play was set in the country. The kind of
country is left to the words. The *Dyskolos* gives most. Pan
distinguishes between the Phylasians and 'the people who can
work the rocks here' and calls his Nymphaion a 'very famous
shrine'. It is the well known cave on Mount Parnes and Knemon's
farm and Gorgias' plot run up the valley through the scrub
(117, 351) from the road below (162) to the pear trees (100).
The Phylasians, including Kallippides, farm the richer land below
the level of the cave, and on the way up to the cave there were
fig trees (395–6).[29]

[27] Cf. *Rylands Bulletin* 45, 1962, 242 ff.; A. W. Pickard-Cambridge, *Theatre
of Dionysus*, 148 f.; A. D. Trendall and T. B. L. Webster, *Illustrations of
Greek Drama*, 9.

[28] Perhaps also Potamioi in the *Didymai* (108 K–T), Trikorynthos and Thria
in unknown plays (652a and 888 K–T); on *Sikyonios* see appendix.

[29] Cf. E. W. Handley, *The Dyskolos of Menander*, 22. Add *Epitrepontes* 66,
82, the scrub, the sheep, the charcoal; *Heros* 26, sheep, fr. 8, pear trees and
hunting. The farm of the boys' father in the *Georgos* (36) with the neighbouring vineyards and farm of Kleainetos (47) sound as if they were in richer
country: the play itself it set in Athens (79).

The two side doors in the façade balance and so would naturally be used for the two houses; (there is no valid evidence for more than two private houses in Menander: see the appendix on *Adelphoi A*, *Perikeiromene*). The central door is larger. If only the two houses are needed, it could be covered, perhaps with a curtain or hanging. But it can be used for a shrine or an inn (*Encheiridion*, *Theophoroumene*, probably also *Perikeiromene*, *Misoumenos*). When it is used for a shrine, a wooden statue of the god would show to whom it belonged. The frequent references to Pan in the *Dyskolos* (401, etc.) imply a statue, and the mosaic of the *Leukadia*[30] shows a statue of Apollo: the central door represents his temple on the wild and stormy shore, which is described in words (Turpilius XI). In the *Apistos–Aulularia* the central door is a shrine, but if the goddess is Pistis this can only have been made clear by words.[31] The central doors of the *Kolax* (fr. 1 K–T) and of the *Hiereia* may have been the shrines of respectively Aphrodite and Kybele, who could have been indicated by statues, but there is not enough text to show. The mosaic of the *Phasma*[32] suggests that the central door was the shrine in the party wall between the two houses, at which the girl appeared; it was marked by greenery and sashes.

When the central door was a shrine the stage altar would naturally be taken as the altar of the shrine, and it is so used in the *Leukadia* (257 K–T), and in the *Dyskolos* (622) Sikon comes out to pour a libation on it. Very curiously in a papyrus fragment (Antinoopolis 55) the altar is used for posting a legal challenge; in that play the central door was perhaps the shrine of the deme Hero to justify this. In the *Dyskolos* the altar does double duty, and is also the altar of Apollo Agyieus outside one of the houses; a little later Sikon swears by 'Apollo here' (659), and Photios says that they were accustomed to call the altar of Apollo, which is set before the doors, Loxias, Apollo or Agyieus. This is the Apollo to whom Demeas prays in agony in the *Samia* (444) and whom Syros greets on his return from Ephesos in the *Dis Exapaton* (*Bacchides* 172). This is the altar from which Polemon snatches a garland at the end of the *Perikeiromene* and

[30] L. Kahil, *Entretiens Hardt*, 16, 1970, 243.

[31] Pistis, to betray the pot of gold belonging to the Apistos, must surely be right (the cult of Pistis in Athens is attested by Diogenianos II, 80). In any case a shrine is needed, and the grove of Pan is off-stage (674).

[32] L. Kahil, *op. cit.*, 245; cf. *J.H.S.*, 91, 1971, 211.

from which Mysis is told to take the myrtle branches in the
Andria (40 K–T).

Two questions may be raised about the side doors. When
Knemon is brought on in the *Dyskolos* after falling down the
well and at the end of his speech asks to be wheeled in (758),
Menander certainly, as Handley says, alludes to the tragic
ekkyklema, but does he use it? The other passage which asks
for it is the prologue of the *Synaristosai*, where both mosaics[33]
show the three women seated. It is true that the old woman says
that the slave has removed the table (385 K–T), but for bringing
the seats on and removing them before the explanatory speech
of Boetheia the *ekkyklema* would be extremely useful. I am
unwilling to suppose, particularly for the *Dyskolos*, that sym-
metry was destroyed by making the central door (where the
ekkyklema was used in tragedy) the door of one of the private
houses, but the possibility of a smaller rolling platform for such
special scenes in comedy may be admitted.

The other question is whether the doors of the private houses
could be distinguished when one of them was owned by a rich
man and one of them by a poor man or woman, as for instance
in *Adelphoi* B, *Georgos* and *Plokion*.[34] The probable answer is
no, and Menander made it clear by his description that the inside
of the houses was different. Demeas describes the inside of quite
a large two-storey house in the *Samia* when he relates his
preparations for the marriage (225), and one gets an impression
that Nikeratos' house is much more cramped (533). The *exedra*
(alcove) mentioned in the *Koneiazomenai* (10) and the back
room where Clitipho shuts himself up with Bacchis (*Heautont.*,
902) are the extra rooms of rich houses.[35]

To speak his parts Menander had three actors, and he could
employ mutes for characters who did not need to speak.[36] The

[33] L. Kahil, *op. cit.*, 238, pls. 2 and 3; A. D. Trendall and T. B. L. Webster,
Illustrations of Greek Drama, 145.

[34] *Cf.* also *Apistos* (*Aulularia*), *Aspis* (if Smikrines counts as a poor man).

[35] Other descriptions: 155–6 K–T, birds in the courtyard; 694 K–T, the
women's quarters, so also *Eunuch* 583; *Perikeiromene* 287, *andron* and women's
quarters; *Heautontimoroumenos*, fr. 129–30 K–T, the poor house of Antiphila,
128 K–T, the rich house of Menedemus (before Clinia left).

[36] Two arguments for Menander having only three actors appear to me
decisive: (1) the inscriptional evidence for three comic actors at Delphi (Soteria)
in the early third century B.C., *S.I.G.*³ 424; (2) the remarkably few difficulties
(in allotting parts) that appear in our texts: on *Dyskolos* 214 (unwanted inser-

obvious advantages of a small number of speakers in a large
theatre outweighed the occasional difficulty of getting a character
off so that the actor could come on in a different part. One of
the ancient illustrations[37] of Menander shows him composing
with one mask held in his hand and the other two masks for the
characters who appear in the same scene on a table by his side.
This may well be how he did compose. The difficulties of the
convention very seldom show, and our perplexities are sometimes caused by a deficient text. But some of the times allowed
for changing mask and costume are so short that one must
assume that the entrances in the wings of the stage building were
used for entrances from off stage; to go into one of the doors,
change, and come out of a door in the wings would take very
little time.

The text of the *Dyskolos* is nearly complete and shows Menander operating with at least seventeen characters. Some of the
sequences are interesting. Towards the end of the second act
Gorgias, Daos and Sostratos go off to work, and Sikon and Getas
come on to prepare for the sacrifice. Daos goes off first to build
his wall (378), and the actor has fourteen lines to prepare for
Sikon's great entry with the sheep (393). Gorgias may be able
to go off before Sostratos finishes his monologue (392), but this
would be unrealistic, as they are going to dig together; whichever
actor takes Getas has nine lines to prepare, and Sikon conveniently asks (402), 'Getas, are you so far behind?' The next
act begins with Knemon, Getas and Sikon in the three speaking
parts, while Sostratos' mother, Plangon, Parthenis, Donax and
Syros (at least) arrive at the shrine, all represented by mutes.[38]
Near the end of the act (595–602) Knemon drives Simike into
his house, leaving Getas on stage to pronounce a monologue of
nine lines; the two actors then come on again as Sostratos and
Gorgias with Daos (mute). For Knemon's apology in the fourth
act mutes are used for Myrrhine and the daughter, and again
when in the last act Gorgias leads them over to the Nymphaion

tion of Pyrrhias), *Misoumenos* 269 (unwanted insertion of Getas) and Professor
Sandbach's elimination of Glykera as *speaker* in *Perikeiromene* 443 and
Sophrone as *speaker* in *Epitrepontes* 759, see L.G.C. 186. On the messenger
scene of the *Sikyonios* see appendix.

[37] Rome, Lateran 487. *Greek Theatre Production*, pl. 24b; Pickard-Cambridge,
*Festivals*², fig. 109.

[38] Cf. E. W. Handley, *The Dyskolos of Menander*, 207 f.

(866). There Kallippides has gone into the Nymphaion at 860; the actor changes into Simike's mask and costume and comes out of Knemon's house just as Gorgias and Sostratos go into the Nymphaion (873). Simike's five-line monologue gives time for one of them to change and come on as Getas at 879; the other comes on as Sikon at 890; here the actors go into and come out of the same Nymphaion door so that a very quick change is possible.

The third act of the *Misoumenos* has quite a complicated sequence which can be reconstructed in spite of the difficulties of the text. It evidently started with Getas taking Thrasonides' swords from his house into the *andron* of Kleinias' house. This gives Krateia and her nurse Phrygia the chance to come out of Thrasonides' house with suppliant boughs, presumably intending to sit on the altar until Kleinias returns from market. Getas comes out of Kleinias' house and drives them back again into Thrasonides' house. His monologue (158?–175) allows the actors to change and become the Old Woman, who comes out of Kleinias' house as soon as Getas enters Thrasonides' house, and Demeas, who follows her about eight lines later. It is not clear when she goes back into Kleinias' house, not before 194 at any rate. This gives the actor time to change and come out of Thrasonides' house as Krateia with Phrygia (now mute)[39] at 208. Demeas recognises Krateia, and Getas bursts out upon them at 216. Getas, when convinced that Demeas is Krateia's father, goes to the inn to fetch Thrasonides (237). Demeas and Krateia go in as Thrasonides comes out (258), so that the actor who played Getas must play Thrasonides and Getas is now taken by a mute. They go in as Kleinias and the cook arrive (270); the actor who played Demeas has twelve lines to prepare to play Kleinias, and the cook is taken by a mute.

These two examples show how Menander uses his actors and his mutes. In particular the monologue at the end of a scene is used to cover the departure of the other two actors when one or both of them has to take another part quickly.[40] Most of these

[39] At 211, 228 Phrygia is asked a question, but the dialogue moves so fast that she does not need to answer it; cf. F. H. Sandbach, *Entretiens Hardt*, 17, 1970, 179.

[40] *Aspis* 433, Smikrines' monologue masks entry of doctor with Daos and two mutes (Chaireas and his servant) and doctor's return with his servant. *Samia* 360, the cook's monologue masks Demeas' entry into the house and

are entirely natural summations of what has preceded; the convention of Greek drama was that the character put his thoughts
into words to the chorus, or to the audience if no chorus was
present. These are merely small-scale instances of the convention.
The most surprising is Getas' sympathetic description of the
Attic farmer after Knemon has driven Simike into the house in
the third act of the *Dyskolos* (603). It is true that sympathy
with Knemon is highly desirable the moment before he falls
down the well and suffers a temporary change of character, but
Getas is not a sympathetic character, and one cannot help feeling
that here he is saying what Menander wanted rather than what
he naturally would have said.

The audience were also accustomed to mutes in two kinds of
role. They could either substitute for an actor when a character
had to be silent in a particular scene (e.g. Pylades at the end
of Euripides' *Orestes*) or play parts which had no words in the
whole play (e.g. Pylades in Sophocles' *Electra*).[41] Menander, as
we have seen, used them for both purposes. They are his only
way of increasing the number of figures on the stage and producing something like a spectacle. When the three women are
drinking in the opening scene of the *Synaristosai* they are served
by a silent slave. When Chrysis is thrown out in the *Samia*, she
takes the baby and the old woman with her. Syros in the *Epitrepontes* (200) can count the baby's trinkets out to his wife. In the
Perikeiromene (71) the moving of Glykera to Myrrhine's house
requires other slaves besides Daos. The moving of Malthake

return with Chrysis. Some other problems: *Perikeiromene* 235, Sosias exits to
play Moschion in 276 (his reference to Sosias in 281 recalls what Daos had told
him earlier; what he sees is the backs of Polemon and Pataikos); 337 is
separated from 338 by seven to fifteen lines, during which Doris returns,
speaks, and exits again, so that the actor can enter as Moschion in 344;
Pataikos has spoken at least one line before 338, so that the minimum time
for change is seven lines. *Aspis*: 213, Smikrines exit, actor returns 233 as waiter
(note that the cook comments on his slowness) the cook's servant (222) is mute;
278 (latest, possibly 275), Smikrines exit, actor returns 299 as Daos. *Sikyonios*
367, Theron exit, actor returns 377 as Stratophanes, 385 Donax mute. *Epitrepontes*: 193, Smikrines exit, actor returns 207 as Onesimos; 433 ff., Karion
probably enters before 433 to borrow a pot (fr. 4, *cf.* Körte on 433) and goes in
again with his helper, Simias (mute), at 455, when Chairestratos comes out.
Theophoroumene: the flute player (27 f. and mosaics) is a mute; the serenade
must be long enough for the actor who takes Parmenon (who may not exit
till after 30) to change and come on as the girl. The tune may be played by
the official flute player, *cf. Dyskolos* 432, *Perikeiromene* 226.

41 Add to the examples given Doris in the *Kekryphalos* 951 K–T.

at the end of the *Sikyonios* (planned 386, perhaps executed 411) and the moving of Bacchis in the *Heautontimoroumenos* (381, 744) are more formidable operations and more spectacular. Similarly mutes make up the procession of captives in the first scene of the *Aspis* and the personnel of the siege scenes in the *Perikeiromene* and the *Kolax*. In the *Perinthia* papyrus, perhaps a scene in the fourth act corresponding to Terence, *Andria* 860, the intriguing slave Daos has taken refuge on the altar and his master Laches (like Menelaos in the *Andromache*) proposes to burn him off. Three mutes, Tibeios, Getas and Pyrrhias, who are fellow slaves of Daos, bring the fuel. Another slave, Sosias (who may correspond to Byrria in Terence), watches and comments. This is the most violent scene in Menander, and as all three actors are engaged and there is no one left to rescue him, Daos must surrender.

The *Synaristosai* starts exceptionally with a drinking scene on the stage.[42] But though actual consumption on the stage is rare, eating and drinking are so firmly fixed in the tradition of Greek comedy that the audience expected to hear about it. I have mentioned briefly the parties held with friends or in the house of a *hetaira* or at an inn and the cooks and their attendants (vocal or mute).[43] These parties, whether they are called sacrifices or marriage feasts or breakfasts (*arista*) or *symposia*, not only carry on the story because things happen at them but set up a time schedule which the audience recognises and expects to see worked out. The full sequence is purchasing, including hiring of cook; preparations, including not only baskets, cakes, etc., but also cooks borrowing pots from the neighbours; libation and slaughter of animal; eating the animal; *symposion*. It is seen clearest in the *Dyskolos* and the *Samia*.

In the *Dyskolos* the sacrifice happens away from home at the Nymphaion at Phyle; instead of purchasing, Menander gives us the arrival of Sikon with the sheep and Getas with rugs and couches at the end of act II. Act III begins with the procession of the household bringing the implements of sacrifice, and the pre-

---

[42] Cf. P. Ant. 55c, 'this watery drink'; perhaps frs. 55–6 *Anepsioi*, 216 *Hippokomos*, 239–40 *Kekryphalos*, 319 *Pallake*, but these may all be from descriptions with passages of direct speech. Probably the slaves at the end of *Adelphoi* A (*Stichus*) drink on stage.

[43] Cf. ch. III, nn. 12 and 18. *Thrasyleon* (III) with 200 K–T may be spoken by a disapproving *paidagogos*: therefore possibly a party with a *hetaira*.

parations of baskets, lustral water and cakes (440) happen in the
shrine. Then comes the borrowing scene.[44] Before the end of the
act Getas is driven out by the smoke (548) so that we know that
the cooking is far advanced. At the beginning of the fourth act
Sikon asks for silence for the libation before the meal. The fifth
act continues the sequence, with separate parties for the women
and the men (855). The theme is continued by Getas and Sikon,
who demand the equipment for a rich feast from Knemon and
then change to describing the party[45] which is actually in
progress before they carry him in to join it.

In the *Samia* the party is a marriage feast to be held both in
the bride's house and in the bridegroom's.[46] In the first act Parmenon tells Moschion to go in and make preparations (74), and
Moschion imagines the sequence to himself while he waits for his
father (122). In the second act Demeas sends him in again to
make preparations (157); then Demeas sends Parmenon to market
and Nikeratos goes himself. At the beginning of the third act
Demeas describes his preparations in the house. Parmenon arrives
back with purchases and cook, a little later the cook rushes out
because he is afraid that Demeas will break his pots, and at the
end of the act Nikeratos arrives back with his scraggy sheep. By
the fifth act Parmenon can report from Demeas' house that the
wine is mixed and the entrails are being roasted (674). Later
Nikeratos says that bathing, pre-nuptial sacrifice and feast are all
completed in his house (713), and Demeas tells Chrysis to send
for the water for the nuptial bath in his house; the play ends
with Moschion putting a wreath on his head to join the procession.[47]

The meal in the *Epitrepontes* is a party held with friends, as

[44] *Methe*, fr. 264 K–T, describes preparations for a rich sacrificial meal, which
is not unlike *Dyskolos* 447.

[45] *Hydria*, fr. 405 K–T, comes from a similar description.

[46] Marriage feasts at home also in *Apistos* (*Aulularia*), where much of the
sequence can be followed (263, 280, 371, 570, 612); *Aspis*, where the cook has
arrived before the play begins (as also in the *Demiourgos*); *Phasma* (cook
borrowing); *Arrhephoros* (cook borrowing); *Paidion* (see appendix). In *Georgos*
the greenery is brought in from the farm and preparations are being made,
but too little remains to show the cook.

[47] In the *Heautontimoroumenos* Chremes' breakfast to celebrate the Dionysia
also takes place at home: he invites Menedemus in the prologue and later
describes the greed of Bacchis (455 = 133 K–T). The dinner in the *Stichus* is
also at home: we hear little of the brothers' meal but much of the slaves' *symposion* at the end of the play.

Charisios has taken refuge with Chairestratos. Kleinias' party in
the *Misoumenos* and the soldier's party in the *Eunuch* are
differently managed. The *Epitrepontes* opens with a scene
between Onesimos and the cook, who talks instead of getting on
with the breakfast. It is not clear whether he has just arrived or
had been brought out from Athens the night before. Late in the
second act (206) Onesimos complains that the cook is so slow that
they have not yet got as far as the *symposion*. At the beginning
of the third act (258) Habrotonon says that Charisios will not let
her sit beside him, so that the meal has begun; and later the cook,
who has come out to borrow a pot (433, with fr. 4) says that they
are all scattering outside (when Habrotonon had claimed to be
the mother of the baby).

The schedule of Kleinias' party in the *Misoumenos* also gets
delayed.[48] He goes to market in the second act and comes back
with the cook at the end of the third act, but his guests are next
door in Thrasonides' house and do not come over until the end
of the fourth act, but with the reconciliation at the end of the
fifth the party becomes a pre-marriage feast (450). The party
with the soldier in the *Eunuch* is off-stage and so instead of
marketing we have the invitation to Thais and her instructions
for Chremes and then the successive returns of her maid with
her jewellery, which she fears will get stolen in a rough-house,[49]
of Chremes, and of Thais herself, each with their own account of
what went on. This is one of a number of accounts of what goes
on at a party.[50]

Where the central door represents an inn, eating and drinking
can go on inside, but I think it is a natural assumption that marketing and the provision of a cook are the normal business of the
innkeeper, and the audience does not expect to be told about it.
So if I am right in claiming an inn for the *Perikeiromene*, breakfast
is naturally happening there and Polemon's friends, including
Pataikos, have naturally gathered there (52). The inn provides
the army, including the flute girl Habrotonon, for the abortive
siege (226), and the cook and the pig for Polemon's sacrifice in the
fifth act (417). Both the *Encheiridion* and the *Theophoroumene*

48 *Trophonios*, fr. 397, is the reception of a guest friend like Kleinias' party
in the *Misoumenos*.
49 Cf. *Karine* II; *Naukleros* III.
50 Cf. *Adelphoi* A, 2; *Arrhephoroi* 61; *Chalkeia* 443 K–T; *Misoumenos* 164.

have a description of what was evidently a fairly rowdy party in an inn. Too little remains of the text of the *Encheiridion* to clarify the relation of on-stage and off-stage. In the *Theophorou-mene* Kleinias and Lysias are waiting outside (after, as I think, stealing the girl's drum and cymbals) for Parmenon to come and give them a full account of what happened, of which just the end is preserved before they move on to the serenade.

We have, therefore, plenty of evidence that Menander did not neglect the audience's traditional expectations that comedy was concerned with food and drink, but he is extremely skilful in adapting scenes and descriptions to the particular needs of the play. The soldier's party in the *Eunuch* is an unattractive muddle, but it moves the discovery of the girl's parents a stage nearer and covers Chaerea's rape. The expensive marketing of the rich men in the *Samia* and *Apistos–Aulularia* is a beautiful foil for the stingey marketing of the poor men, and Sikon in the *Dyskolos* provides a running contrast both to the seriousness of the young men and to the irritability of Knemon himself. And these scenes provide a kind of clock to show how the story is moving forward towards the desired ending, and however great the obstacles, the clock can be seen to move.

4. *Masks and costumes*

The scenic possibilities of the Attic stage are limited, but the scene both on and off stage can be realised by words in the exact form that is needed for the particular play. Similarly Menander has standard masks and what Aristotle calls chance names to give his characters. Do they also arouse expectations in the audience, and how does Menander individualise them?

It is a reasonable view, supported by the archaeological evidence, that the list of masks of New Comedy preserved in Pollux's lexikon goes back to a source in the third century B.C. and codifies the practice of New Comedy. The standard list contains a number of masks that go back to Old Comedy, a number of masks, like the parasite and cook, introduced to meet the changing practice of Middle Comedy, and a number of masks introduced in the period of New Comedy.[51] How far Menander himself was responsible for the new masks we have no evidence.

[51] *Cf. L.G.C.* 119 ff.

If we take the list as representing his practice, he had five masks for old men, eleven clean-shaven masks, seven slave masks, three masks for old women, and fourteen masks for middle-aged and young women. There are three questions which concern us. First, what predictions did the audience make on seeing a mask? Secondly, does Menander use words to go beyond the masks, as we have found him using words to create an individual setting beyond what his scenery shows? And thirdly, do the predictions made on the mask correspond to the actual character? We have, of course, also to consider costumes as well as masks.

The Mytilene mosaics show how Menander was produced in the third century A.D.[52] Details of the costume are demonstrably contemporary, and the number of masks available seems also to have been reduced. Nevertheless it is worth putting our first question to them, particularly for the scenes for which we also have a text. The distinction between old men, young men, slaves and women is absolutely clear, and depends on hairstyle, colour of face, and costume. What is more interesting is the distinctions within these primary categories. The picture of the fourth act of the *Encheiridion* shows two old men; they wear the same costume, but Straton has a rounded beard and a straight stick, while Derkippos has a pointed beard and a crooked stick. It is Derkippos who is unique here; Straton has the same beard and stick as Demeas in the *Samia*, Smikrines in the *Epitrepontes*, and the father in the *Phasma*. I should have expected Demeas to be different, and this is a reason for supposing that the full Pollux list of masks was no longer available.

Young men are differentiated in the *Theophoroumene*. Lysias and Kleinias have the same colouring and the same-coloured hair, so that there is some reason for thinking that they are brothers (as also on the Dioskourides mosaic), but Kleinias' hair is built up higher and he has a large red *himation*, whereas Lysias has a very small green *himation*. The boy in the *Phasma*, according to the publication, has curly dark hair, and Moschion in the *Plokion* has fair hair.

The two slaves of the arbitration scene in the *Epitrepontes* differ in hair and costume: Daos (wrongly labelled Syros) wears the normal slave costume; the charcoal burner (Syros) wears an elaborate *himation*, which evidently signifies higher status. The

[52] L. Kahil *et al.*, Antike Kunst, 6, 1970, 63 ff.

cook in the *Samia* has quite a different mask—bald, dark side locks, and very dark complexion—and he wears a small *himation* round his shoulders.

The three female masks on the *Synaristosai* mosaic are clearly distinguished, as also on the Dioskourides mosaic of the same scene: the old woman with white hair and fat wrinkles, Plangon (Selenium in Plautus) fair hair with a simple parting, Pythias (Gymnasium in Plautus) also fair, but much more elaborate high hairdressing. She is a *hetaira*, and it is not surprising to find Chrysis given the same mask in the *Samia*; what is surprising is to find a very similar mask on a figure which can only be Krateia in the *Misoumenos* (the figures on this mosaic are not labelled). One can only assume that in the *Synaristosai* the producer gave Plangon a mask which showed that she was not really a *hetaira* but would be recognised as a citizen in the end, and the Dios-kourides mask shows that this was third century B.C. practice; but in the *Misoumenos* (where the recognition of Krateia happens early in the third act) he chose a mask which showed Krateia's status at the beginning of the play. The girl on the *Phasma* mosaic also has simple hairdressing like Plangon, and she also achieves full citizen status when her father is discovered late in the play. If, as seems probable, this was Menander's practice, in the recognition plays the audience would know as soon as they saw the girl that she was going to be recognised as a citizen, whatever might be her momentary status, and the mask would confirm the hint given in the explanatory prologue speech.

The list in Pollux has a number of notes which suggest the sort of prediction that the audience might make. Among the old men, No. 4 looks sluggish, No. 6 rather difficult to deal with (Knemon in the *Dyskolos*:), No. 7 meddlesome (Smikrines in the *Epitrepontes*, Chremes in the *Heautontimoroumenos*?), No. 8 is the *leno* or procurer. Of the young men, No. 10 is athletic, No. 11 is younger and more interested in books than athletics, No. 13 is white, lives in the shade (i.e. avoids athletics, not necessarily solely for the purposes of study), clearly delicate, No. 14 is the rustic and No. 15 is the soldier, No. 17 the parasite, No. 18 the flatterer, who looks more malicious than the smiling parasite. Of the slave masks two were reserved for cooks, No. 25 for the native cook and No. 26 for the foreign cook. The female masks

distinguished three old women, one of whom is designated 'little
housekeeper' (Simike in the *Dyskolos?*), two wives with, in
addition, an elderly wife and a concubine (*cf.* 453 K–T, *Pseudherakles*, and the title *Pallake*), a 'maiden' (e.g. Knemon's
daughter) and two 'false maidens' (this may very well be a term
for a girl who is going to be recognised, whether she has been
raped or not: one of these masks is worn by Plangon in the
Dioskourides mosaic of the *Synaristosai*, and it is the mask that
one would expect for Krateia in the *Misoumenos*), and five masks
with different hairstyles and varying amounts of adornment for
hetairai, and finally two masks for servants, one of which is said
to be for the servant of a *hetaira*. This gives some idea of the
range of masks at Menander's disposal, and the kind of predictions that the audience could make.

It is possible also that he could sometimes command special
masks. An obvious case which hardly needs to be called special
is the mask with one brow raised and the other smooth, so that
the character could show haughtiness or equability according to
which side was turned to the audience. Pollux notes this distinction for two of the old men's masks, Nos. 3 and 7, but from the
monuments it is clear that slave masks also often showed it. An
epigram of Kallimachos (49 Pf.) seems to describe a young man's
mask with one pale cheek and one brown cheek, and such a mask
would be admirable for Sostratos in the *Dyskolos*, who complains
of the sun blazing down on him while he is digging (535) and
then is accepted by Knemon as a farmer because he is tanned
(754). Krobyle, the rich and oppressive wife of the *Plokion* is
said to have a very long nose (333 K–T), and this feature can be
recognised on the Mytilene mosaic, but it may be merely the
normal mask for the elderly wife, embellished by the text.[53] A
further possible instance of the special mask is in the *Misoumenos*: Photios preserves the word *enerochros*, which means
'corpse-coloured'. If it is a description of the love-lorn Thrasonides, Menander may have given him a soldier's mask with a
white complexion instead of the dark complexion attested by
Pollux,[54] but again the audience may have only imagined his
paleness from the words. But this description may be of Krateia's
brother, particularly if he has been wounded.

[53] *Sikyonios* 352, Kichesias is snub-nosed, and may therefore have worn mask
No. 4.   [54] *Cf.* 202, 878 K–T, with no context.

The words can call attention to an actual characteristic of the mask or can add something which the mask cannot show. Raised brows are mentioned several times as a sign of haughty disapproval in old men and slaves. The masks of old men and slaves also show the folds of skin above the nose produced by frowning, and this too is several times noted in the text.[55]

Change of colour can, of course, be indicated only in words. The messenger in the Sikyonios (200) describes Moschion as white, smooth and beardless, which suggests that he wears one of the two 'delicate' masks (No. 13 or 16); he turns crimson (208)—this is description of off-stage action, but Aeschinus in Adelphoi B (643; 301 K–T) is on stage when his adoptive father rejoices to see him blush.[56] The messenger in the Sikyonios draws the further conclusion that Moschion is 'adulterous', whereas the soldier Stratophanes in the soldier's mask is 'very manly in appearance'. It is a nice point that later on (264) Stratophanes (who is in fact Moschion's elder brother) is called 'clean-shaven', whereas Moschion is smooth and beardless. The 'democratic' messenger of the Sikyonios makes a hasty judgement of character from Moschion's appearance as a rich and not obviously athletic young man, and Gorgias makes a similar judgement of Sostratos in the Dyskolos (258): 'The man in the chlanis? Certainly a bad lot from his looks.' The rich man's chlanis first arouses suspicion, and the mask of the young man about town confirms it.[57]

The skin of the female mask was normally white, and in this sense Moschion in the Sikyonios calls the girl 'white, very beautiful' (399), but in the Synaristosai Plangon (Selenium) is pale because she is unhappy, and she is untidy too (56, 113). The mask could not be changed, but the way her himation is draped could, and it is this sort of visible untidiness which makes Megadorus tell Euclio to spruce himself up for his daughter's wedding.[58] Similarly in the Dyskolos Gorgias' extreme reluctance to join the women in the Nymphaion (871) is probably because

[55] Raised brows: Andria 34 K–T; Titthe 395 K–T; Sikyonios 160; Dyskolos 423. Frowning: Epitrepontes 18; Samia 129; Sikyonios 124; Aulularia, fr. VI. Cf. also Dyskolos 147; Andria 857.

[56] Cf. Andria 878, perhaps also Eunuch 838. Charisios may have appeared in the doorway while Smikrines tried to persuade Pamphile to leave him, but his changes of colour can only be described (566, 580). Cf. also the other descriptions of emotion, Sikyonios 218 ff.; Misoumenos 295, 320 ff.

[57] For the chlanis cf. Orge 303 K–T; Perikeiromene 392 Aspis 378.

[58] Aulularia 539 cf. Adelphi 755.

he is wearing the countryman's *diphthera* or skin jerkin, such as was given to Sostratos with the mattock in his mother's dream. The *diphthera* is a clear sign of the countryman: it was certainly worn by Daos and Syros in the *Epitrepontes* (53, in spite of the Mytilene mosaic) and by the country son in the *Hypobolimaios*, and probably by the self-exiled countryman Menedemos in the *Heautontimoroumenos*[59] and Kleainetos in the *Georgos*, as well as by Knemon. Other recognisable costumes were the military cloak of the soldier, the black or grey single garment of the poor parasite, who also carried his own *aryballos* and *strigil* (the parasite in the *Sikyonios* wore white because he was going to marry), and the flowered garment of the eunuch.[60]

It is clear that mask and costume did allow the audience to make predictions and that Menander's words added what the mask could not show. If the interpretation given of the *pseudokore* masks is right, Menander did warn the audience of the true status of his lost girls: there he did not want surprise. But it looks as if he did want to surprise the audience with the true character of the *hetaira* genuinely concerned to establish her supposed sister or of the successful soldier genuinely in love with a girl; nothing in the mask distinguished the one from the *hetaira* who simply exploited young men or the other from the boastful womaniser (unless the doubtful evidence of *enerochros* in the *Misoumenos* is accepted). Here he wanted to contrast appearance with reality.

5. Names

If the masks do not distinguish good from bad in soldiers or *hetairai*, neither do their names. The names of the soldiers are all speaking-names which suggest soldiers because they are formed from words meaning violence, war, army and boldness. But nothing in the name distinguishes the bad soldiers of the *Kolax* and *Thrasyleon* from the good soldiers of the *Perikeiromene*, *Sikyonios* and *Misoumenos*. Chrysis was the name of the

---

[59] Menedemus also has a mattock at his first appearance (88). So presumably also the country boy in the *Hypobolimaios* (hence the title Rastrarius). *Cf.* the slave from the harbour with fishing equipment, *Stichus* 289.

[60] Soldier's cloak: *Perikeiromene* 164, *Samia* 659, *Misogynes* 282 K–T. Parasite: *Stichus* 350, 230; *Sikyonios*, fr. 9. Eunuch: *Eunuch* 370, 683 = 856 K–T? Other visible disguises: *Aspis* 377; *Olynthia* 299 K–T; *Pseudherakles* 458 K–T?

good *hetairai* in the *Samia* and *Eunuch* (Thais in Terence) and according to a brilliant conjecture of E. W. Handley[61] of the destructive sisters of the *Dis Exapaton*, and Chrysis was the name of a living *hetaira*. So was Malthake (*Sikyonios*), Pythias (*Synaristosai*; Gymnasium in Plautus), and Thais, the destructive *hetaira* of the *Thais*.[62] I think it is also reasonable to assume that Habrotonon (*Epitrepontes*, *Perikeiromene*), Phanion and probably Paidion (both titles of plays) were recognisable as *hetaira* names.

So far all is clear: *hetairai* are recognisable by their names, but their names do not distinguish them as good or bad. But Glykera and Plangon are also *hetaira* names. Glykera may be a *hetaira* in the *Misogynes* and in the *Glykera* (if there was such a play); she has *hetaira* status in the *Perikeiromene* but is finally recognised as a citizen. Plangon is the heroine of the *Synaristosai* (Selenium in Plautus), the daughter of Nikeratos in the *Samia*, the daughter of Myrrhine who is subsequently found to be the daughter of Laches in the *Heros*, and an unknown girl, possibly the daughter of Kallippides, in the *Dyskolos*. If the name suggests a *hetaira*, one could argue that Menander wants the audience to recognise the *hetaira* status of the girl in the *Synaristosai*, the doubtful status of the girl in the *Heros* (her father is unknown at the beginning of the play), and the precarious status of the girl in the *Samia* (she has been raped); then I think that the only solution for the girl in the *Dyskolos* is that she is another musician, like Parthenis, and this could have been made clear by giving her an instrument to carry. Another name which sounds like a *hetaira* name is Dorkion: both in the *Kekryphalos* and in the *Leukadia* (if Turpilius has preserved the Greek name) it is probable that the girl with this name is in a disadvantageous position and is going to be recognised, but not enough is preserved to make this clear.

It is largely chance if we know that a name in Menander was or had been borne by a historical figure or had already been used in comedy. We can, however, recognise speaking-names, whether they also belonged to real people or had already occurred in comedy or were invented by Menander. All his soldiers, as far as we know, were so named, and of the *hetairai* Chrysis (golden) and Malthake (soft) fall into this class. So do the parasites Gnathon

---

[61] E. W. Handley, *Menander and Plautus*, 21, n. 15.
[62] On *hetaira* names in comedy, cf. *C.Q.*, 2, 1952, 21.

(jawman), Theron (hunter), and probably the flatterer Strouthias (birdman). Of the old men, Knemon suggests irritability and Smikrines miserliness, a characteristic which he lives up to in the *Apistos–Aulularia*, *Aspis* and *Epitrepontes*, and which is attributed to him by the 'democratic' messenger in the *Sikyonios* (162). A young countryman is called Gorgias in the *Dyskolos*, *Heros*, *Georgos*, and probably in the *Daktylios*: his name suggests the rhetorician and in the *Dyskolos*, and probably in the *Heros* and *Georgos*, he justifies it.

Slave names are readily recognisable. Some suggest country of origin, as we have noted above:[63] Daos, Getas, Karion, Lydos, Dardanos, Dryas, Sangarios, Sikon, Syros, Tibeios, Doris, Phrygia; and, of these, Karion, Sikon, Syros and Doris were already in the comic tradition. Some suggest character or function: Dromon, Kantharos, Kerdon, Onesimos, Parmenon, Sosias, Spinther, Philinna, Sophrone, Synete, Mania; and of these Dromon Parmenon and Sosias were already in the tradition. Some suggest appearance: Pyrrhias, Simias and Simike, of which Simias is known elsewhere.[64] Of all these Daos, Syros and Parmenon appear to be the most popular. Menander does not seem to have followed any very obvious principles. Daos has the leading part in the *Aspis*, *Perinthia* and *Eunuch* but a minor part in the *Dyskolos* and *Epitrepontes*. Syros has the leading part in the *Dis Exapaton* and probably in the *Phasma* but a minor part in the *Epitrepontes* and a minimal part in the *Georgos*. Probably mask rather than name showed which slave had the leading part. Doris, on our limited evidence, belonged to girls who were momentarily in the possession of a *hetaira* (*Encheiridion*, *Kekryphalos*, *Kolax*, *Perikeiromene*). Karion and Sikon were cooks. Pollux lists the two masks for native and foreign cooks under the slave masks, but these cooks who were hired in the *agora* may have been freedmen who had kept their slave names rather than slaves.[65]

Little is known about Menander's names for married women. Myrrhine occurs four times, and the name is already found in Aristophanes' *Lysistrata*. The rich heiress wife of the *Plokion* is

---

63 Cf. above, ch. III, p. 41.
64 *Dionysios*, fr. 2 K: a cook's slave, as probably also in the *Epitrepontes*.
65 Cf. L.G.C. 71; G.T.P. 84. A clever combination of frs. 272 and 741 K–T by Headlam shows that the *leno* in the *Messenia* was called Psyllos, a Libyan name, suggesting Flea; he would have the same kind of status as the cook. Cf. above, ch. III, p. 33.

called Krobyle, and possibly the name alludes to the elaborate hairstyle known as *krobylos*.

Old men and young men have distinct sets of names (with one difficulty to be discussed below). Of the old men, Chremes and Laches were already in the comic tradition, and Blepes (if this is the right interpretation of *Sikyonios* 188) has a name very like Blepsidemos in the *Ploutos* of Aristophanes. Of the young men Pheidias, Pamphilos and Chaireas are already in the comic tradition. On our evidence Laches and Demeas appear more commonly than any of the other old men's names; but although Laches is known to us from the Platonic dialogue, Menander simply used them as old men's names: it is clear that no link except age unites the old men called Demeas in the *Samia*, *Misoumenos* and *Adelphoi* B.

Possibly sometimes Menander means his men's names to show a family connection. Chairestratos in the *Aspis* has a stepson Chaireas and a nephew Kleostratos, which would agree with the principles of Greek naming if Chaireas' father was a near relation and if Chairestratos' father also had a name beginning or ending in stratos. (Smikrines, the older brother of Chairestratos, falls out of the picture because Menander wanted to give him a speaking-name.) Simon (in the *Eunuch*) is a good old cavalry name,[66] and Chairestratos is a suitable name for his son; unfortunately we do not know whether Terence, who named him Phaedria, also changed the name of the younger son Chaerea. Sostratos is an old Athenian aristocratic name, and so Kallippides is a fitting father for him in the *Dyskolos*, and the pair make a good contrast to Knemon and Gorgias. If this line of argument is right, then Derkippos and Mnesippos may be father and son in the *Encheiridion*, and, as the masks also suggest, Lysias and Kleinias may be brothers in the *Theophoroumene*. Conceivably also Philinos and Kratinos are father and son in the *Daktylios*.

There are two different cases where Menander seems to use names in two categories. Chaireas is a young man in the *Aspis*, *Koneiazomenai* and *Fabula Incerta*. But in the *Dyskolos* the *dramatis personae* calls him a parasite, and his account of the different treatment to be given to a friend in love with a *hetaira* and a friend who intends to marry (58) sounds like a parasite's

[66] On the other hand I do not think that any allusion to Nikias' family is meant by the name of Nikeratos in the *Samia*.

philosophy.[67] The difficulty is not only that the parasite has a special mask but also that parasites in Menander, as far as we know them, have speaking-names. Sostratos calls him 'both a friend and extremely practical'. I am inclined to think that he is a young man, a more experienced friend, and that an intelligent commentator decided that he was a parasite and put this description in the *dramatis personae*.

Chairestratos is more difficult. In the *Aspis* he has a marriageable daughter and a marriageable stepson, and we should naturally reckon him an old man. In the *Eunuch* he is in love with Chrysis and is the elder son of Simon, so that he is certainly a young man. In the *Epitrepontes* he is in love with Habrotonon and apparently lives on his own, but Syros calls him 'the young master' (201, *trophimos*), so that again he is young. In the *Aspis* he is presumably the youngest of the three brothers, and he calls Smikrines 'very old indeed' (259). If Menander thought about it, he may have supposed that he married very young and was now in his early thirties. Then the gap between him and the Chairestratos of the *Eunuch*, whose younger brother is in the second year of his ephebate and therefore twenty years old, need not be more than a few years. The young masks allow for three ages; No. 11 is younger than No. 10 and No. 13 is younger still (I am assuming that No. 19, which is the oldest of all and has hair sprinkled with grey, is irrelevant, because Pollux says that it was used for foreigners). I feel certain that in the *Aspis* name and mask were meant to emphasise the distance between Smikrines and Chairestratos.

The commonest of the young men's names is Moschion. He is the adopted son of Demeas in the *Samia*, a supposititious son in the *Perikeiromene* and *Hypobolimaios*, the son of Laches in the *Kitharistes*, *Plokion*, *Fabula Incerta* (?*Arrhephoros*) and P.S.I. 1176 (?*Demiourgos*), the son of Smikrines in the *Sikyonios*. The name seems to have come into comedy from a historical parasite.[68] This perhaps suggests a wild young man about town, and such a description suits the Moschions of Menander. According to Choricius,[69] Menander makes us suspect that Moschion will rape maidens. He has in the *Samia* and probably in the *Kitharistes*

[67] Cf. E. W. Hadlney, *ad loc.*
[68] Cf. Alexis, fr. 236 K.
[69] Cf. Kock, C.A.F., III, 494.

and *Plokion*, but not in the *Perikeiromene* or *Sikyonios*, although it might be argued that he had this intention.

6. *Language*

Masks and names both allow the audience to make a preliminary prediction. At the least they show sex, age and status, and sometimes suggest a finer differentiation within the main classes. How far the prediction is true is the task of the words to establish. Before considering further the vocabulary and style of the speeches we may look first at oaths. Greeks invoke the gods to emphasise what they are saying much more commonly than we use exclamations or expletives. It would seem possible that Menander distinguishes his characters by the gods they invoke. Certainly he distinguishes women from men.

We should perhaps expect men to invoke gods and women to invoke goddesses, but it is not quite as simple as that. Naturally women invoke 'the two goddesses' (Habrotonon in the *Epitrepontes* and the old slaves in *Dyskolos*, *Georgos* and *Misoumenos*), Artemis (Simike, who had brought up the girl in the *Dyskolos*; probably Krateia in the *Misoumenos*; the girls who gave birth in the *Andria* and *Georgos*), Aphrodite (Habrotonon; Doris in the *Perikeiromene*). Knemon's daughter naturally invokes the Nymphs, and Habrotonon calls on Persuasion (Peitho) before she puts her plan into action. It is strange that 'O gods' (as distinct from 'By the gods') is used only by Habrotonon (thrice) and Glykera (twice).[70] The four different forms of 'By the gods' are used fifty-three times by men and twice by women: one form of 'By the gods' is used by Knemon's daughter (*Dyskolos* 201), and Sostratos seems surprised at her, and another form is used by Chrysis in the speech which Sostratos (Mnesilochos) imagines her making (*Dis Exapaton* 95). Both instances are therefore unusual. The only other oaths shared with men are 'By Demeter' (Habrotonon) and 'By Zeus' (Glykera; Myrrhine in the *Georgos*, once each against seventy-four uses by men). Although the preserved women's parts are slight, it may not be chance that Habrotonon has more uses (seven) and a wider range than any other women. She is a *hetaira*, and *hetairai* are expected to be free with their oaths.[71]

[70] Cf. F. H. Sandbach, *Entretiens Hardt*, 16, 1970, 131.   [71] Cf. *Dis Exapaton* 21.

Four men let off a string of oaths at moments of emotion. The slave Parmenon in the *Samia* (309) is accused by Demeas of withholding information and expects to be beaten: he swears his innocence by Dionysos, by Apollo here, by Zeus the saviour, and by Asklepios. His other interesting oath is when he returns, realising that he need not have run away (641): then he swears by Zeus the greatest.[72] Getas in the *Misoumenos* (284 ff.) is infuriated by the treatment of Thrasonides by Demeas and Krateia, and starts with 'Much-honoured Zeus', then 'by the sun', then 'Herakles', rather later 'O Herakles', and later 'by Apollo here'; there may be more that we have lost because the text is defective. Earlier in his indignant description of Kleinias (165) he allows himself a 'much-honoured gods'.

In the *Dyskolos* it is the young lover, Sostratos, who shows his emotion in this way. When the girl comes out to get water (191) he invokes Father Zeus, Phoibos Paian and the Dioskouroi—all are unique in Menander. Then when he describes Knemon's rescue (666) he swears 'by Demeter, by Asklepios, by the gods'. In the course of this speech he also swears 'by the gods' and 'by Zeus', and he ends up with 'O Zeus saviour'. He swears elsewhere by Poseidon, by Herakles, by 'Apollo and the gods',[73] and by the much-honoured gods. His total of twenty-three oaths and invocations is the largest in Menander, and Menander must have meant to show that he was emotional. In his oaths as in his general style, as Professor Sandbach has shown,[74] he contrasts with Gorgias, who swears only four times and each time uses the simple 'By Zeus'.

Professor Sandbach also contrasts the high-flown language of the town cook Sikon with the simpler language of the country

---

[72] Also used by Kallippides to reassure Sostratos, *Dyskolos* 835, and by Smikrines in protest against the democratic man, *Sikyonios* 157.

[73] It is curious that this occurs otherwise only in the *Epitrepontes* 220, Syros; 224, 631, Onesimos. Zeus the saviour, Apollo Paian and the Dioskouroi are to save Sostratos from the stormy disease of love (*cf.* 203a, which belongs to Sostratos). P. Oxy. 2826 also a young man in love, appeal to Zeus the saviour. Parmenon, *Samia* 310, and Onesimos, *Epitrepontes* 587, appeal to Zeus the saviour when in physical danger; Parmenon in *Kekryphalos* (951 K–T) appeals to him when he has had a windfall. *Cf.* Demeas' appeal to Zeus tropaios, when he thinks he will find Krateia, *Misoumenos* 45. In the *Androgynos* 49 K–T, the man who calls Zeus philios to witness is probably the youth assuring the father that he will marry the girl.

[74] *Op. cit.*, 118, where he is surely right in giving *Dyskolos* 777 to Sostratos rather than to Gorgias.

slave Getas. He has fourteen oaths to Getas' seven. Getas has perhaps caught 'much-honoured gods' from Sostratos; Earth and Demeter are natural oaths for a countryman. Apollo is more suited to the townsman, and a cook can reasonably swear by Dionysos. Sikon's 'by Heaven', (only otherwise in the young man's first speech in the Daktylios) is presumably part of his high style.

The fourth man to use a string of invocations is Demeas in the Samia (325). This, however, is different because instead of invoking gods he quotes tragedy: 'O city of Kekropian land, O thin-spun aether, O —'. But apart from that he uses sixteen oaths as against Nikeratos' six. He swears four times by Apollo (once as Loxias), twice by Herakles, and once by the twelve gods, Athena, Hephaistos and Helios. Nikeratos also swears twice by Herakles, and once by Apollo, by Dionysos, and by 'Poseidon and the gods'. Demeas' concentration on Apollo is, I think, because he needs the present help of the Apollo outside his house. They are both deeply stirred by the action in progress, but Demeas' emotion goes much deeper, and Menander probably means us to see him as reacting rather like the young Sostratos in the Dyskolos.

The total number of oaths sworn by men is 247, and they divide into seventy-five sworn by old men, eighty by young men, twenty-three by cooks and sixty-nine by slaves. The big blocks, 'By the Gods' and 'By Zeus', and the less frequent 'By Apollo' do not show significant variation between the classes. Athena is not used by cooks because they are not citizens.[75] Cooks and slaves swear by Herakles (because he is illegitimate and a foreigner); the old men still swear by him because they are old-fashioned. This may also account for the virtual restriction of Hephaistos to old men,[76] and the preponderance of Poseidon with old men.[77] On the other hand Dionysos is used more by young men than by anyone else. I do not know why Menander gives an oath by Helios five times to young men and four times to slaves but only twice to old men. But enough in Menander's use of oaths is clear to us to show that he did use them to give a particular colour to his character's speech.

[75] It is, however, once used by a slave: P.S.I. 1176 (? Demiourgos).
[76] Knemon, Demeas, Kichesias, but also Chaireas in P. Oxy. 2533 (? Arrhephoros).
[77] Knemon (twice) but also Sostratos, Sikon, Getas; Nikeratos but also the cook; Pataikos Smikrines (Aspis).

It may be impossible to decide how far Menander's style is
tailored to fit the situation at the moment and how far it is
determined by the kind of character speaking. This difficulty has
already appeared in discussing his use of tragic metre and
language and his use of oaths. Tragic metre and language are
used at moments of crisis in monologues by the old man Demeas
(Samia), the young man Thrasonides, and the slave Daos (Aspis),
and in dialogue by Glykera and Pataikos. They are also used in
quieter passages where an old man philosophises or a paidagogos
advises his young master. In both these uses the situation rather
than the type of character calls forth the language. But the use
of tragedy to baffle elderly men is primarily the privilege of
slaves. Similarly the frequent use of oaths distinguishes the
elderly Demeas from the elderly Nikeratos in the Samia, the
young Sostratos from the young Gorgias and the cook Sikon
from the slave Getas in the Dyskolos, so that oaths seem to be
associated with a character trait rather than a type of character.
On the other hand there is a clear distinction between men's
oaths and women's oaths, and, among women, hetairai and
women in the position of hetairai seem to swear most and to use
a rather different range of oaths.

Habrotonon is the only hetaira for whom we have any considerable stretch of Greek text, except for Glykera in the rather
special recognition scene. There is nothing distinctive, I think,
about her style, but she is very much given to the use of endearments. She calls Pamphile 'beautiful' (308) and the baby 'pretty'
(290). When she takes the baby out to look for Pamphile it is
'dearest child' (536) and she is successively 'dearest . . . sweet . . .
dearest . . . blessed'. And she addresses both Chairestratos and
Charisios as 'sweetest' (17, 633, 659). Otherwise the word
'sweetest' seems to be used by nurses in Menander. But this is
entirely right. The hetaira goes on using nursery endearments

Another character who probably came to Menander with a
tradition of highly-flown language is the cook. Sikon is a superb
example, and his language is not only plastered with oaths but
has a number of unusual compound words contrasting with the
plainer language of Getas.[78] Other cooks who use high-flown or
at least pompous language are found in the Demiourgos, Kolax,

[78] Cf. F. H. Sandbach, Entretiens Hardt. 16, 1970, 119. On the tradition cf.
L.G.C. 66.

Messenia, Pseudherakles, Samia and *Trophonios*. In other plays
too little of the cook's part remains to tell. But the cooks of the
Misoumenos and *Perikeiromene* seem to have been silent figures,
which must have been an effective surprise. The cook in the *Aspis*
has no flights of language. Menander wants a different contrast
here—dishonest realism against the honest but educated and
clever Daos. But the cook's opening sentence (216) is a beautifully
constructed double period, with each section subdivided and the
introductory particles repeated for the main sections and the
subsections; the closing clause balances the opening conditional
clause. He then goes on with a string of sentences in asyndeton.
In English we are so used to leaving out connecting particles that
it is difficult to remember that in Greek asyndeton is surprising
and clearly marks a change of style.[79] The present case might be
called agitated asyndeton and is not particularly striking. It is
the elaborate opening sentence which marks the cook as an
educated man. The other case of very special language in Menander is the bogus doctor in the *Aspis*; again it is traditionally comic
that the doctor should speak Doric and should use the maximum
number of technical terms.

Soldier and flatterer, parasite and friend, and running slave are
traditional, and the audience knows in advance what they will
say. The *Kolax* gives an example of excessive praise showered on
the soldier by the flatterer. Chaireas in the *Dyskolos* may not
technically be a parasite, but he describes the parasite's services
in suitable quick asyndeton (57–68).[80] Pyrrhias in the *Dyskolos*
is the running slave and appropriately says that he is too out of
breath to talk (96). For fifteen lines before that he has described
his fear of Knemon in a string of very short, agitated asyndeta.
Then he goes on to tell his story in longer sentences only occasionally without connections or with quick internal asyndeta,
'letting fly with clods, stones, pears' (120). The arrival of
Pyrrhias is a beautiful adaptation to the present situation of a
traditional figure which we know from Amphitheos in the *Acharnians* (176) more than a hundred years before.[81] In the same way

---

[79] Demetrios, *On Style*, 193, contrasts the reading style of Philemon with
the acting style of Menander: his example of the acting style is a four-verb
asyndeton (fr. 685 K–T): 'I conceived, gave birth, nurse, love.'

[80] The parasite is expected to describe his life, cf. *Stichus* 155, *Eunuch* 232
(flatterer rather than parasite?), perhaps *Sikyonios* 39. Cf. *L.G.C.* 64.

[81] Cf. *L.G.C.* 92–3, 197.

the arrival of a character with an animal for sacrifice is traditional, but Menander has two beautifully different adaptations
of it: Sikon with his refractory sheep in the *Dyskolos* and
Nikeratos with his skinny sheep in the *Samia*, but in P. Oxy. 11
(? *Paidion*) Simon brings the sheep from his farm without
comment.[82]

Nikeratos in the *Samia* (399) starts describing his sheep in
quite a long bipartite period, but even there in the first limb slips
into quick asyndeton: 'for it has blood, enough bile, good bones,
big spleen'. But when he sees Chrysis standing outside the door
he breaks into staccato asyndeton, which carries him through to
the end of the scene. This staccato asyndeton of small units, as
Professor Sandbach has pointed out, characterises Nikeratos all
the way through, and Menander gives him longer sentences or
tragic language only for very special effects. His views on the
sheep are the result of long reflection on the way home. His out-
bursts in the fourth act (507, 495, 517, 533) are due to great
emotion, and there are intentionally no transitions from his
staccato style to his emotional style. His is perhaps the most
individual style of Menander.[83]

Demeas is completely different (as in his use of oaths), and this
is, of course, the point. The one speech in which he comes very
near to Nikeratos' staccato asyndeta is the speech (547) where he
is caught up in Nikeratos' agitation and thinks that Nikeratos is
going to burn the baby. His first great monologue (206) starts
with a long image from tragedy. Then a long sentence of eight
lines,[84] starting with the equivalent of a triple relative clause, the
parts in asyndeton and introduced by the same or a similar word.
'Unsurpassable pain' is high-flown language. For his narrative
he goes over into Menander's ordinary easy narrative style, with
occasional quick asyndeta (222, 227, 244). He ends up with
long sentences. The first (265 ff.) goes into a result clause with
two parts, the second part splitting again into two parts. But
then his emotion overcomes him: 'whether mine or—but I do not
say this to you, I do not suspect, but I tell it and what I heard
myself, not yet indignant'. This sentence is balanced three lines
later (275) by a sentence beginning with a temporal clause

[82] Cf. L.G.C. 197.   [83] Cf. Sandbach, *op. cit.*, 121 f.
[84] The text is uncertain, but probably an anacoluthon in 214, and 216–8
hung on by a relative pronoun.

divided into two parts and each part again subdivided, and
ending 'I went out of my mind'. Demeas' other tragic speech
(325) also proceeds in beautifully formed long sentences between
the emotional outburst of oaths and self-apostrophe at the beginning and the self-apostrophe of the conclusion, which is rein-
forced by emotional asyndeton and alliteration: 'from the house
on her head to hell thrust the handsome Samian'. The very carefully formed sentences, with balancing parts and sometimes
antithesis and echoing beginnings or endings, sometimes tragic
reminiscences, are the mark of an educated man. Oaths, asyndeta,
anacoluthon, self-apostrophe are the marks of emotion, and the
combination brings Demeas nearer to the young Moschion than
to the elderly Nikeratos.[85] We have not enough Greek fragments
to show whether Menander stylised the similar trio, Micio,
Aeschinus, Demea in *Adelphoi* B, in the same way; certainly fr.
11 K–T, attributed to Demeas, 'But I, rustic, hard-working,
sullen, bitter, close-fisted', has a likeness to Nikeratos.

Professor Sandbach[86] has characterised the distinction between
the two young men in the *Dyskolos*: 'Sostratos' speech is easy
and flexible; one can rarely guess what is coming next, so that it
seems to take shape as it is uttered.' Gorgias talks like a book; his
thought takes the antithetical form familiar in the orators, so
that his sentences are determined before they begin. He quotes
Gorgias in the first scene with Sostratos (250–87) and in the last
act (823) for elaborate bipartite sentences, and compares Knemon
(743), the messenger in the *Sikyonios* (176) and the slave in the
Plokion (335 K–T).[87] The point about Gorgias is that he uses this
style, which we have seen already in Demeas, so much.

Sostratos has one passage in this elaborate style when he takes
his father to task on the marriage of Gorgias and preaches him a
sermon on the use of money. Here he uses long antithetic sentences, like Gorgias (797).[88] The other extreme of Sostratos' style
occurs in the scene with the girl: first the stream of invocations
(191, 202) and then self-apostrophe (214–17). Here he reminds us

[85] Moschion: tragic metre, 45 ff., 616 ff., long sentences, 616–22, 623–32;
emotional asyndeta, 47 ff., 624 f., 664 ff.
[86] Sandbach, *op. cit.*, 116.
[87] For this style in the philosophical slave probably *cf.* 198, 251 K–T; in the
philosophical old man. *Theophoroumene*, fr. 1; *Kitharistes*, fr. 1; 276, 401, 416,
581, 620 K–T; P. Oxy. 1239.
[88] Cf. fr, 213, 612 K–T, young men.

of Demeas in the *Samia*. But apart from these two passages the adjectives 'easy and flexible' fit well—particularly his narratives of his digging (522) and of Knemon down the well (666).

The other Sostratos, in the *Dis Exapaton*, shows the same two poles of extreme emotion and controlled emotion. His first monologue (19), when he decides to pay the gold back to his father, has emotional antithesis, anacoluthon, self-apostrophe; then, when he has carried out his decision (91), he is much calmer and speaks in long sentences. This controlled emotional style I think we can see again in Moschion of the *Perikeiromene* and in Chaireas in the *Aspis*.[89] The extreme emotional style occurs again in Polemon in the *Perikeiromene* (256 ff., but we have too little of him to see the whole range), in Thrasonides in the *Misoumenos* (1 ff.; 388, 394), and in the speech of Charisios in the *Epitrepontes* (588 ff.) in spite of his appearance of great control at the beginning.[90]

It is interesting to compare these three with their slaves. We see least of Sosias in the *Perikeiromene*, but he has an indignant loyalty to Polemon which expresses itself in excited asyndeta when he is aroused (196 ff.). Getas in the *Misoumenos* is clearer: all his three speeches are rich in short asyndeta, not unlike Nikeratos (*cf.* particularly 216). The two monologues are so difficult, particularly with a badly preserved text, because they switch so swiftly between self-apostrophe (160), reported speech, comment and apostrophe of others (168, 317). He also has an indignant loyalty to his master, but his breathless reaction is, I think, an uneducated reaction.

Onesimos[91] has a greater range of style, and it may very well be that he was originally the *paidagogos* of Charisios. His education is obvious when he plays with Smikrines in the last act. He can quote tragedy and bogus philosophy. He frames his sentences admirably, with long asyndeta, often subdivided and introduced with echoing words (734 ff.). But when he is afraid for his life (558 ff.) this style vanishes. The description of Charisios is not

---

[89] *Perikeiromene* 276; *Aspis* 248. Cf. above, n. 84, Moschion in the *Samia*. Perhaps also P. Ant. 15, *Daktylios* prologue, though the text is too corrupt for the articulation to be clear, and fr. 656 K–T.

[90] Cf. self-apostrophe of Chairestratos, *Epitrepontes* 652. Also highly emotional fr. 185–6 K–T.

[91] Sandbach, *op. cit.*, 134 ff.

as staccato as Getas, but it has similar patches of reported speech and three considerable asyndeta (558, 573, 585).[92]

This speech of Onesimos is probably the nearest thing in the preserved plays to the monologues where a slave wonders whether he can remain loyal to his master or not. Here we find the same emotional style with asyndeta and frequently self-apostrophe. The best preserved is P.S.I. 1176 (perhaps *Demiourgos*), where the asyndeta, and at the beginning the self-apostrophe, are carried over into the long image of the storm at sea, itself a sign of the slave's education.[93]

In the *Epitrepontes* Syros and Daos are contrasted as the educated and the uneducated slave. Syros may very well have been the *paidagogos* of Chairestratos, as he calls him his 'young master' (201). Daos' speech is by no means to be despised. He tells his story in long sentences, speeds it up with asyndeta and enlivens it with reported speech when he wants to. But Syros knows all the tricks: he makes the baby plead for himself (125), he knows (or at least pretends to know) tragedy, he can use antithesis and word play (particularly 129, 143).

Daos in the *Aspis* is, on his own statement, the *paidagogos* of Kleostratos, but he has no chance either to worry about whether he can remain loyal to his master or, like some of the elderly *paidagogoi*,[94] to advise him in his youthful follies. The tragic reminiscences in his opening lament and in his decepton of Smikrines have been discussed already. The opening is phrased in very long sentences; the second (4) is tripartite and the third is bipartite, with the second part divided again into antithetic sections. Then Daos starts his story and goes on in an easy narrative style. There is nothing very remarkable after that until the planning scene. There Daos rushes out of the house and castigates Chairestratos for giving up so feebly in a string of short asyndeta, mostly imperatives (299). When he starts to plan he goes into long and complicated periodic sentences to express his thought (329). What we do not find in Daos, because he is not in the sort

[92] Cf. the contrast in the *Perinthia* between Daos in fr. 1 and Daos in the papyrus fragment.

[93] Cf. P. Ant. 55, fr. a recto, d recto; P. Grenfell II 8 b; P. Oxy. 10, 12; P. Oxy. 11, 29 (? *Paidion*). Near also Parmenon's speech, *Samia* 641 ff.

[94] Cf. *Kolax* 85 ff.; *Phasma* 27 ff.; fr. 740. Cf. also 250, 264, 538 K–T. 722 K–T and P. Oxy. 2826 are sympathetic. Most of these show long sentences livened by quick asyndeton.

of agitation that produces it in the worried slave or love-sick master, is self-apostrophe. His grief at the beginning is a measured grief, a *threnos*, not a *kommos*.

The messenger speech of the *Sikyonios* is the greatest set piece in Menander. It starts with an enormously long and complicated sentence, which, as far as can be seen from the difficult text, runs for more than twenty lines: 'I was in fact neither ... nor ... (do not suggest that, for I am the sort of person who ...), but, coming from the city to meet ... (I was one of them; for ...), I stopped ... and I see ..., and one of the circle was Euthydemos, and'. This is a monster. It has nothing to do with the character or status of the messenger, although it does in fact sum up his position very nicely and so form a conclusion to the scene before.[95] The carefully framed opening to a long narrative is common technique. Daos' opening lament is another special example. Here Menander is simply telling the audience that a long narrative is coming and incidentally describing the speaker. Then the narrative flows easily, with its occasional patches of excitement: Moschion's first intervention, Stratophanes' first speech, and the quarrel at the end naturally show quick asyndeton.

It is worth while finally to look at Knemon.[96] He, if anyone, should be individual. He certainly has some strange words: *epereasmos, polypletheia*. The staccato style of Nikeratos is not his normal style. He uses it like anyone else when he is irritated —with the procession (431), with Getas (466), with Sikon (500), with Gorgias (750).[97] It is his longer speeches that show something distinctive. His entrance is not remarkable only for its address to Perseus (153). 'Was not Perseus blessed in two ways, that he was winged and met none of those walking on earth, and that he possessed a possession with which he turned to stone all obstructors? Which might it be mine now. For nothing would be more prevalent than stone statues everywhere. But now it is unlivable, by Asklepios. Already they are invading my land to chatter. I am used to spending my time along the road, I, who do not even work this part of the land but escape because of the

---

[95] Cf. above, ch. III. For the introduction of the proper name Euthydemos, cf. E. W. Handley, *B.I.C.S.*, 12, 1965, 50; this is necessary also for the structure of the sentence.

[96] Cf. Sandbach, *op. cit.*, 122.

[97] Cf. frs. 451, 581, 718, 800 K–T; P. Hibeh 6, 39. Frs. 303, 333 K–T have angry asyndeton but longer sentences.

passers-by. But already they are chasing me on to the hills above. Oh, the multitudinousness of the mob.' He starts with an elaborate sentence with two balanced clauses. The wish is hung on by a connecting relative, and he continues adding clause to clause until he gets to the end, with the single exception of the very mild asyndeton in 'Already . . .' (161). But each addition leads a step nearer the climax: 'Oh the multitudinousness of the mob.' On a minimal scale the same style appears in 505: 'I do not have either a pitcher pail or an axe or salt or vinegar or anything else, but I tell the neighbours simply not to come near me.' And the same sort of movement leads him on and on in his great apology (708): the new danger that he has perceived in the solitary life, the exception to the general corruption which had made him choose the solitary life, the adoption of Gorgias, and finally the philosophy of self-sufficiency and his prevision that it will be rejected. He works with a sort of continuing antithesis: 'you could not persuade me . . . but I made a single mistake, who thought that I should need no one. But now . . . I do. But I thought no man was kindly . . . but Gorgias proved the opposite,' etc. And at the very end he does not finish with his philosophy but takes one step further: 'But perhaps you like your way better. Follow it. The difficult and uncomfortable old man will be out of your way.'

On our evidence I should say that Knemon is individual because of the way he concatenates long sentences, Nikeratos is individual among old men and Getas (*Misoumenos*) among slaves because of their staccato use of asyndeton. But staccato asyndeton is used elsewhere as a mark of agitation; what is individual about Nikeratos and Getas is that they are continually agitated. All the stylistic phenomena noted above—long sentences of various kinds, asyndeton, quick, emotional, or staccato, self-apostrophe, anacoluthon—are marks which tell the audience something about the character at that particular moment. He is an educated man expressing himself carefully at the beginning of an utterance or to show off that he is an educated man or to control his emotions for the moment by giving them a well defined shape. Or he is excited with his story or he is agitated by the situation or he is swept away by love or worry or horror. The combination of these marks with each other and with vocabulary, oaths, and tragic reminiscences may be individual (I should like to think that Demeas in the *Samia* was individual, but Micio in *Adelphoi*

B may have been very like) but certainly serves to distinguish characters as belonging to a particular category, and within a category may contrast one character with another: Sostratos and Gorgias, Demeas and Nikeratos, Daos and Syros. But we need more material to be more precise about Menander's style.

7. Conclusion

The characters are what we remember, particularly their inter-actions with each other and their solitary moments of agony. The range of Menander's extraordinarily supple language places them in society, so that the audience can recognise at once where they belong, but also, by approximating to tragedy, shows when they are entirely serious (whether we are meant to laugh at their seriousness or not) and by approximating to Aristotle tells us how we should interpret their action in Aristotelian terms.

Masks and names give the audience a preliminary estimate of the characters, and they may run true to form or they may have a real value out of touch with their face value. If the simple and obvious conventions for the relating of stage space and time to imagined space and time are accepted, the stories are seen to be composed of incidents which are probable in the Aristotelian sense, and the improbabilities often seem more acceptable because they have already appeared in earlier comedy or in tragedy. Menander adopted the five-act form very early and gave it a predictable climax in the fourth act. The plays are set in the present and include sufficient allusions to recent historical events and attitudes to fix them in contemporary reality.

Menander is a conscious technician, like Sophocles before him, and the certainty with which he makes his dramatic points is one of his attractions. But beyond this he has the supreme skill of being able to make this situation in this play completely convinc-ing, immediate and particular, and beyond that again is the humane view of life with which he informs his comedy.

Appendix I

Menander's plays

This appendix summarises what we know or can conjecture about Menander's plays. Where we have long stretches of papyrus or adaptations by Plautus or Terence, the stage houses are indicated and act and scene divisions are given. Plautus and Terence wrote for continuous playing, and in their adaptations the act divisions can be restored only conjecturally by using the criteria indicated in chapter VI. In the Greek texts act divisions, where they survive, are marked. Scene divisions are a modern convenience.

The plays are arranged in alphabetical order of their transliterated titles. I have added the probable date (see chapter I) after each title. Much of the earlier bibliography is cited in the Teubner text of Körte and Thierfelder, and a very complete recent bibliography has been given by H. J. Mette in *Lustrum* 10, 1965; 11, 1966; 13, 1968. I have therefore quoted only what seemed to me relevant. Fragments in arabic numerals will be found in the Teubner text (abbreviated K–T). Fragments in roman numerals will be found under the name of the Roman adapter in Ribbeck, *Comicorum Fragmenta*. Plautus and Terence are quoted from the Oxford text. I have quoted under the relevant plays the recent papyri which are not included in K–T, vol. I. The excellent Oxford text of F. H. Sandbach was published when my manuscript was complete. It was only possible to refer to it in the footnotes of the appendices. The numeration is the same as mine except in *Epitrepontes* and *Perikeiromene*, but there the Körte numeration is quoted in brackets.

The majority of Menander's plays survive in quotations alone, whether of the Greek original or of a Roman adaptation. In many of these the fragments reveal nothing of the structure: *Anatithemene* (unless it is the same play as the *Messenia*), *Anechomenos*, *Aphrodisios*, *Chalkis*, *Chalkeia*, *Chera*, *Dardanos*, *Deisidaimon* (to which perhaps add fr. 754), *Didymai*, *Glykera*, *Halaeis* (unless it is the same as the *Epitrepontes*),[1] *Heauton Penthon* (which cannot be an alternative title for the *Aspis*, as both occur in P. Oxy. 2462), *Heniochos*,

---

[1] C Corbato, *Studi Menandrei*, Trieste, 1965, 69.

Hippokomos, Katapseudomenos, Lokroi, Menagyrtes, Nomothetes, Phanion, Progamon, Proenkalon, Poloumenoi, Pseudherakles, Stratiotai, Synerosa, Synepheboi, Thettale, Thyoros, Trophonios. But the rest have some point or points of sufficient interest to justify inclusion here. *Achaeans or Peloponnesians* was unknown until the finding of the Oescus mosaic,[2] which shows a seated old man with a civilian youth standing on one side and a soldier on the other, perhaps two sons. The title is confirmed by P. Oxy. 2462, and a fragment (*Atti del XI Congresso*, 11) speaks of a poor man made rich by fortune, perhaps the soldier son?

Adelphoi A or Philadelphoi (before 312)

Like the second *Adelphoi*, which Terence translated, the first *Adelphoi*, adapted by Plautus as the *Stichus*, seems to have had an alternative title, *Philadelphoi*. The fragments of the *Philadelphoi* are compatible with the *Stichus*. Besides the fragments given to these two titles the papyrus Didot A has been assigned with some probability to this play.[3] House A is occupied by Panegyris, the wife of Epignomus; house B by Pamphila, her sister, wife of his brother Pamphilippus.

Act I. It would be unlike Menander to give the audience no preparation for the return of the brothers. A prologue speech could tell how they became so poor that they had to seek wealth abroad, warn the audience that they would soon return, and enlighten it on the character of Antipho, the father of the two sisters (fr. 2 describes their wild living).

Sc. 2. Panegyris is visited by Pamphila; they discuss Antipho's desire to take them away from their absent husbands. (1–57)

Sc. 3. Antipho enters with a slave, whom he sends back with instructions to clean his house (this is more likely than Plautus' version, where he has a house on the stage and talks back into it).[4] He considers whether to treat his daughters 'gently or fiercely', and leads up 'gently' to the suggestion that they should come home with him. They refuse. He goes off to consult his friends (in the *agora*). Pamphila goes into her house. Panegyris sends her servant, Crocotium, to summon the parasite Gelasimus. (58–154)

Act II, sc. 1. Antipho's opening suggested that he would also talk

[2] *Monuments illustrating New Comedy*, XM 1; L. Kahil, *Antike Kunst*, Beiheft 6, 1970, pl. 27, 1.

[3] H. Lucas, *Ph.W.*, 1938, 1101. Barigazzi, *Athenaeum*, 43, 1955, 267, again suggests *Epitrepontes*. Bühler, *Hermes*, 91, 1963, 345, denies that it is Menander.

[4] Alternatively, Antiphon had a house on stage, and the brothers shared the other stage house. I am not clear that the 'garden way' is not Plautine.

fiercely to his daughters (79), and the Didot papyrus and frs. 438, 440 (perhaps also 743) seem to preserve traces of another scene in which they resisted him. This should come here. Antipho then goes to the harbour.

Sc. 2. Gelasimus enters with a typical parasite monologue. Crocotium, having returned, and finding him at the door, tells him to go to the harbour, and herself goes in. (155–264)

Sc. 3. Before he can go, the slave Pinacium, whom Panegyris had sent earlier to the harbour (153), arrives running (cf. fr. 690), with the news that Epignomus and his slave Stichus have arrived with much Eastern booty. He tells Panegyris, who sends Gelasimus off and goes in with Pinacium to start a sacrifice. (265–401; fr. 437)

Act III, sc. 1. Epignomus arrives with Stichus, and agrees that Stichus shall have a holiday with his brother's slave, Sangarinus, and his brother's maid, Stephanium. (402–53)

Sc. 2. Gelasimus arrives and tries to get an invitation for dinner from Epignomus, who firmly refuses. (454–504; perhaps fr. 439 belongs)

Act IV, sc. 1. Antipho arrives with Pamphilippus (presumably he had heard in the *agora* of the arrival of the ship and had gone to meet Epignomus and then waited for Pamphilippus, 510). Epignomus comes out of his house. Antipho requests one of the foreign slaves as his concubine, and goes in to greet his daughters. (505–73)

Sc. 2. The brothers remain to make fun of Gelasimus, who returns to greet Pamphilippus in the hope of being asked to dinner. He is again sent off. (574–640; frs. 436, 441 with a change of metre to trochaic tetrameters, perhaps when Gelasimus is left alone)

Act V, sc. 1. Stichus comes out to look for Sangarinus, who arrives (641–72; fr. 1). The rest of the play is given up to the junketings of Stichus, Sangarinus and the girl Stephanium, greatly enlarged by Plautus (673–775).

Every scene preserved has been expanded by Plautus. It is very likely that he cut out a prologue speech and a second scene between Antipho and his daughters, as suggested above. The monologue of Stichus (436–53), after he has twice been told to take Epignomus' booty in, is suspicious, and the reference to the licence of Athenian slaves is Roman. It contains the reference to the garden way, by which he will find Stephanium in the other house and go to do his marketing. By the same garden way Pamphila and Stephanium have arrived in Epignomus' house unseen by us (536; 673). This arrangement does not sound like Menander; I suspect that Panegyris sent a slave to bring Pamphila (and Stephanium?) across to her house as soon as she got the news of her husband's return (*cf.* 147–8). It is also possible that Epignomus went or sent a slave to do the marketing (and hire a cook?), both for his party and for the slave's party, either at the end of the third act, returning in the fourth act, or, less probably, in the fourth act, returning at the beginning of the fifth, but it is possible that Menander simply assumed all this and did not show it.

Adelphoi B or Homopatrioi (305)

Menander's play had alternative titles, *Brothers* or *Sons of one father*. This is shown by the occurrence of fragments ascribed to both plays in Terence's adaptation.[5] Terence himself tells us that he has inserted a passage from Diphilos' *Synapothneskontes*, and this can be defined as ll. 155–95.

The scene is Athens. House A belongs to Micio (Lamprias in Menander); his adopted son Aischinus (the son of his brother Demeas) and slaves Syrus and Dromo also live there. House B is occupied by a widow, Sostrata, her daughter Pamphila (who has been raped by Aischinus), her slave Geta and her nurse Canthara.

Act I, sc. 1. Micio is worried because Aeschinus has not returned from a dinner party the night before. Demeas arrives from the country, where he has left his son, Ctesipho. On his way in he has heard that Aeschinus broke into a house and carried off a woman. Demeas and Aeschinus contrast their methods of bringing up sons. Demeas goes off. Micio goes to the *agora* to find Aeschinus. (26–154; frs. 3, 528, 605, 609, perhaps 654b)

The complicated story of the night before can be reconstructed from later hints, but Menander probably used a prologue figure to tell it and also to warn the audience that Aeschinus had raped Pamphila nine months before.[6] The night before seems to have gone like this: at dinner Ctesipho told that the girl he loved was being taken to Cyprus by the procurer and then went home; in the early morning Aeschinus broke into the procurer's house and removed the girl to a friend's house until Micio had gone out; Syrus had gone to fetch Ctesipho. Two scenes therefore followed the prologue speech. Aeschinus arrived with the girl, and Syrus returned to report that Ctesipho was coming. This completed the first act.

Act II, sc. 1. The procurer comes to complain of his losses. Syrus meets him and promises to provide the purchase price of the girl. (196–251; fr. 4)

[5] *Cf.* K. Gaiser, *W.S.*, 79, 1966, 195, most recently.
[6] The prologue speech may have come at the beginning, as Varro noted a difference between the 'beginning' of Terence and Menander.

Sc. 2. Ctesipho arrives from the country, full of gratitude. Aeschinus comes out to him. Ctesipho goes in to see the girl. Aeschinus goes to the *agora* with Syrus to pay the procurer. (portions of 252–87)

Sc. 3. Sostratos comes out from house B with Canthara (mute), worried about the pains of Pamphila. Getas enters from the *agora*, where he has heard that Aeschinus has fallen in love with the procurer's girl. He is sent to find Hegio, a relative of Sostrata's late husband (in Menander Sostrata's brother), and Canthara is sent for the midwife (288–354; frs. 5–6)

Act III, sc. 1. Terence has probably cut out a brief scene in which Canthara returns with the midwife.

Sc. 2. Demeas enters, having heard that Ctesipho was involved in carrying off the procurer's girl. Syrus follows, having arranged with Micio to pay the procurer and bringing the fish, which he hands over to the slaves in house A. He persuades Demeas that Ctesipho had fiercely criticised his brother and gone back to the country. Syrus goes into house A. (355–434; fr. 109)[7]

Sc. 3. Demeas is going off when he sees in the distance Hegio arriving with Geta. Hegio is incensed at Aeschinus' conduct in deserting Pamphila for the procurer's girl. He tells the story to Demeas. Pamphila is heard crying out in labour. Demeas promises to tell Micio. Hegio and Geta go into Sostrata. (435–510; fr. 7)[8]

Sc. 4. Hegio comes out and also goes off to find Micio (511–16). Possibly in Menander the midwife also left now.

Act IV, sc. 1. Ctesipho comes out with Syrus, afraid that his father will come and find him. Syrus drives him back in again when Demeas in fact arrives, furious because he has not found Micio and his bailiff has told him that Ctesipho is not in the country. Syrus tells him that Ctesipho came back to punish him (Syrus) and that Micio has gone to visit a couch-maker. Demeas goes after him. Syrus decides to go and drink, while waiting for Aeschinus. (517–91)

Sc. 2. Micio returns with Hegio, and together they go into house B. (593–609; fr. 8)

Sc. 3. Aeschinus returns. He has met Canthara and knows that he is suspected of having deserted Pamphila. He is going to visit her when Micio comes out. Micio pretends that Pamphila is being claimed in marriage by her next of kin. Aeschinus confesses, and Micio promises that he shall marry Pamphila. They both go into Micio's house. (610–712; fr. 9; 301–2)

---

[7] Gaiser, *op. cit.*, has strengthened my ascription to 109 K–T to this play; then Terence's Demea was Menander's Demeas.

[8] In Menander Demeas' monologue must have been long enough to cover Hegio's entry and return; Hegio must leave the stage in act III.

Act V, sc. 1. Demeas returns and finds Micio at home. He believes from Micio's account that Aeschinus is going to live with his new wife and the procurer's girl in the same house. Micio goes to house B. (713–62)

Sc. 2. Syrus comes out drunk. Dromo calls to him to come in to Ctesipho. Demeas understands the truth and rushes in. Syrus follows. (763–86)

Sc. 3. Micio returns. Demeas rushes out, furious. Micio argues with him and begs him to come to the wedding party. (787–85; frs. 10, 300)

Sc. 4. Demeas, alone, decides to adopt Micio's policy of giving. (854–81; fr. 11)

Sc. 5. Demeas is polite to Syrus, who comes to call him in, then to Geta, who looks out of house B to see if they are coming to fetch the bride. (882–98)

Sc. 6. Demeas suggests to Aeschinus that the two houses should be thrown into one. Micio comes out, and Demeas suggests that he should marry Sostrata and give Hegio a plot of land, free Syrus, let him marry, and set him up in a trade. (899–997 without Syrus and Geta, who are additions of Terence; fr. 12; P. Oxy. 2534)[9]

Andria (308–6)

Terence says that he took over what suited him from the *Perinthia*, which was similar in plot but different in style.[10] The surviving fragments of both plays gives some guidance as to what in Terence comes from each play, and Donatus gives some help.

House A is occupied by Simo, who has a son, Pamphilus, and a slave, Davus. House B was occupied by an Andrian *hetaira*, Chrysis, who has recently died, leaving a supposed sister, Glycerium, a slave, Mysis, and other female slaves.

Act I, sc. 1. Simo (alone, according to Donatus) tells how he is worried by Pamphilus' apparent love for Glycerium; he hopes to move him and frustrate Davus by pretended marriage preparations with the daughter of Chremes. (48–167)

Sc. 2. Sosias, a freedman, of Simo, arrives with provisions. Simo enlists his aid. (28–47; 168–71)[11]

(Sc. 3. A prologue speech is needed to tell that Glycerium will turn

---

[9] P. Oxy. 2534 summarises the ending; cf. *Essays presented to Franz Blatt.*

[10] Koerte (K–T, I, liii) finds the difference of style in the treatment of the midwife and in the punishment of Daos. I have suggested (ch. I) that the plays are near in date.

[11] According to Donatus, Menander began the play with the monologue of the old man. Hence this rearrangement of Terence.

out to be a lost daughter of Chremes and that she is now in the last
stages of pregnancy by Pamphilus.)

Sc. 4. Simo warns Davus not to hinder the marriage and goes to the
agora. (172–205, fr. 33)

Sc. 5. Davus debates whether he should obey Simo or help Pamphilus; he goes to the *agora* to warn Pamphilus. (206–27, fr. 43)

Act II, sc. 1. Mysis comes out of house B to fetch the midwife. Pamphilus enters from the *agora*, in misery because his father has told
him to prepare for marriage. He protests his loyalty to Chrysis'
memory. (228–300)

The next two scenes in Terence come from the *Perinthia* (301–74);
we do not know, therefore, exactly how Menander wrote the beginning of the scene in which Davus comes back from the *agora* and
finds Pamphilus; but from 375 Terence is using the *Andria* again.

Sc. 2. Davus comes back from the agora. He persuades Pamphilus
to humour his father. (375–403)

Sc. 3. Simo comes back from the agora. Pamphilus agrees to the
marriage, and goes in to get ready. Davus complains that the marketing has been too parsimonious. (404–58, fr. 34)

412–31 are inserted from the *Perinthia*, but Pamphilus must have
made a similar declaration in the *Andria*. It is not clear how Menander worked the end of the act. Mysis' return (459) must be act III, and
Simo and Davus must be on stage. Possibly the act starts with Simo
and Davus setting out for market (*cf.* 456).

Act III, sc. 1. Simo and Davus overhear Mysis talking to the midwife
(mute) as she brings her back to house B. Then Glycerium cries out in
labour, and the midwife goes off, giving her instructions back through
the door (459–88, frs. 35, 36, 37).

Sc. 2. Simo interprets this as a trick of Davus. Davus suggests that
it is a trick of Glycerium, and that he should go ahead with the
marriage. Davus is sent in to make preparations (489–531).

Sc. 3. Chremes arrives, having heard that in spite of his earlier
protest marriage preparations are being made. Simo tries to persuade
him, and calls Davus out to support him. Chremes goes home to make
preparations. Simo goes in to Pamphilus. (532–99, fr. 38)

Sc. 4. Davus is in utter despair at the wreck of his plans, and
Pamphilus comes out and curses him. (607–24, fr. 39)

625–72 come from the *Perinthia*, and again it is not clear how
Menander worked the act end in the *Andria*. Probably both go in, and
at the beginning of the new act come out with something like 670
ff.[12]

[12] Note that 670, like *Bacch.* 692, translates the 'second sailing' of *Theophoroumene* fr. 6 and 205, 244 K–T.

Act IV, sc. 1. Pamphilus and Davus come out and Davus promises a new plan. (670–83)

Sc. 2. Mysis comes out to fetch Pamphilus. He swears his loyalty and goes in to see Glycerium. Davus follows, leaving Mysis on stage. (684–720, without Charinus)

Sc. 3. Davus comes out with the baby and puts it on Simo's doorstep. He sees Chremes coming and tells Mysis to act up to him. (721–39, fr. 40)

Sc. 4. Chremes arrives. Davus maintains that Glycerium is tricking Pamphilus into marrying him. Chremes goes in to Simo. (740–89)

Sc. 5. Davus explains to Mysis. Crito, who is Chrysis' cousin, arrives to claim her estate as her heir. Mysis greets him. Davus follows them into house B. (789–819, fr. 41, 45)

Act V, sc. 1. Simo and Chremes enter. Simo still tries to persuade him to carry on with the marriage. (820–40)

Sc. 2. Davus comes out to them and reports that an old man (Crito) has said that Glycerium is an Attic citizen. Simo sends him in to be punished and calls Pamphilus out of house B. (841–71)

Sc. 3. Pamphilus admits his love for Glycerium and demands that what Crito says shall be heard by his father. (872–903)

Sc. 4. Crito comes out and is recognised by Chremes. In spite of Simo's protests he maintains that Glycerium was an Attic citizen, left as a child with Chrysis by Phania, who said she was his brother's child. Chremes realises that she must be his daughter, as Phania was his brother. Simo accepts the situation, and her betrothal to Pamphilus is arranged. (904–56, without Pamphilus; fr. 42)

It is not clear how much Terence has shortened Menander here because he wants to end the play with a *Perinthia* scene (927 ff.). Donatus' quotation of 919 proves that there the three speakers in Menander were Chremes, Simo and Crito. Possibly Crito went in or off when he had made the essential identification of Phania, then Pamphilus came out, heard the two discussing the girl's name and added his piece of knowledge (945), and then the play ended with his betrothal and the liberation of Davus (956).

Androgynos or Cretan (321–19)

The reference to Lamia (47) and to Chairephon (51) date the play early. It is listed in P. Oxy. 2462 and was adapted by Caecilius. *Androgynos* means a coward in *Samia* 69 and *Aspis* 242, but literally it means 'womanish man', and a twelfth-century Latin comedy, in which a boy dresses up as a girl so as to get introduced to the daughter of a widower, claims to derive from Menander.[13] The father lost his wife when the girl was born and for that reason he has forbidden her male society. Menander has adapted the story of Euripides' *Skyrioi*, but the twisted old man recalls his own Euclio and Knemon. The old man is amazed when the girl becomes pregnant (46 goes with Alda 546), but the boy confesses (49) and the play ends in marriage (52). The dressing up and whatever help the boy had from slave, nurse or sister (Alda) was prehistory, told partly in the boy's confession and partly in a prologue speech, which also described the mother's tomb (Caecilius I). Mette[14] has explained the alternative title *Cretan* as a reference to an obscure Cretan legend in which a girl grew a male organ. This seems far-fetched, and the Cretan is more likely to have been a mercenary soldier. A soldier is needed to explain the reference to the battle of Lamia (47) and to an utterly worthless enemy (50, perhaps *cf.* also 942). How he came into the story we do not know: possibly he and the boy were rivals for the same *hetaira* before the boy found that the girl was pregnant and asked to marry her. The father's name was Kraton (49).

Anepsioi (probably late)

Listed both in P. Oxy. 2462 and in P. British Museum 2562. Adapted by Afranius. This may have been a play not unlike the second *Adelphoi*, with the young men cousins instead of brothers. The problem of bringing up sons was discussed (Afranius I, *cf. Adelphi* 57). One of the young men was deeply in love (53). The fragments about making light (55–6) probably belong to the description of a symposion. There was a *hetaira* (IV), and a brave Thracian (?) slave (57), who presumably intrigued. The other young man had probably raped a poor girl: a father complains of a troublesome daughter (54); there was a drunken midwife or nurse (II); the boy was perhaps interrogated by his father (VI, V). The word 'valuation' occurred:[15] conceivably the poor man's house was bought by the rich man. (*Cf.* also fr. 925.)

Apistos (Aulularia) (318/7)

The parallels with the *Dyskolos* make the case for the *Aulularia* being based on an original of Menander even stronger than it was before.[16]

---

[13] So G. Neumann, *Hermes*, 81, 1953, 491.

[14] *Hermes*, 90, 1962, 383.

[15] Mette, *Lustrum*, 11, 140 from Photios.

[16] See E. W. Handley, *The Dyskolos of Menander*, London, 1965, 12, etc., and *Entretiens Hardt*, 16, 1970, 100; W. G. Arnott, *Phoenix*, 18, 1964, 232.

The likeness of the suspicious hero to Theophrastos' Apistos (cf. particularly Characters, XVIII, 7) makes Menander's Apistos a likely candidate, and the one fragment (58) could belong to the prologue if Menander told rather more about Euclio or his father than Plautus has preserved.[17]

House A is occupied by Euclio, his daughter, and the maid Staphyla; house B belongs to Megadorus and his sister Eunomia and her son Lyconides, who has a slave, Strobilus. In Menander Euclio's name was Smikrines (Choricius, R.P., 1877, 288). Between the two houses is the shrine of Pistis.

Act I, sc. 1. The prologue speech is very like that of Pan in the Dyskolos. The speaker in Menander was probably Hestia, as Euclio's grandfather had hidden the pot of gold in the hearth. She describes Euclio's miserly character. She has let him find the gold so that he may have a dowry for his daughter, who has been raped by Lyconides. She will help by making his uncle ask to marry her. (I–39)

Sc. 2. Euclio drives Staphyla out of the house and, while she worries about the pregnancy of her young mistress, goes back to make sure that the gold is safe; then he tells Staphyla to bolt the doors and keep out all intruders while he goes to collect money from a (deme?) distribution. (40–119)

These scenes cannot be divided from each other, and the likeness of the prologue to the Dyskolos makes it unlikely that a scene preceded it. One would expect in the first act to see Lyconides and his slave; Menander may have inserted such a scene here. Lyconides evidently went to the agora and there heard the news of Megadorus' proposal to marry Euclio's daughter, but it is not strictly necessary that we should have seen him go.

Act II, sc. 1. Megadorus and his sister Eunomia come out of his house and discuss marriage. Megadorus proposes to marry Euclio's daughter. (120–77)

Sc. 2. Megadorus crosses over to Euclio's house, but before he can knock Euclio returns and immediately suspects that Megadorus has heard of the gold. In the following scene while Megadorus presses his proposal of marriage Euclio twice runs into the house to see that the gold is safe. At the end they agree, and Megadorus summons Strobilus from his house to go with him to market. (178–264)

Sc. 3. Euclio tells Staphyla of the marriage and goes to market. She comments on the impossibility of concealing the girl's pregnancy. (265–79)

---

[17] Gaiser op. cit. n. 5, accepts my identification with Apistos, but associates 58 K–T with Aul. 496–7.

Act III, sc. 1. Strobilus returns with two cooks, who gossip and squabble as to which shall cook for Megadorus and which for Euclio. Anthrax is sent into Megadorus' house. (280–349)

Sc. 4. Strobilus then calls on Staphyla to take the other cook, Congrio, into Euclio's house. (350–62)

Plautus has inserted a little soliloquy by another slave here to cover a major cut of Menander scenes. It looks as if Lyconides returns at this point, having heard of Megadorus' proposed marriage, and agrees with Strobilus that Strobilus shall tell Staphyla that it was Lyconides who raped the girl. (This she knows in 807; and Lyconides says in 815 that Strobilus must have visited her.) So Plautus has cut two scenes: Sc. 5, Lyconides and Strobilus; then Lyconides goes into Megadorus' house. Sc. 6, Strobilus and Staphyla; they retire into their respective houses as they see Euclio coming.

Sc. 7. Euclio returns with incense and flowers from market. Congrio calls to one of his assistants to borrow a pot from next door. Euclio rushes in. (371–96)

Sc. 8. Anthrax, from Megadorus' house, proposes to borrow a pot from Congrio, but goes back when he hears the shouting in Euclio's house. (397–407)

Sc. 9. Congrio dashes out of Euclio's house. Euclio pursues and stops him. Euclio goes in again. Euclio comes out with his pot of gold and drives Congrio in again. (406–59)

Sc. 10. Euclio cannot get away with his pot because Megadorus comes back from market. Megadorus discusses the disadvantages of rich marriages and invites Euclio in to drink with him. Euclio refuses, and when Megadorus has gone into his own house takes his pot of gold and puts it in the shrine of Pistis. (460–586)

Act IV, sc. 1. Strobilus comes out to report to Lyconides how the marriage preparations are going forward. (587–607)

Sc. 2. Strobilus overhears Euclio, who comes out of the shrine saying that the gold is in the shrine, and goes in to look for it. Euclio is frightened by a crow and goes back to the shrine, where he finds Strobilus and searches him. He tries to drive Strobilus away. (608–60)

Sc. 3. Strobilus watches while Euclio fetches the gold and goes off to hide it in the grove of Pan. Strobilus follows him. (661–81)

Sc. 4. Lyconides comes out with Eunomia, having confessed that he raped Euclio's daughter. Euclio's daughter is heard crying out in her birth pangs. They go in to ask Megadorus to allow Lyconides to marry the girl. (682–700, greatly shortened by Plautus)

Act V, sc. 1. Strobilus comes back with the pot of gold and goes into Megadorus' house. (701–12)

Sc. 2. Euclio enters distracted. Lyconides comes out, hearing his wailing. They misunderstand each other because Euclio is talking about the gold and Lyconides is talking about his daughter. Finally Euclio understands and goes in to see his daughter. (713–807)

Sc. 3. Strobilus comes out in triumph and tells Lyconides that he has found Euclio's pot of gold. (808–32)

Here the text breaks off. According to the second argument, Lyconides gives a report on the theft to Euclio and is presented with gold, wife and son. In fact this is what must happen; Euclio betroths his daughter to Lyconides with the gold as her dowry, and says that now at last he will be able to sleep (fr. IV). P. Oxy. 1239 preserves the last few lines of a play by Menander with a badly preserved final speech of a man who contrasts his happiness with others who have much more (wealth?)—this, apparently, involves friends, laughter, tears, change and fears for the future. He then says that though he wishes to say much more, he sees that he is speaking at the Lenaia (i.e. seriousness is out of place in comedy, cf. *Dysk.* 746; *Ad.* 991). He is going in to see his daughter. Then the play ends with the usual demand for applause. C. Corbato[18] has suggested that the man is Euclio (or rather Smikrines, as Choricius gives his name) at the end of the original of the *Aulularia*, and this is very attractive.

Arrhephoros or *Auletris* (?321–19)

The second title occurs in P. Oxy. 2462. Adapted by Titinius. The girl was probably seen performing her duties by a young man and bore him a child, as a talkative nurse (Myrtile) is mentioned (60). Conceivably the flute girl played the part of Habrotonon in the *Epitrepontes*. A slave, Sosias, conceives an over-daring intrigue (63). The young man's father has been on a public mission (Titinius I) to Byzantion, and has given a young friend a Byzantine party on his return (61) and advised him against marriage (59), but as a cook appears (65) and tries to borrow a pot from next door (67), he has probably arranged a marriage for his own son, which will be upset by the liaison with the Arrhephoros.

It is possible that this play is the so-called *Fabula Incerta*,[19] which probably brings with it P. Oxy. 429 and 2533.

[18] *Studi Menandrei*, 91. The word suggesting Lenaia in P. Oxy. 1239 may be used in a general sense of 'connected with comedy' and does not necessarily conflict with my ascription of the play to the city Dionysia (ch. V, n. 1), even if the word has been read correctly, which is doubtful.

[19] On this see below, p. 201. It is appropriate that Kleainetos the Areopagite should have a daughter who was Arrhephoros. On 59 K–T, see Gomme, C.R., 8, 1958, 4.

Aspis (314/3)

The scene is two houses in Athens; one belongs to Smikrines and the other to his younger brother, Chairestratos. Smikrines lives alone in house A with an old female slave. Chairestratos, in house B, has a wife, a daughter, a stepson, Chaireas, and a niece, the daughter of an elder brother, whose son Kleostratos is campaigning in Asia to recoup his fortunes. On the day the action opens Chairestratos proposes to marry the niece to Chaireas. Cook and waiter are already in the house; he and Chaireas are in the *agora* making arrangements.[20]

Act I, sc. 1. Daos, the *paidagogos* of Kleostratos, enters with his master's shield, captives male and female, and pack animals with considerable booty. He tells that his master has been killed on campaign, and that he has brought the booty home. His long 'messenger speech' is interrupted by comments from Smikrines, who shows more interest in the booty than in the loss of his nephew. It is not clear whether Smikrines has met Daos on his way from the harbour or is standing at the doorway of his house as Daos arrives. At the end of the scene Daos and his train go into house B; Smikrines, saying *sotto voce*[21] that he will see Daos later, goes into his own house to consider the situation. (1–96)

Sc. 2. The goddess Tyche tells the audience that Kleostratos had changed shields with another soldier, was captured and soon will arrive safe home. She also describes the two households and particularly points out that Smikrines is a miser, whose plans to get hold of Kleostratos' property will leave him exactly where he is. (97–148)

Sc. 3. Smikrines enters from his house. He wants to stop the marriage. He calls Daos out. (149–63)

Sc. 4. He wants to stop the marriage and thinking (rightly) that he is legally entitled to marry Kleostratos' sister himself, consults Daos how to do it. Daos refuses to be involved: he is a Phrygian slave, with his own standards. Smikrines goes off to the *agora* to look for Chairestratos. (164–215)

Sc. 5. The cook enters from house B, complaining that if there is a death in the family he will be out of a good job. He is followed by the waiter, who tells Daos that he is a fool if he has not made off with some of Kleostratos' property—a contrast of Thracian and Phrygian morality. Daos sees the chorus coming and drives cook and waiter back into the house. (216–49).

[20] First published in *P. Bodmer* 26, 1969, and immediately afterwards by C. Austin in *Kleine Texte* 188a, Berlin. Austin's *Kleine Texte* 188b, 1970, contains many alterations to the text, including excellent suggestions by F. H. Sandbach. See now his O.C.T.

[21] 'Sotto voce' is given by the text here and at 467.

I am not sure whether Daos' first reaction (220, 235) is to send the cook away. Both verbs can equally mean 'Get away from me', i.e. into the kitchen. The normal procedure at the end of the first act, when the chorus of drunks is sighted, is for anyone on stage to go indoors. So here Daos has no knowledge that after a period of mourning the marriage will not go on, and no status to order Chairestratos' hired servants away; he has just learned that technically he himself now belongs to Smikrines.

Act II, sc. 1. Smikrines comes back from the *agora* with Chairestratos and Chaireas. He says that he is going to marry Kleostratos' sister in spite of Chairestratos' objections. He goes into his own house, telling Chairestratos' to send Daos to him with an inventory of the booty. Chairestratos rushes into his house, threatening suicide. (250–83)

   Sc. 2. Chaireas soliloquises on the cruel upsetting of his happiness. (284–98)

   Sc. 3. Daos, in the doorway of house B, summons Chairestratos to come out and console Chaireas (this must be the sense of l. 300).[22] Daos then produces a plan. They should take advantage of Chairestratos' melancholia. He is to pretend to die, and then Smikrines will find it much more profitable to marry Chairestratos' daughter, as she will be worth four times as much as Kleostratos' sister. He explains the plan condescendingly to the other two, who accept it. Chaireas goes off to find a friend who will dress up as a doctor. Daos and Chairestratos go in to make arrangements in house B. (299–390)

Act III, sc. 1. Smikrines comes out of his house, complaining that Daos has not brought the inventory. Daos comes out of house B, shouting of the terrible illness which has fallen on Chairestratos, reinforcing his news with a string of quotations from tragedy. Smikrines asks about a doctor. Daos points to Chaireas (mute), the pseudodoctor and his attendant (mute), who now arrive. Daos escorts them into house B. (391–432)

   Sc. 2. Smikrines soliloquises: they will not want to see him. How is he to find out about the inventory? (433–36)

   Sc. 3. The pseudo-doctor with his attendant comes out, describes in pseudo-Sicilian Doric[23] the desperate condition of Chairestratos, and makes off, saying that Smikrines looks like death himself. Smikrines surmises that the womenfolk are already making away with Chairestratos' property. (437–67)

   Sc. 4. Daos enters and says *sotto voce*, 'I will confound him.' Here the text breaks off, and apparently 205 lines are lost. At least we can

[22] See Lloyd-Jones, G.R.B.S., 12, 1971, 183; Del Corno Z.P.E., 8, 1971, 29.
[23] Cf. Gigante, P.P., 127, 302.

be certain that there must be a long scene in which Daos confounds Smikrines. The strategy must be to put Kleostratos' property as low as possible and possibly to magnify Chairestratos' property. Daos will therefore produce his inventory and all the items will be as undesirable as possible. Daos may also enlarge on the situation of Chairestratos' daughter, who is likely to become an extremely rich heiress. We must then see Smikrines decide that she is much more desirable than Kleostratos' sister and that the law would allow him to marry either. But Smikrines, although he has no shame (118), has some respect for appearances and a good deal of caution. He cannot move until Chairestratos is dead, and he probably wants to consult his friends again (*cf.* 184), so that he presumably goes off to the *agora*, and this probably ends the third act.

In making the plan Daos pictured Chairestratos' sudden death: 'we cry "Chairestratos is gone," and we beat our breasts in front of the doors' (343). This is what seems to be happening when the text resumes with beginnings of lines some fifty lines before the end of act IV. Smikrines is there and asks if Chairestratos is dead. It looks as if he has only recently arrived. If this is right, the beginning of act IV may be a planning session between Daos, Chairestratos and Chaireas. Daos reports progress with Smikrines. Arrangements are made to conceal Chairestratos safely. The dummy corpse has to be prepared convincingly (345). Presumably Chaireas is instructed how to behave when Smikrines gives him Kleostratos' sister; that must be the signal for letting Chairestratos appear.

The choice for the speaker who informs Smikrines of the fictional death lies between Chaireas and Daos. On the analogy of *Alcestis* 86 one would expect Daos, and it may be that Daos watches, sees Smikrines coming and then send Chaireas out to deal with him. The last speech (484 ff.) has 'to betroth ... perhaps ... when (something) has happened to you (plural) ... I am ready to ... whatever he orders ... in the presence of ... you (singular)'. This sounds like a speech of Smikrines to Chaireas, saying that it is perhaps too soon to make a betrothal when the house is involved in such tragedy but that he is going to consult someone else (and perhaps bring him as witness?). (469–90)

Here there is a difficulty. The stage is empty for a moment, and then Kleostratos arrives. Parallels for an empty stage between scenes are *Epitrepontes* 557 (where Pamphile and Habrotonon go into one house and Onesimos comes out of the other), 704 (where Charisios goes inside and Smikrines arrives from off stage). Here Chaireas certainly goes into house B. One would expect Smikrines to go to the *agora*, but can he exit towards the *agora* without meeting Kleostratos, who is coming from the harbour? Perhaps, therefore, Smikrines has already brought his friend with him (mute), and now takes him into his own house. Kleostratos greets his native land and then bangs on the door of house B. Daos plays the part of the house slave driving away strangers from a dead man's house, and then recognises his master. After ten lines of explanation they go in, and the act closes. (491–515)

For the fifth act we have only the ends of the first thirty lines; the metre has changed from iambic trimeters to trochaic tetrameters. Someone announces what has happened between the acts. A double marriage is happening; it involves 'his own daughter' and 'the niece'.[24] The speaker, therefore, cannot be Chairestratos, since he is here reported, and is unlikely to be Kleostratos or Chaireas, as they are included in the report. Daos is obviously possible. But in 526 occurs the phrase 'the neighbour'; it must refer to Smikrines but is a most unlikely word for Daos or any of the family to use. On the other hand the cook could very well use it, particularly if he wanted to borrow a pot, and the cook has two marriages to cater for instead of one. There are two speakers on stage very soon afterwards, possibly from 528. I do not think it is possible to decide whether Daos or the cook begins the scene, but it seems probable that they are both on stage in 528 or soon after.

The next clear point is 540 ff., 'betrothal ... and in the presence of witnesses ... and to Chaireas what he wishes ... for I (will give up) this property'. This must be Smikrines announcing what he will do, completely ignorant of the return of Kleostratos. His arrival is marked in 536 and possibly already in 532. Lloyd-Jones has suggested that the end of the Aspis may have been parallel to the end of the Dyskolos: Daos and the cook bullied Smikrines (and perhaps carried him in to the feast at the end). The same thought had occurred to me. Perhaps we even have evidence for it in the text. Someone is to be 'made more orderly' in 538, and it is very tempting to restore l. 539 from the corresponding line of the Dyskolos (903): 'I must soften the man up somehow.'

This play is a study of a miser, just as the Dyskolos is a study of a misanthropist. Here too there is at this stage nothing more for the other chief characters to do: the double marriage has been arranged, and we do not need a formal betrothal because it is all in the family and has been expected all the time. But Smikrines is still in a world of his own, expecting to give Kleostratos' sister to Chaireas and to marry Chairestratos' daughter himself. A ragging by Daos and the cook will

[24] Lloyd-Jones's emendation of sister to niece is necessary for scansion. So Sandbach.

return him to his former status, which is what Tyche had promised (146).

Boiotia (no date)

The title occurs in P. Oxy. 2462. An elaborate description of a textile (86) suggests a recognition play. Fragments about slander (82) and about the advantages of wealth for concealing misfortunes (83–4) recall the *Kitharistes*.

Daktylios (no date)

The title shows that this was a recognition play. Five fragments survive in quotation, but one and possibly two papyri may belong to it. P. Antinoopolis 15 consists of a single page from the beginning of the play.[25] The first page has the author's name plausibly restored as Menander, a title ending in -os, a list of eight characters and then the text. A young man laments his misfortunes to the night: he has been a faithful husband to the wife he married five months ago, whom he has come to love. Then he shows some distaste as a woman brings him a box of recognition tokens sealed with his wife's ring. He says that he will seal them up again; he is too distraught at the moment to go into the problem. There the text ends.

It is unique to have recognition tokens at the beginning of the play, and obviously there is going to be a long process of unravelling. The general situation must be that of the *Epitrepontes*. The wife has had a baby after five months of marriage. Whether this is the cause of the young man's distress or whether, as in the *Hecyra*, the wife had gone back to her parents to have the baby and he did not know why she had deserted him is unclear. But two safe inferences from this page are, first, that the ring is what makes the tokens significant and, secondly, that the back-history needs telling by a divine or abstract figure.

The title ends in -os. The letter before could be τ, and Austin has suggested *Apistos*, but this title fits the original of the *Aulularia* too well to be lightly transferred. The papyrus is in such a bad state that I am convinced that -ιos is as likely as -τos, and that leads to *Daktylios*, 'the ring'.

The list of characters is in a short column of three on the left and a column of five on the right: Lysippos, Kantharos, Gorgias, Philinos, maidservant. They are not in alphabetical order. On the analogy of

[25] Cf. Lloyd-Jones, *J.H.S.* 84, 1964, 21; Austin, *C.R.*, 17, 1967, 134; Webster, *Essays presented to Franz Blatt*; Sandbach, *O.C.T.*, p. 327.

the *Dyskolos* and the *Heros* they should be in order of appearance. The first is illegible; the second is restored to Kratinos, and he must be the young man. The third has three letters ending in A; Bia (Violence) would be a suitable abstraction to speak the prologue in a play in which rape certainly formed part of the past history. The first name must be that of the woman in the first scene; it is inexplicable why her name is put first; the only clue is the abbreviated speaker's name (three letters ending in R) before her first words (this clearly must not be expanded into THERAPAINA, maidservant, because she is last in the list).

The book fragments are not incompatible. 'We have found a bridegroom who feeds himself and does not need a dowry' (89) could be said by Kratinos' father-in-law, perhaps Lysippos, when the pair are reunited. He also could have been surprised that Danaos was not pleased to marry off his fifty daughters (88). 'It was a wind-egg' (90) could be an ironic reference to the wife's pregnancy and child. 'Autolekythos' (91), used of a wild young man by Demosthenes, might refer to Kratinos' conduct when he raped his wife long before marriage. Finally, 'the young master' (92) should be used by a slave of his young master; of course, the word may have only been used in a report made by someone else, but a comedy without a male slave is very unlikely. The one name in the list which might be a slave name is Kantharos, whether it is interpreted as 'cup' or 'beetle' (the fact that it is found as a free man's name is irrelevant).

The other names in the list do not tell us much. Lysippos may be the father-in-law. Philinos should be an old man and Kratinos' father (Menander likes common endings in family names; perhaps fr. 781: 'he married the girl I wanted him to' belongs). Gorgias is normally a poor countryman, and it is at least possible that he found the baby when it was exposed (perhaps cf. fr. 676, 'they pity this shepherd and call him very sweet'). The maidservant, who entered last, may have belonged to the father-in-law's house and clinched the recognition.

In the original publication of P. Ant. 15 C. H. Roberts suggested that P. Berlin 13892 may be a fragment of the same codex. This has since been doubted, but the fact remains (whether it belongs to the same codex or not) that on its verso a character described as THERAPAINA appears and on its recto Kantharos. If it belongs to the same play it is a late scene, as the maidservant is the last character in the list.

A trace of a page number may put the recto first. Someone interrogates Kantharos about a sword which he has abandoned in confusion, and something about a nurse and 'having wronged'. On the verso someone is amazed that the maidservant has a sword rusted into its scabbard, and when he succeeds in drawing it he evidently recognises it as one that he bought. It seems possible that when Kratinos raped his wife before marriage he gave his sword to Kantharos, who in some disturbance dropped it, and it was found by the girl and preserved by her nurse in her father's house. In the present scene the nurse of the recto is probably the maidservant of the verso, who is summoned out of the house of the girl's parents. The other speaker, who bought the sword, as distinct from possessing it, must be Kratinos' father (Philinos?), and he proceeds from interrogating Kantharos on the recto to interrogating the nurse on the verso.

However the plot unfolded from the first finding of the sealing, which pointed to the mother of the baby, this is probably the main recognition in the fourth act, which identifies Kratinos as the father.

The prologue shows that Kratinos occupied one of the stage houses. The Berlin papyrus shows that the girl's parents occupied the other.

Demiourgos (? before 306)

The title occurs in P. Oxy. 2462 and in P. British Museum 2562. Adapted by Turpilius. The *Demiourgos* is a woman who makes the cakes for a marriage feast: here she is congratulated by the cook and says that she has been up all night (100). In Turpilius the young man loathes the prospect of this marriage (III, VII). He or another is involved with a *hetaira* who knew him for her profit (IV), left him stripped bare (V) and is advised by someone else to treat her lover well if she wants him to stay (I).

The end of a papyrus hypothesis which precedes the Dis Exapaton (P. IFAO 337) has been attractively connected with this play by Borgogno.[26] According to his restoration a hired servant (the cook) was extremely useful, without the need of a slave (intriguer?); there were good old men, and a *hetaira* who was brazen but not wicked; the play took two days—this is regarded as an allusion to the fact that the preparations had started the day before (100). If the identification is right, it follows that the *hetaira* must have been something like Thais in the *Eunuch* and she may have been protecting the girl with whom the young man was in love; her own lover may have been his brother or another. In that case Turpilius VI, 'trials, impediments, long speeches', may perhaps be compared with Crito's unwillingness to be involved in the identification of the girl in the *Andria* (810).

Turpilius VIII, 'Nor when sailors are surrounded by winds on an uncertain course, needing harbour', is very like the sea image in P.S.I.

26 *Aegyptus*, 49, 1969, 82.

1176, 10.[27] There Moschion has objected to a marriage proposed by
the girl's father, acting on instructions of Moschion's father, given
when they were both abroad. This situation is not incompatible with
the *Demiourgos*, particularly if the girl whom Moschion finally
marries turns out to be the lost sister of the girl whom the two fathers
intended him to marry.

Dis Exapaton (321/19)

The Dis Exapaton was adapted by Plautus as the *Bacchides*; since
1968 we have had about 150 lines of the original to compare. In what
follows, references with B. are to lines of Plautus' play; references with
D.E. are to columns and lines of the papyrus of the *Dis Exapaton*, to
a Cairo papyrus, and to the fragments.[28]

The setting is two houses in Athens. House A is occupied by Chrysis (Bacchis), a *hetaira*; house B by Nicobulus, the father of Sostratos
(Mnesilochus), who is at present travelling from Ephesos with a slave,
Syros (Chrysalus). The other family—a father, Philoxenus, a slave,
Lydos (Lydus), a son, Moschos (Pistoclerus)—live off stage. (We do
not know what names Menander gave to Nicobulus or Philoxenus,
and in what follows their Plautine names are retained).

Act I, sc. 1. Moschos and Lydos arrive at Chrysis' house in search of
her twin sister, with whom Sostratos has fallen in love in Ephesos; she
has a contract with a soldier, who is going to meet her in Athens:
Moschos is to try and keep her for Sostratos. Chrysis sends them into
the house. (P. IFAO. 337: B. 20–24,7)

Sc. 2. Chrysis soliloquises outside.

Sc. 3. The soldier's slave arrives with the twin sister (presumably
also 'Chrysis' in Menander) and states his terms. (B. 14–15)

Sc. 4. The sisters discuss the situation and decide to make use of
Moschos. (B. 35–9)

Sc. 5. The sisters send Moschos and Lydos (mute) to buy provisions
for a homecoming. (B. 39–108)

Act II, sc. 1. Moschos and Lydos return with provisions; Moschos
goes into Chrysis' house; Lydos goes away to tell Philoxenus into
what dangers his son is falling. (B. 109–69; D.E. fr. 114; B. 368–84)

Sc. 2. Syros arrives from the harbour. (B. 170–7)

---

[27] Cf. below, p. 203.
[28] The Oxyrrhynchus papyrus was first published by E. W. Handley,
Menander and Plautus, London, 1968. The Cairo papyrus gives a summary of
Demiourgos (cf. n. 26) and the first line of Dis Exapaton spoken to a youth by
a man (cf. *Studi Cataudella*). The play began, therefore, with Moschos and
Lydos visiting Chrysis. On 109 K–T, see n. 7. Sandbach, O.C.T., p. 39.

Sc. 3. Moschos comes out and tells Syros that Chrysis is found and that there is need of money. He goes back into Chrysis' house. (B. 178–234)

Sc. 4. Nicobulus comes out of his house to go to the harbour. Syros tells him a false story that the gold which they were sent to collect in Ephesos was nearly stolen so that they deposited it with Theotimos instead of bringing it home. Nicobulus goes off to the *agora* to meet Sostratos. (B. 235–348; D.E. fr. 112)

Sc. 5. Syros ponders on his success and goes off himself to tell Sostratos that the money can now be spent on Chrysis. (349–67)

Act III, sc. 1. Sostratos enters, having met Syros. (B. 385–404)

Sc. 2. Lydos brings Philoxenus to see his son's corruption. Sostratos overhears. Lydos sees him and draws him into the conversation. Sostratos defends his friend by saying that Moschos was finding Chrysis for him. Lydos (who does not distinguish the twins) insists that Moschos has fallen in love with Chrysis. Philoxenus appeals to Sostratos to save his friend. He then goes off with Lydos. (B. 405–99; D.E. I–II, 5 = 11–17)

Sc. 3. Sostratos, believing Lydos, decides to hand over the gold that he has brought from Ephesos to his father. (B. 499–520; D.E. II, 6–18 = 18–30)

Sc. 4. Nicobulus enters from the *agora*. Sostratos tells him the true story of what happened in Ephesos, and they go off to where Sostratos has deposited the gold. (D.E. II, 19–51 = 47–63)[29]

Act IV, sc. 1. Nicobulus and Sostratos come back after Sostratos has handed over the gold. They discuss the punishment of Syros. Nicobulus apparently leaves it to Sostratos and goes off to the *agora* (D.E. III, 1–28; cf. B. 520–5)

Sc. 2. Sostratos, alone, reflects on Chrysis and does not blame Moschos. (D.E. III, 29–40; B. 430–3)

Sc. 3. Moschos comes out from house A. Together Sostratos and he sort out the misunderstanding. (D.E. III, 40–51 = 88–112; B. 534–572)[30]

(From this point we only have Plautus. It is clear that, as he has shortened Menander in the first part of the play (omitting the end of act III and the beginning of act IV), he has lengthened him greatly in the second part. Menander's act divisions are fixed by the reappearance of characters who have gone some distance off-stage, to the *agora* or, in the case of Lydos, to a house off-stage: these fix the boundaries of acts I (also Plautus preserves the standard formula for the first arrival

[29] 661 K–T, on double interest.
[30] 653 K–T may be from Moschos' description of the two *hetairai*.

of the chorus in 107), II, III and IV; Nicobulus cannot return till act V, and only then can the second deceit be put into operation. I think, therefore, that we have to go back to the old view that the third deceit is Plautine. Any reconstruction is hazardous, and what follows is offered only as a possibility.)

Sc. 4. Either the soldier or his parasite arrive to demand money or the return of Chrysis. Moschos comes out and chases him away. (B. 572–611)

Sc. 5. Sostratos and Moschos are in despair. Syros returns in triumph. He is told the whole story and makes a new plan, probably the writing of the second letter, in which Sostratos confesses but calls Chrysis the soldier's wife, the letter is prepared during the interval between the acts. (B. 611–702; *cf.* 700 with D.E. III, 22 ff.)

Act V, sc .1. Syros comes out with the letter. Nicobulus returns to punish Syros. (B. 770–98)

Sc. 2. Nicobulus calls a slave out of house B to punish Syros. Only then does Syros hand over the letter, which Nicobulus reads. (B. 799–824; D.E. frs. 111, 113; B. 995–1052)

Sc. 3. Nicobulus sends Syros to the *agora* to pay the soldier.

Sc. 4. Philoxenus arrives to see what has happened to his son. (B. 1076–86)

Sc. 5. Philoxenus and Nicobulus discuss their sons. Philoxenus had come to find Sostratos, whom he assumes to be at home in house B. Instead he finds his father, and Nicobulus learns from him that Chrysis is a *hetaira* and not the soldier's wife and that she lives next door, in house A. Together they decide to visit Chrysis (B. 1086–116; D.E. fr. 110)

Sc. 6. The final scene of the temptation of the old men is played with one of the sisters mute. (B. 1117–206)

Dyskolos (317/16)

The place is Phyle, on the north-western slopes of Mount Parnes. House A is inhabited by Knemon, his daughter and his maidservant Simike; house B by Myrrhine, Knemon's wife, Gorgias, her son by an earlier husband, and their slave, Daos. Between the two houses is the shrine of Pan and the Nymphs.[31]

Act I, sc. 1. Pan enters from the shrine and describes Knemon the misanthrope, his separation from his wife, and the present arrangement. Pan has rewarded the daughter's piety by making the son of

[31] Text and commentary E. W. Handley, London, 1965. *Cf.* also J.-M. Jacques, Paris, 1963; Sandbach, O.C.T., p. 47.

a rich father (Sostratos, son of Kallippides) fall in love with her. (1–49)

Sc. 2. Sostratos enters with a friend, Chaireas, who, he hopes, will help him. His hunting slave Pyrrhias, who has been sent to see Knemon, runs in, saying that the old man is chasing him. Chaireas advises waiting till the next day and goes off. (50–134)

Sc. 3. Sostratos comments on the uselessness of his friend and the misconduct of Pyrrhias. Pyrrhias sees Knemon coming and makes off. (135–44)

Sc. 4. Knemon enters, cursing all people who disturb him, including Sostratos, and goes into his house. (145–78)

Sc. 5. Sostratos thinks of fetching Getas, his father's slave, to help him. The daughter enters, needing water: Simike has dropped the bucket down the well. Sostratos takes her jug into the shrine of the Nymphs. (179–206)

Sc. 6. Daos, leaving house B to help Gorgias with digging, sees Sostratos give the full jug to the daughter and go off to fetch Getas. He goes to tell Gorgias his suspicions. (206–32)

Act II, sc. 1. Gorgias and Daos enter, discussing the girl's situation and Knemon's lack of care for her. (233–58)

Sc. 2. Sostratos enters, having failed to find Getas. Gorgias attacks him as a rich man trying to seduce a poor girl. Sostratos convinces him that he wants to marry her. Together they plan that Sostratos shall work beside Gorgias, and when Knemon comes discuss marriage. Daos hands over his mattock and goes to build a wall. (259–378)

Sc. 3. Sostratos impresses Gorgias again with his earnestness, and they both go off to the field. (379–92)

Sc. 4. The cook Sikon enters, dragging a sheep. (393–402)

Sc. 5. Getas enters, laden with rugs. They say that Sostratos' mother is coming to sacrifice to Pan because of a bad dream about her son. They go into the shrine. (402–26)

Act III, sc. 1. Knemon comes out of his house to do a day's work. He sees a procession arriving, Sostratos' mother, Plangon (possibly her daughter or a musician), a flute girl, Parthenis, and two male slaves (all mutes). They are hurried into the shrine by Getas and Sikon. (427–41)

Sc. 2. Knemon decides that he dare not leave his house undefended and goes in. (442–55)

Sc. 3. Getas comes out of the shrine to borrow a cauldron, knocks on Knemon's door and is roundly abused. He returns to the shrine. Knemon goes into his house. (456–86)

Sc. 4. Sikon comes out of the shrine to borrow a cooking pot, knocks on Knemon's door and is roundly abused. He returns to the shrine. (487–521)

Sc. 5. Sostratos comes back from the field, frustrated by digging and no Knemon. (522–45)

Sc. 6. Getas comes out of the shrine, weary of helping Sikon, sees Sostratos and tells him about the sacrifice and his mother. Sostratos goes to invite Gorgias. (546–73)

Sc. 7. Simike has dropped Knemon's mattock down the well and comes out to escape Knemon, who chases her back into the house. Getas comments on the hard life of the Attic farmer. He sees Sostratos coming and goes into the shrine. (574–611)

Sc. 8. Sostratos persuades Gorgias to accompany him to the sacrifice in the shrine. Daos is to look after Gorgias' mother till he comes. (611–19)

Act IV, *sc. 1.* Simike comes out of Knemon's house, shouting for help. Sikon comes out of the shrine, complaining of the noise. Knemon has fallen down the well. Simike cries out for Gorgias; Gorgias summons Sostratos (mute), and they go into Knemon's house. (620–38)

Sc. 2. Sikon rejoices at Knemon's discomfiture and goes into the shrine (639–65)

Sc. 3. Sostratos describes the rescue. (666–90)

Sc. 4. Knemon is wheeled out by Gorgias and his daughter. He sends Gorgias into house B to fetch his mother. (691–703)

Sc. 5. Knemon announces his dispositions and defends his life. Gorgias introduces Sostratos as a suitor. Knemon, his wife and his daughter go into house A. (708–58)

Sc. 6. Gorgias praises Sostratos as a suitor. (758–75)

Sc. 7. Kallippides, Sostratos' father, arrives for the sacrifice. He and Sostratos go into the shrine; Gorgias into house A. (775–83)

Act V, *sc. 1.* Kallippides and Sostratos come out of the shrine, discussing the marriage of Sostratos to Knemon's daughter and of Gorgias to Kallippides' daughter. (784–820)

Sc. 2. Gorgias comes out of house A, and the double betrothal is made. Gorgias goes to fetch the party from house A. (821–55)

Sc. 3. Kallippides goes into the shrine to make preparations. (855–865)

Sc. 4. Gorgias brings his mother and sister, and with Sostratos they all go into the shrine. (866–73)

Sc. 5. Simike comes out of house A. Getas comes out of the shrine. She goes into the shrine, telling him to look after Knemon. (874–88)

Sc. 6. Getas calls Sikon out of the shrine and proposes that they should carry Knemon out and bully him. (888–906)

Sc. 7. They carry Knemon out of his house and rag him. Finally they persuade him to come into the shrine with them, and the play ends. (906–69)

Empimpramene (not dated)

The title, 'The girl who is set on fire', suggests a similar key scene to the opening scene of the *Perikeiromene*, when Polemon cut off Glykera's hair. The lover perhaps is told by his slave that his act is unjustifiable violence (143) and that he will be destroyed by his arrogance (144). Someone deplores marriage (142), and there is a council at a *symposion* (146–7). The girl is perhaps recognised (145).

Encheiridion (317–307)

The title occurs in P. British Museum 2562. The fourth act is illustrated by a mosaic at Mytilene,[32] on which an old man, Straton, moves left, holding stick and dagger; Kerdon in slave's costume moves left with something in his right hand which might be a sheath; an old man, Dersippos, (presumably Derkippos) moves right with crook and dagger. This is likely to be a recognition scene and the dagger a recognition token; but why are there two daggers? The point must be a confusion between the two daggers, and this was sufficiently important to give the play its title. Probably, as in the *Aspis* and the *Daktylios*, one of the daggers appeared at the beginning. The names bring in two fragments not previously attributed to this play. In 639 someone tells Derkippos and Mnesippos that friends are the only refuge when one has been slandered or maltreated. As Menander likes common endings in family names, Derkippos and Mnesippos may be father and son. In three of the book fragments these ideas seem to be followed out: 137, evidently the Korykaean heard him (proverbial for an ill-intentioned listener); 136, my misfortunes do not come from where I would expect; the surprise is always shattering; 140, topsy-turvy.

The names Straton and Kerdon recur as speaker with Doris in P.S.I. 99.[33] The scene is an inn, which was presumably represented by the central doorway. Doris should be the maid of a *hetaira* or of someone who at the moment has the status of a *hetaira*; her mistress will therefore presumably be recognised. The early part seems to be an account of what had happened in the inn, and fr. 138, 'I will force the accursed woman to drink', may belong. At the end Straton seems to have made some discovery from Kerdon, and there is a disturbance. This may be leading up to the scene of the mosaic. The reference early on to Egyptians, with which goes the fragment (139): 'How holy a god is Sarapis', may refer to travels of Straton or of the owner of the girl or of a rival. Possibly P. Grenfell II 8 b, in which a slave (Kerdon?) has found the house where his master's girl is, and apparently fears an Egyptian rival, also belongs.

Ephesios

Adapted by Caecilius. Fr. 171, a slave envisages the possibility of his being sold. 172–3, a marketing scene, with a comment on the high price of fish. 176, a man of Tenedos, in the sense of a man of terrifying aspect. Caecilius: 'I judge this most hateful in old age, to feel that one is hateful to another.' K. Gaiser[34] has identified this play with the original of the Miles Gloriosus; there the helpful old bachelor Periplectomenus prides himself on being born in Ephesos (648). The Menander fragments can be placed in Plautus' play, but the parallels are not nearly strong enough to clinch the identification. The original of Plautus' play must have been written at the end of Menander's life and it is difficult to conceive of the soldier as one of Menander's latest creations. The later date suggested in ch. I for the Kolax may be quoted in favour of the identification, it is true. On the other hand the other plays which mention Ephesos seem to be early: Dis Exapaton, Kitharistes.

Epikleros

Menander wrote two plays called Heiress. Frs. 155–6, about shooing birds away, come from the first, and 160, a word for a wine press, from the second. One of them was called 'The good heiress' (fr. 152), and this was listed in P. British Museum 2562 and translated by Turpilius. A young man was awake early and told his life story; his slave interrupted him (152 and Turpilius I). It is presumably he who objects to a marriage arranged for him, although he dislikes opposing his father (IV, V, VII). He has raped a poor girl, since someone is asked to take pity on Calliphon's children (II; cf. 153–4, 157); he tells his father the truth, and the father consents to the marriage (IX–XI). There is also a slave intrigue (158), and the slave gets drunk (XII–XIII). It is not clear how the dispute between mother and father, which the son adjudicated in favour of the father (III, VI, VIII), fits in. This play may have been the play called the first Heiress, as the description

[34] Gaiser, Poetica, 1, 1967, 436.

of the woman objecting to birds in the courtyard sounds rather like a description of an overbearing wife.[35]

Epitrepontes (after 305)

The scene is two houses in the deme Halai Araphenides. House A belongs to Chairestratos and at the moment houses also Charisios, the estranged husband of house B, his slave, Onesimos, and a *hetaira*, Habrotonon. House B belongs to Charisios and houses at the moment only his wife Pamphile.[36]

Act I, sc. 1. The cook Karion takes time off to gossip with Onesimos, who tells him that Charisios has deserted his wife because he has learnt from Onesimos that she has had a baby five months after their marriage and has exposed it (frs. 1-3; 5). The audience must be told that in fact Charisios had raped her at a night festival before their marriage and is the father of the child; only a prologue figure can do this, and this may have been the second scene.[37]

Sc. 3. Chairestratos comes out of his house, probably to say that he is in love with Habrotonon. Smikrines enters from the city, where he lives, deploring the rumour that his daughter Pamphile has been deserted by Charisios. Habrotonon comes out to summon Chairestratos in to Charisios, and they listen to Smikrines' complaint. He goes into see his daughter. They quarrel and go into house A. (1-35; P. Oxy. 2829, frs. VI and VII; fr. 6)[38]

Act II, sc. 1. Onesimos comes out of house A, reflecting on his master's position, before Smikrines comes out of house B. In the gap between ll. 41 and 42 he probably persuaded Smikrines that Charisios was going back to Pamphile (cf. 403), and Smikrines commented on the situation after Onesimos had gone back into house A. (36-41)

Sc. 2. Daos, a shepherd, and Syros,[39] an outside slave of Chairestratos, who comes on with his wife carrying a child, ask Smikrines to arbitrate; Daos found the child exposed and gave it to Syros; he does

[35] I assume that in 155 K-T the wife is giving orders to the maid and the husband disapproves (cf. *Plokion*). A fragment of Caecilius' *Heiress* seems to describe an unreliable friend, but the original may not be by Menander.

[36] K-T, II, 279 f. gives a number of additions to K-T, I. Sandbach, O.C.T., p. 94, renumbers the lines, but gives the K-T, I numbers, which I use, in brackets.

[37] The prologue speech may have been before or after the cook scene. I have assumed that the cook had been hired for the preceding evening.

[38] Chairestratos' partner must be Habrotonon here; tone and language are wrong for a friend or a slave.

[39] Arnott, C.Q., 18, 1968, 227, rightly argues for Syros as against Syriskos. Syros' name appears on the Mytilene mosaic though wrongly given to Daos, L. Kahil, op. cit., pl. 4 (*Entretiens Hardt*, pl. 1b).

not want also to give up the trinkets found with it. Smikrines adjudicates the trinkets to Syros, and goes off. Daos soon follows, after a last complaint. (42–199)

Sc. 3. Onesimos enters as Syros is counting out the trinkets to his wife. He recognises among them a ring lost by Charisios. Syros allows him to keep it until he can show it to Charisios. They all go into house A. (200–42)

Act III, sc. 1. Onesimos comes out, having failed to show the ring to his master. Habrotonon comes out, furious that Charisios will have nothing to do with her. Syros comes out, asking for the ring. Onesimos tells him that Charisios lost it at the Tauropolia. Syros goes off, saying that he must consult someone in the city. (243–87)

Sc. 2. Habrotonon has overheard and says she saw a rape at the Tauropolia. They plan that she shall confront Charisios first, pretending to be the victim, and then look for the mother. (288–380)

Sc. 3. Onesimos reflects on the situation and goes back into house A as he sees Smikrines coming. (381–406)

Sc. 4. Smikrines enters, complaining of Charisios' conduct. Possibly he has met Syros on the way and drawn the obvious conclusion from the story of the ring. (407–32; fr. 659)

Sc. 5. The cook comes out: the party scattered when Habrotonon came in with the ring. Probably he tells Smikrines that Charisios is going to make Habrotonon mistress of his house. He goes off (or in?) with his helper, Simias, as Chairestratos comes out. (433–55; fr. 4)[40]

Sc. 6. Smikrines wants to use Chairestratos and his friends as evidence that Charisios has treated Pamphile badly; Chairestratos attempts to defend him. Smikrines goes into Charisios' house to see his daughter. Chairestratos goes back into his own house. (456–509)

Act IV, sc. 1. Not very much is left of the big debate in which Smikrines tries to persuade Pamphile to desert her husband and she refuses. Charisios overhears part of this from the door of Chairestratos' house (cf. 564, 600 f.), and perhaps comments unseen. Smikrines goes off to fetch Pamphile's old nurse, Sophrone. (510–32; fr. 7)

Sc. 2. Pamphile, alone, laments her position. Habrotonon comes out with the child, recognises Pamphile, and tells her that she is the mother and Charisios the father. They go into Charisios' house. (Fr. 8; 533–57)

Sc. 3. Onesimos comes out, terrified by Charisios' behaviour. He seeks refuge in Charisios' house. (558–87)

---

[40] Here and Aspis 246 the cook goes away from the door rather than off. In both he will be needed later. Fragment 4 fits neatly in l. 433; the cook comes out to borrow a pot. Simias is the cook's helper (mute), as in Dionysios, 2 K.

Sc. 4. Charisios comes out of Chairestratos' house, bitterly repentant of his treatment of Pamphile and determined to prevent Smikrines' taking her home. (588–612)

Sc. 5. Onesimos brings Habrotonon out of Charisios' house, and together they convince Charisios that the child is his and Pamphile's (613–48). All go into Charisios' house.

Act V, sc. 1. Chairestratos, still believing that Charisios is going to live with Habrotonon, decides to give her up and be loyal to his friend. Onesimos comes out and presumably tells him what has happened. The text is very unclear here, but at the end Charisios evidently says that he will free Habrotonon and be her patron, and then goes back into his own house. (649–703)

Sc. 2. Smikrines arrives with the old nurse, Sophrone (mute).[41] Onesimos comes out in answer to his knock, and mocks at him before telling the truth about the child. (704–73)

The text breaks off at this point. Presumably a final scene gives a reconciliation between Smikrines and Charisios and perhaps the manumission of Onesimos.

Eunuch (308–6)

Terence says that he has transferred the parasite and the boastful soldier into the Eunuch from Menander's Kolax; the relevant passages are partly noted by Donatus and partly marked by quotations. There is no suggestion that the two plays were alike in plot, but the Eunuch had a soldier as a character, and the transferences could be hung on to him.[42]

The scene is Athens. House A is owned by Simo, who has two sons, Phaedria (Chairestratos in Menander) and Chaerea, and a slave, Parmenon (Daos in Menander). House B is occupied by a hetaira, Thais (Chrysis in Menander), with a female slave, Pythias.

Act 1, sc. 1. Phaedria and Parmeno enter from house A and discuss the miseries of being in love with a capricious hetaira. (46–80; Persius, v, 161 ff.; fr. 161–2)

Sc. 2. Thais enters and explains that she must exclude Phaedria for a few days because his rival, the soldier, is going to give her a girl, who had formerly passed as her sister and whom she believes is an Attic citizen. (81–206; fr. 658)

The complicated story of the girl, the certainty that she will turn out to be Attic, and the true good-heartedness of Thais were probably

[41] Cf. Sandbach, P.C.P.S., 1967, 45; O.C.T., p. 129.
[42] On Eunuch see most recently Brothers, C.Q., 19, 1969, 314.

explained by Menander in a prologue speech either before or after these scenes, and Terence may have transferred some of the information from it into these scenes.

Act II, sc. 1. Phaedria comes out of house A, ready to go away, and orders Parmeno to give the Ethiopian girl and the eunuch, as he has promised, to Thais. He goes off. (207–24; 207 is not a doublet of 189 but a genuine repetition)

Sc. 2. While Parmenon comments on Phaedria's character, someone arrives with Thais' supposed sister. In Terence it is Gnatho, the soldier's parasite, but he and his opening speech come from the *Kolax*. In Menander it may rather have been a slave, as on his later appearance he appears to be played by a mute. Both go into the house of Thais. (225–31; 265–88)

Sc. 3. Chaerea arrives; he has been held up pursuing the girl and has lost her. Parmenon tells him that she has gone into Thais' house, and suggests that he should change places with the eunuch. They go into house A. (289–390; fr. 170;? fr. 169)

The soldier's slave must go back to report; Terence has omitted this.

Act III, sc. 1. The soldier returns, talking to his slave (mute). Terence has introduced another *Kolax* scene here. Parmenon comes out with the Ethiopian girl and Chaerea dressed as the eunuch (both mute). He presents them to Thais in the presence of the soldier and goes back into house A. Thais hands them over to Pythias (mute) with instructions and they go into house B. Thais goes off with the soldier to dinner. (Portions of 391–506)

Sc. 2. Chremes, the girl's brother, arrives, very suspicious of Thais' questions. Pythias takes him to where Thais is dining with the soldier (Dorias is an unnecessary addition by Terence). (507–38)

Act IV, sc. 1. Chaerea comes out and describes how he had put the girl to sleep and raped her. Donatus tells us that Terence converted the monologue into dialogue by introducing Antiphon. But Chaerea has to try and find somewhere to change his clothes, and he is afraid to go home (610). Antiphon is therefore necessary,[43] and his opening (589) is excellent; probably, therefore, he comes on at the end of the monologue (549–57; fr. 165), which may have been longer in the original (539–614).

Sc. 2. Pythias comes back from the dinner with Thais' jewellery and goes into her house. (615–28)

Sc. 3. Phaedria has been unable to keep away and comes back. (629–642)

[43] Cf. E. D. M. Fraenkel, M.H., 24, 1968, 235. But he is wrong in rejecting Donatus altogether.

Sc. 4. Pythias bursts out of the house, having discovered what has happened to the girl. She sees Phaedria and tells him that the eunuch is responsible and has vanished. (643–67; fr. 167)

Sc. 5. Phaedria fetches the eunuch out of house A, and forces him to admit before Pythias that he has changed clothes with Chaerea. They go back into house A. (668–717, fr. 163)

Sc. 6. Pythias decides to keep silent. As she goes in, Chremes arrives, drunk, from the dinner. (718–38)

Sc. 7. Thais returns. She shows Chremes the girl's recognition tokens and persuades him to tell the soldier the relationship when he comes to claim the girl. (739–70;? fr. 168)

Sc. 8. The soldier arrives. He regards Chremes as a rival and claims the girl back. Chremes states his case. The soldier retires and Chremes goes off to fetch his nurse, who will recognise the tokens. (Portions of 771–816, but Terence has inserted here the siege scene from the *Kolax*.)

Act V, sc. 1. Thais interrogates Pythias, who tells her that the supposed eunuch was Chaerea. She sees Chaerea coming, still in the eunuch's clothes. Chaerea confesses to Thais and says he wants to marry the girl. Thais takes him into her house. (817–909)

Sc. 2. Terence has cut out a short soliloquy of Pythias here. Then Chremes arrives with his nurse and goes into Thais' house. (910–22)

Sc. 3. Parmenon comes out of house A to see what has happened to Chaerea and congratulates himself. Pythias comes out of house B and tells Parmenon that Chremes is punishing Chaerea as an adulterer. (923–70;? fr. 166)

Sc. 4. Simo arrives from the country. Parmenon tells him the story and he goes into Thais' house. (971–1001)

Sc. 5. Pythias comes out and tells Parmenon that he will certainly be punished. (1002–24)

Terence has introduced *Kolax* characters here and through the rest of the play, so that how Menander finished the play is uncertain; the following sequence is possible:

Sc. 6. Chaerea comes out and tells Parmenon that he is to marry the girl.

Sc. 7. Parmenon fetches Phaedria from house A and he is told the story.

Sc. 8. The soldier arrives and Phaedria arranges to share Thais with him?

Georgos (before 306)

The scene is two houses in Athens: the house of Myrrhine, who has a daughter, Hedeia, and an old servant, Philinna, and a son, Gorgias, out at work with a rich farmer, Kleainetos; and the house belonging to the father of the young man who has raped Hedeia; he has a slave, Daos.

Two overlapping papyri give the last ninety lines of the first act and about thirty half-lines at the beginning of the second. In the surviving scenes of the first act (A) the young man describes how he returned home from Corinth the night before to find that his father had made preparations for him to marry his half-sister. He does not want to desert Hedeia, and he is afraid to knock on Myrrhine's door because Gorgias may be at home. He decides to go away to think out a plan of escape from the marriage.

The opening page is numbered 6, which means that we have lost 220 lines. This, however, might include summary, *dramatis personae*, production notes, and possibly a life of Menander. The actual loss of text is likely to be between 100 and 150 lines.[44] The young man has certainly given an account of the rape; according to Quintilian (XI, 3, 91) he quoted a woman's words, perhaps Myrrhine, when he confessed to her, and he must have given some reason for his fear of Gorgias. But this would hardly account for the total number of lost lines. The young man had evidently promised to marry Hedeia, and he passes over 'the other marriage' very briefly. In particular we need to know that his father's slaves, Daos and Syros, have been sent to the country, where the family farm is next to Kleainetos' farm, to get supplies for the marriage. Either this was made clear in a prologue speech or they were sent out in an opening scene before the prologue speech: they cannot go out and return within the first act, unless there is a prologue speech to function as an act end between their going out and their return.

This suggests a further possibility. We are almost driven to assume a prologue speech, and it must tell us something beyond what we learn from the fairly full information given in the first act, something more than the marriage preparations. The play is certainly going to end with the marriage of Hedeia and the young man. The two possible patterns are given by the *Adelphi* and the *Heros*: either *Myrrhine* was a widow and Kleainetos acts as the friend of her late husband, or Kleainetos had raped Myrrhine in his youth and turns out to be the father of her children. The text may give a hint that

[44] Koerte assumes that we have the end of the first act and this is probably right; but (1) the first act of *Samia* was only just over 200 lines, (2) not enough remains to show whether the standard introduction of the chorus was there or not, (3) Quintilian, describing a young male character quoting a woman in the *Georgos*, does not attribute this to the prologue (but prologue for him may mean only the opening speech). See now Sandbach, O.C.T.

Menander adopted the second pattern: Daos says that Gorgias helped the injured Kleainetos 'as if he considered him his own father' (59). This is almost a quotation of the Sophoclean Oidipous when he says, 'I will fight for him as if he were my own father' (O.T. 264), and Daos, like Oidipous, may be speaking more truly than he knows. If this is the pattern, a prologue speech is certainly necessary to explain it.

After the speech of the young man, scene A, comes scene B: Myrrhine enters with Philinna, who rages against the young man.[45] Daos and Syros arrive from the country, bringing supplies for the marriage. Daos tells Myrrhine that Kleainetos had cut his leg, Gorgias had looked after him, and he had decided to marry Hedeia; they are coming soon to take her away to his farm. Daos then goes in to his master's house, and Myrrhine tells Philinna that Hedeia is going to have her child very soon. The act comes to an end in another eight lines, of which the last two are presumably the customary warning of the arrival of the chorus, if this is the first act.

Something like twenty-five lines are completely lost at the beginning of the next act; then we have the beginnings of thirty lines. Gorgias arrives. Philinna greets him; he asks her to call Myrrhine out. The words 'in the neighbourhood' at the beginning of one line followed by 'Artemis' at the beginning of the next may mean that he heard the cries of Hedeia as he arrived.[46] It is possible that Philinna went to fetch a midwife at the end of the preceding act and returned with her just in time for the birth at the beginning of this act. Gorgias has presumably come from Kleainetos to tell Myrrhine that Kleainetos is going to marry Hedeia (cf. 76). Gorgias and Myrrhine must discuss the situation. It seems to me possible that Gorgias in fury goes to try and have it out with the young man. The young man is out, but Gorgias may have found Daos, and in this way Daos learns that Hedeia has had a child. Then Gorgias goes back to find Kleainetos or to meet Kleainetos, if Kleainetos has already set out.

A fragment in trochaic tetrameters (4), 'Are you mad? It is absurd when you have fallen in love with a free-born girl to keep silence and do nothing when a marriage is being arranged for you,' must be Daos talking to the young man when he returns, and somehow an intrigue must be set on foot to stave off the marriage with the half-sister: the first attempt may be to tell the father the truth about the love affair with Hedeia.

In the next act, probably, Kleainetos arrives. The very scrappy

45 Maehler, M.H., 24, 1967, 77, gives a new text of 24–31 from a Berlin papyrus.
46 Cf. the servant in Plokion, 335 K–T.

papyrus (129 ff.) and two quotations (1–2) show that he argued against Gorgias' excessive anger and pointed out the disadvantageous position of the poor man, who is thought to be only out for money. This must mean that he takes on the defence of Hedeia himself, and fr. 3, 'I am a rustic and not completely *au fait* with city behaviour, but age gives me some experience,' should come from his defence: it sounds like a speech to the young man rather than to his father.

We have no hint of how the recognition of Kleainetos as the father of Gorgias and Hedeia was brought about, if it was. It is not entirely necessary. As a rich neighbour farmer, Kleainetos has the status to persuade the young man's father to allow the marriage, and he himself can marry Myrrhine instead of Hedeia to get support for his old age (*cf.* 73). But it would have the neatness of other Menandrian solutions, and Gorgias could marry the half-sister.

Halieus (308–6)

The title is quoted in the singular in P. Oxy. 2462, but in several quotations is plural. It has been suggested that the fisherman or fishermen caught a box of recognition tokens in the net (25–7;[47] *cf.* also 654a, 696).Two old men, probably the fishermen, live on stage (17; *cf.* 14). One of them has a difficult daughter (18 *cf.* 16). It is not clear how this fits in with the exiles from Herakleia on the Pontos, who describe the luxury of the tyrant Dionysios (21–3) and have brought booty from the East. (20, 24, 29)

Heautontimoroumenos (298)

House A is occupied by Menedemus, who has a son, Clinia, away at the war and a slave, Dromo. House B is occupied by Chremes, who has a wife, Sostrata, a son, Clitipho, and a slave, Syrus. The place is Halai Aixonides, a deme near Athens.[48]

Act I, sc. 1. Chremes stops Menedemus working in his field to invite him to dinner on the festival of Dionysus. Menedemus refuses, explaining that he is punishing himself for the absence of his son Clinia, who has gone to the wars because his father would not let him marry a poor girl, Antiphila. Menedemus goes in. Chremes goes on to remind another guest. (53–170; frs. 127, 128, 475)

Antiphila will turn out to be a daughter of Chremes, exposed by

[47] Bernhardy *ap.* Kock, C.A.F., fr. 26.
[48] I have included fr. 134 as the original of l. 672 and fr. 135 as the original of l. 968; both, like frs. 127, 133, show how Terence flattened out the sharpness of the original.

his wife or rather given to an old Corinthian woman. This must have been told by a prologue figure. The fragmentary papyrus hypothesis (P. Oxy. 2534) shows that the scene with the two old men opened the play. I suspect that Terence has also cut out a scene in which Clinia arrived from the harbour with Clitipho and entered Chremes' house.

Sc. 4. Chremes returns, and Clitipho tells him of Clinia's arrival and then, when his father has gone in, complains of his own miserable situation, in love with a *hetaira*, Bacchis. (171–229)

Act II, sc. 1. The two young men come out; Clinia is worried because Antiphila has not arrived. Syrus and Dromo (mute) enter to say that the women are somewhere behind them; he is bringing not only Antiphila but also Bacchis, who is to be passed off as the girlfriend of Clinia. Syrus drives Clitipho inside. (230–380; frs. 129–30)

Sc. 2. In Menander Clinia must have stayed on stage to cover the period while the actors of Clitipho and Syrus changed to become Bacchis and Antiphila. The two women enter, Bacchis comparing her life with Antiphila's. Clinia greets Antiphila, and they all go into Chremes' house. (381–409)

Act III, sc. 1. Chremes tells Menedemus that Clinia has returned, and warns him not to appear yet; he is frightened by the extravagance of Bacchis. (410–511; frs. 131, 133)

Sc. 2. Chremes encourages Syrus to intrigue for Bacchis. Chremes goes into his house. (512–561)

Sc. 3. Chremes brings Clitipho out of the house, horrified at his behaviour with Bacchis. Syros pretends to side with Chremes, and Clitipho is sent away. (562–90)

Sc. 4. Syrus tells Chremes his plan for robbing Menedemus. (591–613)

Sc. 5. Sostrata comes in, talking back to her nurse. She has recognised Antiphila's ring. She tells Chremes that she had not exposed the baby but gave it to an old Corinthian woman. (614–67)

Act IV, sc. 1. Syrus is in despair; he needs a new plan to help Clitipho. (668–78; fr. 134)

Sc. 2. Clinia comes out in high joy. Syrus persuades him to help by having Bacchis transferred to Menedemus' house. (679–722)

Sc. 3. Bacchis comes out prepared to celebrate the Dionysia with a soldier if she is given no money. She is persuaded to go into Menedemus' house. Clinia leads the way; Dromo (mute) aids the removal. (723–48)

Sc. 4. Syrus makes Chremes believe that Clinia is proposing marriage with Antiphila only as a way of getting money for Bacchis.

Syrus persuades Chremes to bring money to recompense Bacchis for the (supposed) loss of Antiphila. (749–804)

Sc. 5. Clitipho returns and is told the new situation by Syrus. Chremes brings out the money. Clitipho and Syrus go into Menedemus' house. Chremes laments the waste of his money. (805–41)

Sc. 6. Menedemus comes out to talk to Chremes about marriage. Chremes persuades him that he has misunderstood the situation, but agrees that he should tell Clinia that the marriage is being arranged. (842–73)

Act V, sc. 1. Menedemus comes out and meets Chremes and convinces him that Clitipho is in love with Bacchis. Chremes disinherits his son. (874–953)

Sc. 2. Clitipho comes out, followed by Syrus. Chremes reaffirms his view and goes in. Syrus tells Clitipho to talk to his mother. Syrus takes refuge with Menedemus. (954–1002; fr. 135)

Sc. 3. Sostrata pleads with Chremes for Clitipho, and Clitipho finally agrees to give up Bacchis and marry. (1003–67)

Heros (308–6)

Two papyrus pages and nine quotations of the Heros are preserved. The first page begins with a summary of the plot and a list of characters in order of appearance. The summary, with the names added, runs: 'An unmarried girl (Myrrhine) gave birth to twins (Plangon and Gorgias) and gave them to a guardian (Tibeios) to bring up. Then later she married her raper (Laches). Tibeios, who was ignorant of this, put the twins into service with Laches (when the play opens, Tibeios is dead and they are working off his debts in Laches' household). A servant (Daos) fell in love with the girl, believing her to be a fellow slave. But a neighbour (Pheidias) had already raped her. Daos wanted to take the blame on himself. The mother (Myrrhine), not knowing the truth, was excessively angered. When things came clear, the old man (Laches) discovered his children, and the violator (Pheidas) took the girl willingly.'

The play opens with Daos telling Getas, slave of Pheidias, that he is in love with Plangon, whom he believes to be the daughter of Tibeios. Laches has promised her to him but is away in Lemnos. (1–52)[49]

One of the stage houses belongs to Laches; the other to the father of Pheidias. Between them is the shrine of the Hero, who is next in order of appearance and therefore gives the prologue speech after the

---

[49] Line 52 is part of the local colour; perhaps the line restored by Mette, Lustrum, 13, 1968, 552, from P. Oxy. 2741 belonged here.

first scene. As Tibeios is said to have lived 'here in Pteleai' (21), the scene is the Attic deme of Pteleai, and the Hero is presumably the deme hero. He tells the story that we know from the summary: Myrrhine was raped in a shrine (84), and presumably in his shrine. Heroes were often healers, and possibly a fragment (4), 'My dear, you were cured with difficulty and were under the influence of drugs,' may belong to Sophrone's later explanation of why Laches was there and what happened.[50] It seems clear that Laches did not recognise her when he married her, and probable that she did not recognise him.

The Hero knows also about the rape of Plangon by Pheidias, perhaps when she was performing in a chorus in his honour: probably Pheidias knows her, but Myrrhine at least does not know his identity, or she would not have believed Daos. Myrrhine is the next character in the list, and then Pheidias. After the Hero's speech there is likely to have been another scene in the first act. Conceivably Daos, who seems to be ignorant of Plangon's pregnancy in the opening scene, learnt of it during the gap covered by the Hero's speech and now planned to accept responsibility for it and ask Myrrhine to hurry on the marriage.

The scene between Myrrhine and Daos may begin the second act, and Daos uses the well-worn example of Zeus to aid his plea (fr. 1). Myrrhine presumably threatens punishment as soon as Laches returns. This may be followed by a further scene between Daos and Getas, and Getas perhaps offers the comfort of a jug of wine (fr. 3). Getas will have learnt from Daos of the pregnancy, and may pass on the news to Pheidias. The fragment (8), 'Now I will lead the huntsmen from the city round the pear trees', suggests that Pheidias arrives with a party of huntsmen: like Sostratos in the Dyskolos, he lives in the country but frequents the city. This I take to be his exit line: the huntsmen, if they come on stage at all, are extras; there is no reason to suppose that Menander had a special chorus for this play.

Three more characters appear before Laches. Laches' arrival can be fixed in the third act because in the second papyrus page, after an act-end, Laches comes out of his house (55) and the scene develops into a recognition scene, which is likely to come in the fourth act. Laches arrived back from Lemnos, therefore, late in the third act. Before him Sophrone, Sangarios and Gorgias appear. Sophrone is a nurse in the Epitrepontes, and here is probably Myrrhine's nurse; possibly Myrrhine sends her for a midwife in the second act and she returns in the

---

[50] On Heroes cf. 394 K–T; Dodds, Greeks and the Irrational, 77. Fr. 4 was so explained by Van Leeuwen, Menander, 10; the vocative 'sweetest' sounds more like the nurse than Myrrhine.

third. Sangarios is a slave name; his chief or only purpose may be to announce Laches' arrival in harbour, also in the second act. Gorgias is Plangon's brother, who is working off Tibeios' debt to Laches. Two suggestions can be made for the part that he plays. A fragment (2), 'Honour should have the privileges of high birth, and the free man should everywhere hold his head high,' sounds very like the Gorgias of the *Dyskolos* in his debate with Sostratos (272 ff.). This Gorgias may have had a similar debate with Pheidias when Pheidias returned from the pear trees in the third act. The second suggestion is that either before this or immediately after it Sophrone returned with the midwife, and Plangon gave birth and Gorgias (like his namesake in the *Georgos*) heard her cries.[51]

This is the situation which Laches finds when he returns.[52] He opens the fourth act with a brief monologue: he wants to talk with no one overhearing, then something about a bride and something about unbridled. He may be talking about the marriage of Daos and Pheidias' conduct, or conceivably he had been proposing to marry a daughter either by Myrrhine or by an earlier wife to Pheidias and is now disturbed by Pheidias' rape of Plangon. Then Myrrhine comes out to him, and he tells her that he has decided to turn out Plangon, Sophrone and possibly also Gorgias. The parallel in language with the scene in the *Samia* where Demeas throws out Chrysis, the nurse and the baby (369 ff.) makes this the obvious interpretation of the broken scene here. It must have run something like: *Laches*. 'She shall take the Thracian (Sophrone) and go.' *Myrrhine*. 'You will be thrown out unhappy one?' *Laches*. 'What? Certainly, wife— to the devil.' *Myrrhine*. 'You are mad to say things like that.' *Laches*. 'I shall do it, and my mind has long been made up. I was a fool to take on a shepherd who only knew how to look after sheep and allowed his sister to be raped.' At this point, where there is a gap of ten or more lines, Myrrhine must confess that the two are her children and that Tibeios was not their father. When the text resumes she is saying that she has to suffer her misfortune alone (i.e. she does not know who raped her). Laches asks about the rape, and it comes out that she was raped in a shrine sixteen years ago. Laches is beginning to see the truth when the text breaks off (97). He had raped her in the shrine of the Hero.

How much more is necessary we do not know. Perhaps Sophrone can provide recognition tokens. The summary says that Pheidias marries Plangon. Pheidias' father is not one of the characters; this suggests that a marriage with a daughter of Laches had already been

[51] In P. Oxy. 862 a Pheidias returns and is informed by a slave of the birth of a child. This may well belong here.

[52] On what follows cf. Gomme, C.R., 61, 1947, 72; C. Dedoussi, *Hellenika*, 180, 1964, 3; Webster, J.H.S., 93, 1973.

arranged, and that all that has to be done is for Laches to substitute his newly found daughter.

Hiereia (? before 306)

The *Heireia* (priestess) is known from an ancient summary (K–T, I, p. 146; Sandbach, p. 305), which is badly preserved, and two fragments. The priestess had two children; she kept the girl but the boy (A) she gave to a neighbour, who was married and had a daughter but only later gave birth to a son (B). The father of the priestess's children had deserted her but left her tokens, which she buried so as to keep them safe until the children grew up. The summary calls him 'he who was formerly the husband of the priestess', so that this was not a case of rape; it has been suggested that he deserted her because she became a priestess. This fits with a fragment (fr. 210) where someone tells Rhode that people who think they can control the gods by cymbals and rites make man greater than god and are guilty of *hybris*; this is clearly a criticism of a priestess of Kybele. It does not follow that Rhode is the priestess; Rhode may be the neighbour, who is being told by her husband what a bad neighbour they have. Father A may have taken the same view of his wife's profession.

Sixteen years or so after his desertion, father A fell ill (?) and apparently came unrecognised to the priestess for a cure. He overheard her discussing her son and guessed that he was the father. When he got better, he tried to find this son. He persuaded a slave to pretend to be possessed and brought him to the priestess for a cure. The slave tracked down the truth, i.e. that the son had been given to the neighbour.

I think that the play probably started with the scene in which the slave reported to the father or rather that the slave reported to the father in the first act.[53] There is no need for a prologue speech by a god or an abstraction: the father can tell the whole story except for the whereabouts of young A and the existence of young B. The slave supplies the whereabouts of young A, and young B appears after the father has gone off. Probably a long monologue by the father followed by the entry of the slave from the priestess' house opens the play.

[53] Conceivably P.S.I. 847 gives the beginning of the play: someone is interrogated and appears (or feigns) to be ignorant of his identity and where he comes from, Bartoletti, *S.I.F.C.*, 34, 1962, 21, suggested the girl in the *Theophoroumene*, but the accompanying illustration seems to show a male, and ignorance of identity does not appear to be a normal phenomenon of possession in Greek literature. The slave in the *Hiereia* must, however, have concealed his identity. If this is right, the scene preceded the cure and the report to father A.

House A is the house of the priestess and house B is the house of the neighbour. Körte suggests that father A had a third house on the stage. I am inclined to avoid assuming three private houses on stage unless it is necessary, and here it raises two difficulties: if father A is a neighbour, why does the priestess not recognise him? And why does he not know that there are two boys in house B? The central door, whether used or not, may be the shrine of Kybele.

One more scene (at least) belongs to the first act. Young B proposes to marry the daughter of the priestess, and sends his mother in to talk to the priestess about himself. If fr. 210 is rightly ascribed to his father, his father is against it, and in any case he is unlikely to favour marriage with the daughter of an unknown father. Probably, then, the father is away in the country when the son acts, but it is possible that he expresses his views on the priestess before he goes.

The second act probably begins with the two women talking on the priestess's doorstep. According to the summary father A, getting an idea from their conversation and well instructed by his slave, making a mistake in the character, addressed the younger son of the neighbours as his own son. This should mean that the father had discussed the matter with his slave at home and came back to hear the two women talking, and waited while wife B summoned young B out of the house to tell him the position, and then, when she had gone in to her own house, spoke to young B and discovered that he had found the wrong boy. The essential information which the priestess gave to wife B and which wife B passed on to young B must have been 'the father is unknown', and father A, overhearing it, did not realise that they were speaking of the priestess's daughter and applied it to young B.

The summary goes on: young B, realising the mistake, warned his brother (A) that the old man was mad and claimed all young men as his sons. This may be either a further scene in act II or the beginning of act III. Young A is called young B's brother because neither of the young men knows that in fact young A is the son of the priestess.

The next scene is certainly in the third act. Father A discovers the truth and addresses young A as his son; young A sends him away as a madman (cf. fr. 211). After this the summary gives very little until father B returns from the country and the play ends with a triple marriage: father A and the priestess, young A and the daughter of household B, young B and the daughter of the priestess.

A move towards recognition seems to come just before the text breaks off. 'The son of the neighbour (young B) . . . by the slave'. The only slave mentioned in the assessment of characters at the end of the summary is the slave of father A, so that it would seem that he was sent back after the old man's second rebuff and found young B. Two possible restorations in the text give the words 'suspicion' and 'mother'. Young B may have decided that there must be some basis for the claims and have interrogated his mother, perhaps asking if he is himself a bastard. This she would, of course, deny, but she might decide that the time had come when she had to put the slave's statements before the priestess: she faced disclosure for herself and young A, but the discovery of the father would also mean that the daughter of the priestess could marry her son. This must be the fourth act, and the slave must have overheard or been told enough to go and fetch father A to arrange the marriages in the fifth act.

But before he came back, father B returned from the country. A fragment (592) not ascribed to any play contains the rare name Rhode, which, we have seen, may be the name of wife B. A husband rebukes his wife for gossip and says that a free woman should not be seen outside her house. This may be father B's opening words. Probably late in the fourth act rather than at the beginning of the fifth he returns, to see his wife coming out of the priestess's house. (Whether fr. 210, the abuse of the priestess, also belongs here or whether it is his farewell speech when he goes off to the country in act 1, there is no evidence.) He abuses her, but he has to listen to her revelation. They probably go into the house to discuss it, and he finds no objection to father A as a brother-in-law. Then in the fifth act, with the return of father A, the marriages can be arranged.

Hydria (before 306)

In the prologue a youth quoted the speech of an old man. (This by itself rules out the suggestion that the play was the original[54] of the Aulularia, where the prologue was spoken by Hestia.) The play probably had a double plot. One old man indeed had the hydria which contained treasure stolen from him by an enterprising slave (403–4). Another old man, who preferred the country to the town (401), was reminded of an ancient misery (402), which probably means that a child lost in infancy was restored to him, as in the Sikyonios (357). The play ended with marriage or a pre-marriage feast (405).[55] (This excludes P. Oxy. 1239 as the end of this play.)

Hymnis (not dated)

Adapted by Caecilius. A new fragment:[56] 'he was a famous harpist'

[54] W. Kraus, Serta Aenipontana, 1962, 185.
[55] I take 405 K–T as description of an impending dance, cf. Dyskolos 953.
[56] Mette, Lustrum, 10, 1965, 108.

may describe the father of the girl (whether he or his daughter was called Hymnis). He may have been not unlike Phanias in the *Kitharistes*, and I should associate 407 and possibly 414 with him. The girl herself is in the hands of a *leno*, who will not sell her to the impoverished young man (II *cf.* VII). He lives the life of a prodigal (410–11), and his slave intrigues to get him six more months of bliss, whatever his father may say (III, IV, VI–VII). The father buys the girl, who passes for a Milesian (I), and gives or sells her to someone whom she can regard as a rich patron (408–9) and whom the son regards as a debauchee (412, 415). I think it is possible that this is in fact her father, the harpist, so that the girl is recognised and can be married.

Hypobolimaios or Agroikos (before 306)

Agroikos is listed in P. Oxy. 2462. Adapted by Caecilius with alternative titles *Hypobolimaeus* and *Rastraria*. According to Cicero a father had one son in the city whom he disliked and one son in the country whom he loved: the country son wore a leather tunic. Moschion, who was seen by the mother of the girl taking part in the Little Panathenaia (428), was the city son. Moschion in the *Perikeiromene* was supposititious; he is probably the supposititious son in this play and his mother's (or supposed mother's favourite; hence the enmity between his father and his mother (418, 422). He probably quarrelled with his brother (V), who must have come to town (? II); Herzog suggested that the Didot B papyrus was the prologue spoken by the country boy; if so, he also embarked on a course of love; but the ending, 'in the present sunshine I see you, the air, the Acropolis, the theatre', sounds very unlike Menander.[57]

A scheming slave, who took money from his master ostensibly for lessons in music and geometry (430a), probably worked for Moschion; 426 recalls Chremes to Syrus in *Heautontimoroumenos* 610. 417, 420, 427, and 429 probably also belong to the slave. But the father turned against him (III; *Rastraria* V), and when the truth came out sent Moschion back to his own father in spite of someone's objections (*Rastraria* II, IV; 519). Perhaps the country son married the girl (430 mentions the marriage bath, and 425 may be a dialogue with a quibbling cook).

Another character is an unhappy and tritely philosophical old man with a faithful slave, Parmenon (416, 419, 423; *Rastraria* III, perhaps translating 620). *Rastraria* I, 'this worry has now grown numb with misery', recalls the old man in the *Hydria* and Kichesias in the *Sikyonios*, and suggests that this old man too discovers a child that

[57] *Cf.* Gomme, *C.Q.*, 10, 1960, 103; Hemmerdinger, *Aegyptus*, 36, 1956, 24.

he lost long ago. He may, then, be the father of Moschion and the girl. Somehow the train of events which led to the discovery of Moschion's true parents must have been started when he was seen by the mother of the girl (cf. VII) taking part in the Little Panathenaia (428).[58]

Imbrians

The papyrus summary (K–T, I, p. 149; Sandbach, p. 306) gives the date of composition, 302/1, the first line, 'How long, Demeas my friend, (since I saw) you?', and the beginning of prologue information: two poor friends made a common life, settled in Imbros, married twin sisters, and held their property in common; they worked hard by land and sea. Presumably they became rich, and the play deals with the love affairs of the next generation; it was adapted by Caecilius. In 213 a young man pleads with his father to use reason (cf. 552, and Sostratos to Kallippides in Dyskolos 797). He may want to marry a girl who bears a child in the play (II); 'she was leaning back and fanning herself with her tunic' may describe the occasion when he raped her (V, cf. Eun. 595). His brother is drunk and disorderly (VII, cf. III) and probably assaulted a leno (VIII). Possibly he goes, or pretends to go, to the wars (VI).

Kanephoros

Adapted by Turpilius. Alkiphron's reminiscence (III, 31) shows that a youth fell in love with a girl when she was a basket-bearer in a procession; his passion was so violent that he forgot who he was (cf. Eun. 306). A likeness to the Synaristosai is 'he begged you to lend your daughter as a substitute' (220, cf. Cist. 104). The 'you' of this fragment may be the 'slanderous old woman with two parents from Aixone' (222; cf. Cist. 536).[59] The young man is faced with another marriage, perhaps with an heiress, which he dislikes (II–IV). But he has a clever slave (221).

Karchedonios (310/9)

Two papyri, P. Oxy. 2654 and P. Koeln 5031, have made it almost certain that Menander's play was not the original of Plautus' Poenulus. The likelihood therefore remains that the original of the Poenulus

---

[58] Cf. also G. Zuntz, P.B.A., 42, 209; M. Kokolakis, Athena, 66, 1962, 9.

[59] A new Photios fragment, Lustrum, 11, 1966, 141, comes from this sort of context.

was the *Karchedonios* of Alexis, who outlived Menander by twenty years: to the parallels between Menander and the *Poenulus* which had already been noted—the general likeness to the *Poenulus* and the particular likeness to Demeas' recognition of Krateia in the *Misoumenos* (1296 with *Mis.* 216)—is now added correspondence with the *Sikyonios* (1099 ff. with *Sik.* 343 ff.), where also an old man is persuaded to claim as his daughter a girl who in fact turns out to be his daughter. We can only suppose that Alexis was working very much in the tradition of Menander.

The forty-five lines of P. Oxy. 2654, which are identified because they include fr. 228, are extremely obscure. In the first column a slave comes out and is overheard by another man talking about someone who has suffered a severe tossing and finds it very difficult to be rid of a long-engrained folly in a single day. Then there is something about a brother and something about a father and possibly something about a metic. Then a third character appears and is interrogated by the slave; he gives his mother as the daughter of the Carthaginian general Hamilkas. To this the slave says, 'If you are the grandson of Hamilkas, why do you bother us and think that you will get a girl who is a citizen?' This situation is completely incompatible with the *Poenulus*, where the girls are Carthaginians and this is known before the Carthaginian arrives. It is possible that in Menander's play the Carthaginian has to prove that the girl is Carthaginian, unless he turns out himself to be an Athenian.

All that can be usefully read in P. Koeln 5031 is a line in which a slave is told to follow with military equipment. The master may be a soldier or may be a young man pretending to go to the wars, like Moschion in the *Samia*. (See now Sandbach, p. 152.)

Karine

Adapted by Caecilius. The title may mean simply a Carian woman rather than a professional dirge singer, but a special kind of flute was mentioned (225). There was certainly a rich and shameless *hetaira*, who demanded presents (223–4). Perhaps one of her lovers steals her ear-ring (II, III). A girl, who, I suspect, will be thereby recognised as a citizen, wants to redeem her mother's jewellery and dress, which her mother had pawned in her lifetime (I).

Kekryphalos (318/7)

Our knowledge of the *Kekryphalos* depends on a Hamburg papyrus and a number of fragments. Two of the fragments (239–40) come from a description of a *symposion*. One contains an invitation (242). One speaks of the list of cooks held by the *gynaikonomoi* (238). A feast must therefore have played a considerable part as in the *Eunuch* and the *Theophoroumene*. It was an intrigue play (244), and as 'chance helped' (241) it was probably a recognition play, as the title (*Kerchief*) suggests.

The papyrus starts[60] with a slave, Parmenon, calling Moschion's attention to the arrival of two women, Doris (mute) and another who is not named. They have garments and gold ornaments, which can be pawned to help Dorkion and should fetch 1,000 drachmai. This is the woman's contribution to the 'salvation' of Dorkion. Parmenon calls her a noble lady; she has appeared like a *deus ex machina*; the rest can be done by ordinary human means. Somebody, probably the woman, proposes to go in to Dorkion, as had been recently arranged, and tells Doris to bring all the things with her, and 'good luck go with it'. Moschion speaks for the first time, saying that he wants to go in and see her too. Parmenon tells him to go in and comfort her. He remains on stage for a soliloquy; only the first words of just over twenty lines remain. He is evidently troubled about what Moschion's father will say: 'the better the reason, the more he will dislike it'(II, 28, as probably completed by Kock, III, 444, No. 187); and he thinks of running away. (Thierfelder convincingly compares Syrus' speech in the *Dis Exapaton* after his first deceit, *Bacch.* 358 ff., but here Parmenon probably has to think of a plan to get the rest of the money.) Possibly the fragment about the list of cooks (238) comes in at the end, but 'from' at the beginning of the line is too little to hang it on.

It is clear that Parmenon has been told by Moschion to provide 1,000 drachmai for Dorkion. This may be part of her price as a slave or to buy off the rest of the time for which she has been hired by a rival or repayment of a loan. In any case, it implies that she is a *hetaira* or at the moment has the status of a *hetaira*. This accounts for the fragments about a feast: she was probably guest or entertainer and Moschion's rival was present.

Moschion speaks only once in the whole scene and never addresses the woman. The woman cannot, therefore, be his mother or the wife of a friend of the family. Parmenon's phrase 'noble lady' (or it may rather be 'You were noble, lady') is either politeness or gratitude or irony. We should not in any case expect Moschion's mother or a friend of the family to do anything to help a *hetaira*. The phrasing is significant here: the woman is contributing garments and gold, for

[60] 951a K–T; Hamburg 656; Siegman, N. 120; Sandbach, O.C.T., p. 335. Identified as *Kekryphalos* by occurrence of fr. 243 in l. 12.

which she knows she may not be repaid, to the 'salvation' of Glykera. The same word is used in the *Epitrepontes* (163): to deprive the baby of its trinkets is to destroy its hope of 'salvation', i.e. of being restored to its parents. It is difficult to avoid the conclusion that the woman is knowingly giving Dorkion her recognition tokens. Two patterns in Menander come to mind: the rich *hetaira* and her supposed younger sister in the *Andria* and the *Eunuch*, and the old *hetaira* Melaenis and her supposed daughter in the *Synaristosai* (*Cistellaria*). The second seems more likely: Dorkion is not living with the woman; she is out on her own. And the woman acts as a *deus ex machina* for Parmenon: her generosity is unexpected.

If this is right, the woman took Dorkion in as a baby, kept her recognition tokens and brought her up as her daughter. I think that, like Melaenis when she brings Selenium and her recognition tokens to Phanostrata, the woman is in a corner: she knows that she is going to have to give Dorkion up and so she hands over the recognition tokens without telling Parmenon what they are. It is possible that Parmenon is the Lampadio of the *Synaristosai* (*Cistellaria*) and has been led to the woman as the supposed mother of his mistress's lost daughter; the woman sees what is happening and to his surprise offers him garments and gold for Dorkion, whom he is trying to get for Moschion. Moschion goes in with the woman to see Dorkion, and the result will presumably be known only in the next act.

If Moschion, inspecting the recognition tokens, turns out to be the brother of Dorkion, then the situation is like the *Perikeiromene*, and when she is recognised as a citizen the rival can marry her. It is, on the other hand, possible that Parmenon turns to the woman simply as the supposed mother of Dorkion, and someone else, possibly the rival, turns out to be Dorkion's brother. There must be a clue in the invitation to the *symposion* (fr. 242)—one thinks of Chremes in the *Eunuch* and Demeas in the *Misoumenos*—and in the official register of cooks (fr. 238): does Parmenon need to find out the name of one of the guests, who may be Dorkion's brother?

We do not even know what the houses on stage are. It is certain that Dorkion, who is inside, is visited by the woman and by Moschion. The woman does not live there, but she may live in another stage house. Moschion has not set up house on his own, like Alcesimarchus in the *Synaristosai* (*Cistellaria*); he is too short of money for that. But his father may have had one of the stage houses. Unless Moschion has extracted Dorkion from a brothel and for the moment planted her in his father's house, she is probably either in an inn or, less likely, in the house of the rival.

Kitharistes (? 321–19)

The scene is Athens. Laches lives in house A. He has a wife and a son, Moschion. Phanias, the kithara player, lives in house B.

An act end (probably not the first act) divides the papyrus fragment at l. 27. Before it one of the speakers is a woman (2). Marriage is mentioned and an act of violence and a mother. Possibly Moschion has raped a girl and confesses to his mother, who persuades him to send for his father from the country (*cf.* 54).

The next act starts with a short scene (31–52) between two men, one of whom fears that a woman who has not arrived may have been shipwrecked. At the end they go off to the *agora*, sending someone to take 'these things' into the house. The house must be B rather than A, because immediately afterwards Laches arrives and Moschion comes out of house A to meet him; one of the speakers is, therefore, likely to be Phanias and to have just arrived from abroad.

Laches and Moschion discuss marriage and the criteria for marriage. Laches is prepared to give up a match for Moschion which he wanted (76 ff.), if Moschion's choice comes up to his standards. Moschion says that he fell in love in Ephesos with the daughter of Phanias, who was there to collect debts. In a fragment a son appeals to his father to help the wronged (fr. 3), and this fits with the suggestion above that Moschion has raped the girl. (The similar appeal to Laches by name in fr. 4 must rather be made by Phanias or Phanias' friend).

The scene helps to explain the preceding scene. Apparently Phanias has sent an Ephesian woman (39) and his daughter home separately, because he feared for his reputation if he brought the Ephesian woman with him. It is not clear whether she was somehow connected with his debts or whether she was coming as a pupil (*cf.* frs. 5–6). He fears that he may be regarded as a procurer (I think this must be the meaning of l. 41).

The obvious solution is that the women have come to Athens on the same ship as Moschion and that, knowing that he has raped the daughter, he has brought them home, and is hoping to persuade his father to arrange a marriage.

Fr. 1, in which someone expresses to Phanias his surprise at the troubles of the rich, and fr. 2, 'poverty is the lightest of evils', should belong to the return of Phanias and his friend from the *agora* in the next act.[61] How the plot worked out we cannot say.

---

[61] The rare name Phanias occurs in 544, 797 K–T, and in two lines in P. Vindob. 19999A, Borgogno, *Hermes*, 99, 1971, 374. All are addressed to a despondent Phanias and should belong to this play. See now Sandbach, O.C.T., p. 164.

Kolax (after 302)

Our knowledge of the Kolax depends, besides fragmentary quotations, partly on three papyri, partly on passages in Terence's Eunuch: he tells us in the prologue that he transferred the flatterer and the boastful soldier from Menander's Kolax. Plautus' Colax and Naevius' Colax also provide a few fragments. The chief papyrus (P. Oxy. 409 with 2655) has 120 lines but consists of excerpts, not continuous text; but it clear where one excerpt ends and another begins. P. Oxy. 1237 gives fragments of about thirty lines, of which the first two overlap with the end of one of the excerpts. The problem is to fit the fragments and the passages from Terence into and round the excerpts provided by the chief papyrus.

The third papyrus is a tiny fragment[62] but settles an important problem. It gives Bias and Strouthias as speaking characters. Frs. 2 and 3 show that they were the soldier and flatterer transferred by Terence into the Eunuch; fr. 3 has been rightly identified with Eun. 498, but there it is spoken by Gnathon. Gnathon appears as a speaking character in P. Oxy. 1237. It was therefore suggested that Gnathon was the helpful friend of the young hero, and called himself Strouthias only to deceive the soldier, his rival. This suggestion is ruled out by the third papyrus, which shows that the name of the flatterer was in fact Strouthias. The play therefore had a parasite, Gnathon, who may have been a friend of the hero, and a flatterer, Strouthias; Terence switched the names, perhaps because he thought Jawman was more intelligible than Birdman. (Possibly the pun on Gnathon and Plato in Eun. 263–4), which is more likely to be Menander than Terence, belonged to Gnathon's speech in the original play and was transferred by Terence to Strouthias' long description of the art of flattery.)

The two houses belonged to the young lover Pheidias (his father was away at the beginning of the play; he has a slave Daos and probably a second slave (mute) Sosias) and to the procurer, who owns at least one hetaira and probably a slave girl, Doris. The girl with whom Pheidias and the soldier are in love is probably an Attic citizen: this would account for the procurer's fear of lawsuits (121) and the break-up of the siege (Eun. 805). In that case a prologue figure must explain that a recognition is coming. And Pheidias' father must return for the betrothal, but we have no trace of him.

Act. I. The first excerpt (1–14) is exposition: a slave tells that his young master has been kept short of money by his father, who is away, and he is the host at a sacrifice to Aphrodite Pandemos (cf. fr.

---

[62] I owe my knowledge of this fragment to Professor E. W. Handley. On the rest see now Sandbach, O.C.T., 166.

1). As Pheidias refers back to marketing later (47), Pheidias and Daos presumably set out to the *agora* now.

Act II, sc. 1. The entry speech of the flatterer explaining his philosophy may well begin the act; he probably bring gifts for the girl from the soldier, as in the *Eunuch*. Daos also, as there, may meet him on his return from market (*Eun.* 232–64; fr. 5). Daos presumably brings the cook for the sacrifice; from fr. 1 it appears that he is pompous in the manner of comic cooks.

The flatterer must return to the soldier after handing over his gifts, and Pheidias in the second excerpt has returned from marketing. 'Doris' (probably the name of a slave girl in the procurer's establishment) has come into the text against metre in l. 19. It is possible that Doris saw the flatterer off and soliloquised until Pheidias came on.[63]

The second excerpt (15–54) overlaps with P. Oxy. 1237, which runs with fragmentary lines on to l. 84. Pheidias is addressed in l. 20. Daos speaks l. 68 and addresses Gnathon, and Daos speaks l. 73. Probably, therefore, Gnathon comes on with Pheidias at the beginning, and Daos enters from the house in l. 68. The second excerpt is largely taken up with Pheidias' description of the soldier as a monster of ill-gotten wealth, whom he has seen in the *agora*; Gnathon asks an occasional question; possibly he reproaches Pheidias with inactivity (63–4), and later the procurer is mentioned (72).

The third excerpt (85–94) is Daos telling Pheidias that flatterers are disastrous, particularly to kings and generals. If this is not the prudent old slave warning his young master against his own parasite, Gnathon, then it must be Daos' reaction to the great scene between Strouthias and Bias, and Strouthias having gone off in the second act, cannot get back on stage until the third act. This gives the following sequence.

Act III, sc. 1. Strouthias comes back with Bias. Bias praises himself and is egged on to further extravagance by Strouthias. Daos overhears from the doorstep of Pheidias' house. Possibly Strouthias is sent into the procurer's house to invite the girl to dinner and is refused. They go off, threatening violence. (*Eun.* 391–498, portions; frs. 2, 3, 4, 8; Plautus, fr. III?)[64]

Sc. 2. Daos comments to Pheidias on flatterers. (85–94; Plautus, fr. II)

Sc. 3. In the fourth excerpt (95–108, with the eleven new lines of P. Oxy. 2655 between 98 and 99) Pheidias reacts to a 'startling propo-

---

[63] Doris may have been a speaker's name which has come in from the next column.
[64] 745, K–T may belong here.

sal', which he does not understand. It seems likely that Gnathon, having heard Daos' account of the flatterer, has come up with a plan. The text is difficult, but in what follows Gnathon seems to be urging that even a strong man can be upset if he is off his guard—even an Olympic *pankratiast* like Astyanax; it is no good approaching the procurer with a small sum of money (*cf.* Plautus, fr. 1) Then something about the soldier. Then a call to 'slaves' (103), which can only mean that he is knocking on the door of the procurer's house, and a final summing up: 'You have the man off his guard, you can do what you like.'

Sc. 4. The next excerpt is a soliloquy of the procurer (109–21): he contrasts the soldier and his neighbour, Pheidias. He is afraid of the soldier's forces. But he is evidently also afraid that if he sends the girl to the soldier, Pheidias will carry her off and he will have legal proceedings.

We can only guess at what proposals Gnathon and Pheidias had put up in the preceding scene. As mentioned above, a suggestion that the girl could be recognised as an Attic citizen would account for the procurer's fears, and an invitation, either to her or to the procurer or both, to the celebrations in honour of Aphrodite in Pheidias' house would pick up the theme announced in act I; from the procurer's point of view acceptance of the invitation would divert the soldier's attack from him to Pheidias.

Act IV. The siege scene of the *Eunuch* must belong to this act (771–816). The rather pompous prayer of the cook (fr. 1) marks a stage in the sacrificial meal to Aphrodite. It seems possible that, as in the *Dyskolos* (622) the cook's libations are disturbed by Knemon falling down the well, so here the cook's libations are disturbed by the arrival of the soldier and his army. If so, the cook goes in, and the actor later comes out to parley with the soldier and the flatterer. He takes the part either of the relation who claims that the girl is a citizen or conceivably of Gnathon pretending to be the relation.

Act V. The only trace of the last act is the scene in the *Eunuch* (1025) where the soldier comes to surrender to Thais like Hercules to Omphale; Naevius' *Colax* (fr. 1) also has a comparison of the soldier to Hercules, which rather supports the suggestion that Terence was following the *Kolax* here.[65] In Terence it is the flatterer who negotiates with Phaedria to give the soldier a share of Thais; one would gladly derive this too from the *Kolax*, but nothing in the fragments as we know them suggests how this theme could be worked in, and if this girl is an Attic citizen it is impossible.

[65] 907 K–T may belong here.

Koneiazomenai (no date)

The title shows that in the course of the play women, perhaps a mother and daughter, too, intended to take or pretended to take hemlock; presumably the daughter had been raped and the prospect of marriage was hopeless. The mention of Epimenides (fr. 2) may be connected with this. In the papyrus fragment (Sandbach, p. 176) a youth, to his astonishment, is being informed by another that his marriage is being arranged with a dowry and a dress allowance, and that his future father-in-law is talking to Chaireas. He gives thanks to Fortune for saving him, and then goes in to see them. Fr. 1 may be the reflection of a slave (cf. Aspis 191): conceivably he suggested the daring intrigue. [66]

Kybernetai (not dated)

Illustrated on a mosaic from Mytilene:[67] a very strange scene from the third act; a young man approaches a girl kneeling on the seashore; an old man comes up, perhaps to restrain him. Conceivably the girl has been rescued from the sea, or the seashore merely alludes to her being the daughter of the sea captain. This may be the young man 'who forgot who he was' (254), presumably an effect of love, as in the Kanephoros, and is reproached, perhaps by the captain, with putting too much trust in the power of money (250). The captain also probably complains of being kept waiting for his pay (252), and he or a slave describes the father of the young man as regarded as happy in the agora but ruled by his wife at home (251).

Leukadia (? 308–06)

Adapted by Turpilius. The prologue is illustrated on a mosaic from Mytilene:[68] a slave arrives from the left, the priestess, a temple servant, a statue of Apollo. The priestess opened the play with a song in anapaests to Apollo at Leukas (258, perhaps also 259–61) and instructed the temple servant to put fire on the altar (257). The white-haired slave of the mosaic presumably comes to consult the god on behalf of his master. Conceivably the priestess turns out to be the mother of the girl, Dorcium. The girl seems to be jealous of the

---

[66] The attractive combination of Koneiazomenai with Fabula Incerta has become less likely since the discovery of P. Oxy. 2533, which fits Fabula Incerta more easily. The situation in P.S.I. 1176 is compatible with Koneiazomenai, but there is no positive link between them. Cf. above on Arrhephoros.

[67] Cf. L .Kahil, op. cit., n. 2, pl. 7,2.

[68] Cf. L. Kahil, op. cit., pl. 7,3.

young man (X) and to accept the advances of a foreign soldier (II), reducing her rejected lover to extremes of misery (I, III, IV, V, XII, XIII). Possibly the soldier carried her off and was shipwrecked with her; the youth rescued her (XIV, XI, XV; cf. 806, 880), and they were reconciled (XVI). Two fragments refer to a drunken slave (XVIII, XIX).

Messenia

The Mytilene mosaic[69] illustrates the fifth act: a young man, Charinos, between two slaves, Syros and Tibeios, who seem to be pulling him in opposite directions, perhaps a struggle between temptation, represented by Syros, and sobriety, represented by the older Tibeios (*paidagogos?*). The prologue was spoken by the Messenian woman and was full of *non sequiturs* (268). This sounds as if she was an old woman and perhaps the mother or supposed mother of a girl kept by the *leno Psyllos* (272), who was described introducing his girls to the young men at a *symposion* (741). There was also a talkative cook (269, 271).

Methe (produced before Kallimedon was condemned to death in absence in 318)

Methe (Drunkenness) spoke the prologue and excused the young man for rape (?). A parasite had a part. There was marketing for a rich meal (264). One of the young men was delayed by Chairephon (265; cf. *Eunuch* 323 ff.). A cook fails to borrow from a miserly or impecunious old man (267), who, perhaps, invokes Nemesis and Adrasteia (266; cf. *Samia* 503): he may be the father of the girl.

Misogynes

280 is the first line of the play: someone visits Glykera after a long time. Glykera is a *hetaira* name, but is the name of the girl who is later recognised as a citizen in the *Perikeiromene*. 276, Simylos complains to someone about his wife; the other speaker admits the disadvantages of an extravagant wife but notes the advantages of having children. The name in one quotation is not Simylos but Demeas; it is not safe to conclude from this or from the occurrence of Simylus as an old man in Terence (Ad. 352) that the misogynist is an old man— he may be a man of forty rather than a man of sixty. 277, we used to sacrifice five times a day, etc. This, with 283-4, is his complaint against his wife, and the past tense implies that he is already living

[69] Cf. L. Kahil, *op. cit.*, pl. 4.4.

apart from her. Desertion, then, is the chief item in the suit of damages which someone swears he will bring against him (279, cf. 278).[70] The speaker is unlikely to be the wife, because no woman in Menander swears by the sun; it is probably the wife's father. 282 is a list of a soldier's equipment, but it may be evidence of a threat to go campaigning rather than of a soldier's presence. It is at least possible that Simylos has deserted his wife for Glykera. There is no clear link with P. Ant. 55, which has been attributed to this play.

Misoumenos (305)

The houses on the stage are occupied by Thrasonides and Kleinias. Possibly, as will be suggested below, there is an inn (*pandokeion*) between them. In house A is the soldier, Thrasonides, the girl Krateia, her nurse Phrygia, and the slave Getas. In house B is an old woman who looks after Kleinias.[71]

The setting may be Rhodes. It is a place where one is expected to come to ransom captives who have been captured in Cyprus. Demeas 'comes here from Cyprus' and his home is somewhere else. His home may be Athens; Menander uses both Demeas and Kleinias as names for Athenians. Demeas is continually called *xenos*, 'stranger', but this merely means that he does not live here, and Kleinias is evidently his host, i.e. an Athenian living in Rhodes. If Demeas is an Athenian, Thrasonides must also be an Athenian to marry Demeas' daughter.

Act I, sc. 1. The play opens with Thrasonides addressing Night. He is madly in love with Krateia, but he will not go and take her. (P. IFAO 89; frs. 6, 5, 3)

Sc. 2. Getas comes out and reproaches him for night-walking (fr. 9).[72] Thrasonides goes into the inn; Getas acts as his scout.

Sc. 3. Thrasonides only knows the story from when he captured Krateia. The rest only a prologue figure can tell, and we can only guess it. The following reconstruction seems possible: Demeas, Krateia and his son were Athenians living in or visiting Cyprus. In the confusion of war they became separated: Demeas escaped or was away (cf. fr. 2); Krateia was captured with Phrygia (cf. 228) and was ultimately bought by Thrasonides (233–6); the brother fought, was

[70] 679 K–T, in which someone turns a woman out for having dyed hair, might belong to this play.

[71] See now Sandbach, O.C.T., 180. The main text is given in P. Oxy. 2656–7. E. G. Turner's preliminary publication in B.I.C.S., supp., No. 17, is still very useful. Comments on the prologue, P. IFAO 89, in Z.P.E., 1971, 97 (Koenen and Handley); a new P. Oxy. is promised. On fr. 13 see Arnott, C.R., 18, 1968. 11.

[72] 722 K–T might be Getas' opening speech, but the tone is perhaps too soft and disagrees with the description by Arrian (fr. 3). Cf. G.R.B.S., 1973, 287.

wounded, and ultimately escaped; in the confusion he had exchanged
swords with a comrade, who was killed by Thrasonides (this theme
we now know from the *Aspis*). The sword was inscribed, and
Thrasonides therefore listed the brother among his casualties, whom
he recounted to Krateia (*cf.* fr. 1). This caused her hatred, which
gives the play its name, a hatred based on misunderstanding, like the
fury of Polemon described by the prologue figure of the *Perikeiromene*.
(Fr. 7 probably comes from this speech and describes Thrasonides'
successes in Cyprus, perhaps as a soldier of Demetrios Poliorketes.)

A fragmentary text is provided by P. Oxy. 2657, which probably
belongs to act II. No suggestion can be made for the end of act I;
conceivably there was a scene with Kleinias, in which he too expressed his love for Krateia.

Act II, sc. 1. There are traces of a scene between Thrasonides and
Getas, and probably Getas is sent into house A (9). Thrasonides
sees Demeas arrive; he has writings, and Thrasonides directs him to
Kleinias' door and goes into his own house (17–22).

Sc. 2. Demeas is received by Kleinias (24 ff.; fr. 2). He evidently
asks for help in finding his daughter. He gives her name, and
Kleinias tells him that there is a Krateia living with the soldier. He
asks Kleinias to call her out so that he can see her. Possibly Kleinias
already asks for her hand (77). A general parallel is given by the
arrival of Hanno in the *Poenulus*; he has a letter to his guest friend
(958), and when he arrives in a town he tries to find his daughters
by seeking out all the *hetairai* (103). But his daughters were lost in
infancy: Demeas knows Krateia by sight but cautiously wants to see
her before he gives himself away.

Another gap follows before the text picks up in act III with the
long but difficult P. Oxy. 2656; here we can only reconstruct from
later hints.

Sc. 3. Demeas has gone into Kleinias' house. Kleinias goes to
Thrasonides and asks him to bring Krateia to dinner. Thrasonides
refuses and perhaps now, perhaps later in the act, goes into the inn
to drown his sorrows.

Sc. 4. Kleinias somehow, perhaps through the nurse, conveys his
invitation to Krateia. He then summons a slave from his own house
and goes to market (this must happen in act II for him to return in
act III, 270).

Act II, sc. 5 or Act III, sc. 1. Getas brings out Thrasonides' swords
and deposits them with the old women in Kleinias' house. Earlier, not
necessarily on stage, Thrasonides had threatened suicide and Getas
had refused to give him a sword (fr. 3 *cf.* fr. 12). It would clearly be
easier to remove the swords if Thrasonides, as suggested, is now in

the inn. Kleinias hears about the swords only after he has come back (276).

Act III, sc. 2. Here P. Oxy. 2656 begins. Krateia and her nurse come out of Thrasonides' house, carrying suppliant boughs. Presumably Getas' absence gives them the chance, and they propose to take asylum at an altar until Kleinias comes back and finds them. But Getas, having deposited the swords catches them and they go back into the house. (109–156; fr. 10)

Sc. 3. Getas soliloquises: the woman object to his spying; he suspects Kleinias; Krateia thinks that Kleinias, unlike Thrasonides, knows how to behave in the symposion; why did Kleinias come and then go back home and then set out again for market unless he means some harm? Getas goes in to watch what the women do. (157–175)[73]

Sc. 4. The old woman comes out of house B, surprised that Demeas has been inspecting the neighbours' swords in the *andron*. Demeas follows and asks her to knock on Thrasonides' door and ask about the sword. She refuses and goes in. He knocks himself. (176–207)

Sc. 5. Krateia and her nurse (mute) come out, again carrying suppliant boughs. Krateia and Demeas immediately recognise each other. Getas bursts out of the house, expecting to catch Krateia's lover, and is presented with her father. Demeas explains, and Getas goes to fetch Thrasonides. (208–37)

Sc. 6. Demeas is alone with Krateia and asks about his son. Krateia says that he is dead, killed by Thrasonides. Demeas does not give his own evidence. They go in to make a plan. (238–57)

Sc. 7. Thrasonides enters with Getas (mute): Demeas will make him blessed by giving him his daughter or 'Thrasonides is done for'. He goes in trembling to discover the truth (258–69). (It is this passage which makes it probable that the central stage door is an inn. If Thrasonides had stayed in his own house he would have run into Demeas and Krateia as they went in. On the other hand if he had gone to a house off stage, an act end would be necessary between the summons and his return.[74] But he can be summoned from the inn on stage and so follow Demeas into his own house.)

Sc. 8. Kleinias arrives back from market with the cook (mute) and tells him that the party will be himself ,Demeas and Krateia—'if she has arrived. I am worried about that myself too.' (This shows that there were difficulties about the invitation and that he, as well as Demeas, has an interest in Krateia.) They go into house B. (270–75)

Act IV, sc. 1. Kleinias comes out of his house, speaking back to the old woman. He is surprised that Demeas has recognised the sword

---

[73] Cf. *Essays presented to Franz Blatt*, 135.
[74] The special cases quoted in ch. VI are different.

and gone to Thrasonides, and he asks when the neighbours deposited the sword. Then he hears someone coming out of Thrasonides' house. (276–82)

Sc. 2. Getas comes out and for forty lines describes with commentary the conversation between Demeas, Krateia and Thrasonides, while Kleinias vainly tries to break in. Thrasonides has accepted a ransom for Krateia, but Demeas is deaf to all his entreaties to be allowed to marry her. There is a short conversation between Getas and Kleinias before Kleinias goes in, presumably convinced that his chance of getting Krateia is good. (283–341)[75]

Sc. 3. The text is very unclear here, but suggests a conversation between Thrasonides and Getas, followed by a monologue of Thrasonides. He answers Getas' criticism that he has been faint-hearted; he is afraid that drink will strip the plaster from his wound; he refuses to stand on his rights over Krateia; if she hates him because of some misfortune he is prepared to pity her; he thinks that he may win her by kindness and gifts. The remark about drink may mean that he goes into the inn until Krateia has left his house. (342–408; fr. 4; 479)[76]

Sc. 4. There is a gap here of nearly 160 lines. Probably what happens is that Demeas, Krateia and the nurse move over to Kleinias' house and are admitted, perhaps by the old woman.

Sc. 5. Demeas probably remains outside and so sees the arrival of his son (fr. 13). The son, I assume, like Demeas before him, is looking for his sister and comes, like his father, to the house of the family friend, Kleinias. Son and father recognise each other and go inside to join Krateia.

Act V. Here the interpretation of the Mytilene mosaic[77] is the best lead. It names act v, but not the characters. It gives, from left to right, (*a*) a slave moving left fast, (*b*) a man in *chiton* and *himation* moving left, (*c*) a woman looking left. The slave is Getas and the woman Krateia. The man cannot be Demeas because he has not the distinctive *himation* worn by all old men on this set of mosaics. He could be Thrasonides in civilian dress (like Polemon in the *Perikeiromene* (57, 164); but it is difficult to imagine in the fifth act a scene in which Krateia sends Thrasonides away. Kraus[78] has taken the

[75] 650 K–T, 'One should bear misfortunes as a human being, stranger,' seems to pick up Getas' beginning in 302, and may be a quotation of Thrasonides speaking to Demeas later in Getas' report.

[76] After 403 Thrasonides may quote the 'immortal gratitude' which Demeas promised if Krateia was ransomed, i.e. 479 K–T may belong.

[77] Cf. L. Kahil, *op. cit.*, pl. 8,1.

[78] *Rh. Mus.*, 114, 1971, 1 and 285. If the brother was wounded (which would provide an admirable contrast in fr. 13, 'they wounded me, father, but they

central figure for Demeas' son, and this seems the best solution. It gives the following run of scenes.

Sc. 1. Getas comes out to discover what is happening; he may bring gifts for Krateia.

Sc. 2. Krateia and her brother come out from house B. Getas overhears enough to understand who he is and the meaning of the sword story, and goes back to report to Thrasonides. Krateia bids her brother farewell and goes in.

Sc. 3. Getas and Thrasonides come out. Getas goes into house B with gifts and congratulations from Thrasonides. Thrasonides soliloquises. (410–28)

Sc. 4. Getas comes out and tells Thrasonides that they are giving him a wife. (429–422)[79]

Sc. 5. Demeas comes out and makes the formal betrothal. They go into house B to feast before the marriage, which will take place on the next day. The play ends. (443–66)

Naukleros (before 306)

The title occurs in P. British Museum 2562. Adapted by Caecilius. The shipowner is Straton, and someone announces the return of his son Theophilos (286): Straton is more interested in the ship than his son. Someone, probably a slave, greets the earth on his arrival from the voyage (287). The son, probably, is in love (290), and the father threatens to curse him for disobedience (288). In Caecilius a girl gets her jewellery stolen, presumably in a rough *symposion* (III). A fragment (II) in which some one is cursed for an ill advised recollection (*cf.* 402), taken with (I),'you will hear if his daughter returns', suggests that the girl was lost in infancy and is finally recognised.

Olynthia

This play is dated about 314 by the reference to the naval expedition of Aristoteles (297): it is probably a scornful reference, like Daos' reference to 'four-obol men' in the *Perikeiromene*, 190. There is also a reference to a *symposion* (298) and to a wig (299), probably a disguise, *cf. Aspis* 377. Olynthos was destroyed in 348, so that the Olynthian woman must be the mother of the young heroine or a *hetaira*.

have not killed me'), he may have been described as 'corpse-coloured', a new fragment from *Photios, Lustrum*, 10, 1965, 106.

[79] Fragment 11 (Getas tells Thrasonides to go in because he is going to marry) should belong here, but there seems to be no place for it. It must therefore come before 410.

Orge

Menander's first play, Lenaia, 321. Anger spoke the prologue and was responsible for the trouble, like Methe in her play. Little can be made out. A man called Lamprias (307) complains of the extravagant behaviour of his wife (303). There is a reference to an adulterer (306) and several to a meal (304–5, 309–10).

Paidion

Produced in 311 and adapted by Turpilius. Probably Paidion is the name of the *hetaira* who demands gifts (314–5, VIII, II) and from whom the father seeks to separate the young man, probably vainly (IV, VI, VII) even at the cost of the marriage which he has arranged and which is far advanced (IX, XII, *cf.* P. Oxy. 11, 43 f., rather than *Samia* 449). The young man regards his father as a monster (XI) and has a bachelor friend (313, X) and a slave (312, 317) to help him; it is probably he who invokes Aphrodite (I). The girl who has been brought up ignorant of vice (V; *cf. Dyskolos* 384) is probably the love of another young man, perhaps a brother.[80]

Pallake (before 306)

Adapted by Naevius, whose single fragment, 'stop (abusing?) your father-in-law, my brother on the father's side', shows that one of the young men of the play was married. Otherwise we have only evidence of a drinking scene (319), and perhaps the concubine reporting that someone runs up to her with presents (318).

Parakatatheke (not dated)

Adapted by Afranius, *Depositum*, which gives the sense of the title. 323, a quarrel between friends. 324, an unhappy soldier. 325, a talent of gold weighed out to a slave, apparently for an extravagant son. 327, probably an unhappy father. 329, *hetaira* grateful for the purchase of jewellery. 331, perhaps instructions to raid the establishment of a *leno*.

[80] P. Oxy. 11 (Daos reprimands a young master, who is abandoning a marriage already arranged for a foreign woman; a father, Simon, making marriage arrangements), P. Cairo 65445 (a cook waiting for a slave and Simon), P. Vienna 29811 (Daos and Simon talk, possibly of rape and recognition, *cf.* Turpilius V) may belong.

Perikeiromene (314/13)

The scene is Corinth. House A belongs to the soldier Polemon, who has a mistress, Glykera, a slave, Sosias, and a maidservant, Doris. House B belongs to a man who is probably called Philinos, his wife, Myrrhine, an adopted son, Moschion, and a slave, Daos. Between them is an inn.[81] Pataikos, who turns out to be the father of Glykera and Moschion, is one of the kindred souls who gather to help Polemon in his misery (54 f.; cf. fr. 1). If it is an inn rather than the house of Pataikos, it would naturally have a cook (418) and a flute girl (226).

(Act I, sc. 1. The play opened with the return of Polemon from a campaign. He is met by Sosias, who says that on his return the night before he had seen Glykera being embraced by an unknown young man (Moschion). Polemon summons hcr out, cuts off her hair, and then goes off with Sosias to the inn.)

Sc. 2. Agnoia (Ignorance, or rather Misunderstanding) tells the story. Some eighteen years ago Pataikos' wife had born him a son, Moschion, and a daughter, Glykera, and died; he had lost his fortune in a shipwreck and exposed the children. They were found by an old woman, who gave the boy to Myrrhine and brought up the girl, later giving her to Polemon as her daughter. Before she died she told Glykera the truth, but Glykera said nothing to Moschion. (1–51)

Sc. 3. Sosias has been sent to spy by Polemon. He sees Doris come out of Polemon's house before he goes in himself to fetch Polemon's civilian clothes. As he comes out again and goes off he sees Doris knocking on Myrrhine's door. (52–70)

(Sc. 4. Myrrhine comes out and agrees to Doris' request for an asylum for Glykera. Doris returns to tell Glykera.)

(Sc. 5. Glykera comes out and meets Myrrhine. Daos is sent across with other slaves to fetch her baggage. The women go in to Myrrhine's house.)

Sc. 6. Daos sends the slaves in with the baggage and goes off to the *agora* to report to Moschion. (71–6)

Act II, sc. 1. Daos comes back with Moschion. He is sent in to see what is happening, and reports that the women seem to be waiting for Moschion. He is sent in again to say that Moschion has arrived. and is told to get out. With difficulty he persuades Moschion to go in and keep quiet. (77–163)[82]

---

[81] Cf. *Essays presented to Franz Blatt* on P. Oxy. 2658, which gives the inn. The text of the whole play is now in Sandbach, O.C.T., p. 198 (he gives the line numbers of K–T, I, in brackets).

[82] Cf. Whittle, C.Q., 9, 1959, 57, on ll. 87–8.

Sc. 2. Daos sees Sosias arrive with Polemon's sword and cape and go into Polemon's house. Sosias comes out, cursing the slaves, who have let Glykera escape. He threatens Daos with a siege. Daos goes into Myrrhine's house. (164–206)

Sc. 3. Doris comes out of Polemon's house and tells Sosias that, Glykera has fled to Myrrhine in fear. (207–16)

(Here the text breaks off, but the following sequence seems likely:

Sc. 4. Polemon comes out of the inn to receive Sosias' report. They discuss the situation with Pataikos. Sosias suggests a siege, Pataikos negotiations.

Sc. 5. Pataikos goes across to Myrrhine's house and is admitted as a friend of Glykera.

Act III, *sc.* 1. Polemon and Sosias prepare a siege with the soldiers in the inn and the flute girl Habrotonon (all mute).)

Sc. 2. Pataikos comes out of Myrrhine's house, and persuades Polemon to dismiss the army. The rest go into the inn; Sosias probably into Polemon's house. (217–35; P. Oxy. 2830)

Sc. 3. Pataikos points out the legal position to Polemon. Polemon persuades him to act again as an ambassador, but first takes him into his house to show him Glykera's clothes and jewellery. (236–75)

Sc. 4. Moschion comes out of Myrrhine's house, frustrated because no one except Daos has been near him. (276–300)

(Again the text breaks off, but a sequence can be reconstructed from what comes later:

Sc. 5. Daos comes out and tells Moschion that Glykera has sworn to Myrrhine not to reveal that she is the brother of Moschion.

Sc. 6. Philinos arrives from the country. Moschion tells him the story. They go in to question Myrrhine as to his parentage.

Act IV, *sc.* 1. Pataikos comes out of Polemon's house (possibly carrying the robe, which he has recognised as of his wife's weaving). He summons Glykera out of Myrrhine's house.)

Sc. 2. Glykera refuses to consider going back to Polemon. She asks Pataikos to get her the robe which she had from her mother and father. Pataikos calls Doris out of Polemon's house. (The text goes off here; I think Doris may say that the robe has been taken from her and go back in. Pataikos shows Glykera the robe that he is carrying.) (301–37)

Sc. 3. As they are examining the robe, Moschion comes out of Myrrhine's house and overhears the recognition taking place and the recital of his own recognition tokens. He breaks in. (338–97)

(Again the text breaks off, but we can guess at what must happen:

Sc. 4. Glykera and Moschion have gone in to tell Myrrhine.

Pataikos summons or meets Sosias, tells him that he is the father of the two, and then goes in to Myrrhine and Philinos.[83]

Sc. 5. Sosias reports to Polemon. Polemon sends Doris with congratulatory gifts for Glykera. He thinks his case is hopeless and retires again to the inn.

Act V, sc. 1. (It is possible that P. Oxy. 2658 belongs here. It has a scene in front of an inn. Someone, who later claims not to be drunk, speaks of a 'brother-loving disposition' (Polemon on Glykera) and says that Doris is inside (which may refer to Myrrhine's house). Then Doris comes in, and he greets her.)

Sc. 2. Doris reports that Glykera will come back to him. He sends her in again to find out more. She says that Glykera is getting ready to come out. Polemon is so moved that he runs back into the inn. Doris follows him to make arrangements for a feast. (406–27)

Sc. 3. Pataikos comes out with Glykera (mute?).[84] The betrothal is made. Pataikos goes back into Myrrhine's house to betroth Moschion to the daughter of Philinos. The play ends after Polemon has reflected on the situation. (428–48)

Perinthia (? 308–6)

Terence says that the *Perinthia* was similar in plot to the *Andria* but different in style. The girl presumably, like the girl in the *Andria*, turned out to be an Athenian citizen;[85] it is certain also that she gave birth to a child,[86] since a fragment describing a drunken old woman (fr. 5) corresponds to the description of the midwife in the *Andria* (229). Donatus says that Terence transferred the first scene of the *Andria* from the *Perinthia*, 'where the old man talks with his wife as in Terence with his freedman'.[87] This surely implies more than dialogue instead of monologue; it suggests that the pretended marriage preparations and the story of the funeral were common

[83] Fragment 2, 'Nevertheless show these things to your wife and', may imply an actual meeting on stage between Pataikos and Philinos, if 'these things' are recognition tokens. Perhaps Kock, C.A.F., III, adespota 131, should also be considered: someone (Myrrhine?) asks Philinos for a return of the gratitude which he owes her for happiness.

[84] Cf. Sandbach, P.C.P.S., 1967, 40.

[85] Cf. ch. 1, p. 2, on the chronology. The Perinthian woman may be the supposed mother of the girl. The text is now in Sandbach, O.C.T., p. 224.

[86] Fragment 4 may be the occasion of her rape, cf. ch. V, n. 1.

[87] See K–2, II, 288, for fr. 1a: 'Menander used prostates of the patron of a metic at the beginning of the *Perinthia*.' This suggests that Laches was the patron of the Perinthian woman. Barigazzi, *Hermes*, 88, 1960, 379, suggested that P. Hibeh 181 belonged to the Perinthia on the basis of a note, 'about to fetch the prostates'. The name Daos is insufficient as a link.

to both plays. The papyrus fragment shows that the old man was called Laches and his slave Daos; another slave, presumably of another household, was called Sosias.

The *Perinthia* started with a dialogue between Laches and his wife. The second scene of the *Andria* starts with Simo overhearing Davus; perhaps in the same position, certainly early, in the *Perinthia* Laches heard Daos saying that it is easy to cheat an easy-going master (fr. 1), which Laches quotes in the papyrus fragment. A prologue speech is also necessary: in addition to the recognition and the pregnancy this play has the further complication of an extra young man —Charinus is in love with the daughter of Chremes, whom Laches is trying to get for his son.

Laches and the Perinthian girl must have house A and B; Charinus and Chremes live off-stage. This gives some guide as to how the act divisions must fall. Terence has preserved a structure which surely comes from Menander; Charinus uses Byrrhia (probably the Sosias of the papyrus) as a spy, and if he lives off-stage an act end must fall between each appearance of Charinus and/or Byrrhia. Their first appearance (301) may be in the first act. They come on because Byrrhia has heard from Daos that Pamphilus is to be married. Menander uses the prologue speech as the equivalent of an act end, so that it can, so to speak cover, Daos and Byrrhia meeting in the forum and returning. Here Charinus reproaches Pamphilus, and Pamphilus reassures him; Charinus sends Byrrhia home (possibly 336 f. translates fr. 3). Terence has shortened here; a further conversation between the two young men must have preceded Daos' entry. Daos now suggests that the marriage preparations are only a pretence; this scene is secured for the *Perinthia* by a quotation (369, fr. 6). Daos tells Charinus to go and pay his court to the two old men if he wants to marry Chremes' daughter, and he says he will. This suggests a *Perinthia* scene of which we have lost all trace.

Byrrhia's return (412), when he hears Pamphilus tell his father that he is prepared to marry, must belong to the second act; Terence has conflated an *Andria* and a *Perinthia* scene here.

As a result of this report, Charinus returns in the third act (625) to upbraid Pamphilus, and Daos proposes a new plan. The Charinus sections of the next *Andria* scene (691, 702–14) probably come from the *Perinthia*. Charinus then goes home.

In the papyrus fragment Laches is making preparations to burn Daos off an altar on which he has taken refuge. Pyrrhias, Getas and Tibeios are mutes, slaves of Laches who help. If this is a much more violent version of the punishment of Davus at *Andria* 860, Daos has caused the trouble by saying that someone has arrived who claims that the Perinthian girl is an Athenian citizen; he may have expected gratitude for this news (19). The third actor in this scene is Sosias (col. i, 17, col. ii, 21). As long as he is present, no one can release Daos: I suspect, therefore, that Daos surrenders and is taken into the house to be punished. Sosias is a slave name; another speaking slave in Laches' household is unlikely; Sosias may therefore be Terence's Byrrhia, who has come back in the fourth act to spy for Charinus.

The report that the Perinthian girl may be a citizen brings Charinus back in the fifth act (957), when she has been proved to be the daughter of Chremes. Chremes is in fact in house B (951), meeting his lost daughter, so that it is possible that the *Perinthia* ended, like the alternative ending in Terence, with the betrothal of Charinus to the other daughter of Chremes, who had originally been designed for Pamphilus.[88]

Phasma (before 306)

Our knowledge comes from a summary by Donatus, a papyrus in Leningrad, a mosaic and P. Oxy. 2825 (fixed by frs. 1 and 2).[89] I give Donatus' summary, with letters for the names of the characters, none of which is known with certainty. The step-mother (wife A) of a youth (young A) had with her continually without anyone's knowledge a daughter, whom she had conceived from a neighbour (B); the girl was brought up in secrecy in a hiding place in the neighbour's house (B). She had had the wall between the two houses perforated so that the passage looked like a shrine; it was adorned with wreaths and foliage; when she sacrificed there, she called the girl to her. When the youth saw this, the first sight of the beautiful girl struck him with horror as if it were the apparition of a god (hence the name of the play). Then gradually he discovered the truth and flamed into such love for the girl that there was no remedy but marriage. The play ends with a marriage that suits the mother and the girl, answers the lover's prayers, and is consented to by the father.

One column of the Leningrad papyrus agrees so closely with this summary, down to the word 'apparition', that it must be the ultimate source, which suggests very strongly that this column is a prologue

---

[88] On the alternative ending cf. P. Oxy. 2401 and O. Skutsch, *Rh.Mus.*, 101, 1957, 53.

[89] The mosaic, L. Kahil, *op. cit.*, pl. 8,2. On P. Oxy. 2825 and the whole play, Sandbach, O.C.T., p. 288; E. G. Turner, *G.R.B.S.*, 10, 1969, 307; Webster, *J.H.S.*, 93, 1973. C. Garton, *Latomus*, 31, 1972, 150, argues for Terence, *Phormio* 6–11 deriving from *Phasma*. Possibly a dream of young B, who thinks of the apparition as pursued by young A.

speech. The other column is a dialogue between a youth, probably called Pheidias, who suffers from a rich man's melancholy, and is told by his slave to try a rich man's cure, a ritual purification by the women. There is nothing external to settle the order of these two columns. E. G. Turner has argued for slave dialogue as the first column and then a column containing according to him dialogue between youth and woman, followed in l. 9 by the prologue speech of a god. There are two major obstacles to this arrangement. The first is space; even if the papyrus had a forty-eight-line column, only twenty-six lines separate the entry of the god from the preserved end of the slave's speech. The slave is still in full flow. According to Turner, the young man has to accept his advice, summon out wife A, and tell her that he has seen an apparition and wants to be purified. She has to dissuade him (or at least in an aside express her fear of this investigation of the apparition) and tell him to keep quiet; which he accepts. The second difficulty is the absence of transition to the speech of the god. In the *Aspis* we are told what Daos and Smikrines are going to do and where they are going; then Tyche enters, saying, 'If they had really had a disaster; it would not have been likely for me, a god, to follow them. But in fact they are all astray and have misunderstood,' and then her narrative follows. Here the young man ends, 'I will do it. For what harm can it do?' and the next line (which must be something like 'she is not an apparition but a real girl') starts the narrative of the god without any introduction.

The alternative is to accept the traditional order of the columns. This has become more attractive since we now know that in the *Samia* Moschion himself gave the prologue speech. What we have preserved is the end of youth A's advice to himself: the broken lines contain the words 'bridegroom yourself . . . mother of the girl . . . to her step-brother . . . do not give any (handle) against yourself. Act thus. Yes, I shall. For what harm can it do?' Then he goes over to narrative and explanation of the arrangement of the passage; starting, 'She is not an apparition, but a real girl, living in the same house as my future bride.' In the earlier part of his speech he must have told us that he is utterly miserable because his father, who is away, has ordered him to marry the daughter of his neighbour, B. He has seen the apparition, which frightened him so much that he consulted his stepmother. She told him the truth, and he is now desperately in love with the girl. But he can only keep quiet about it so as not to give his stepmother away.

A maximum of twenty-three lines separate the description of the shrine in the party wall, which seems to be running out in l. 25, and the dialogue of the slave and the young man. It has been assumed that the young man here, whose name is restored as Pheidias (50), is the young man A, who is in love with the apparition, but, as I hope to show, the Oxyrrhynchus papyrus throws considerable doubt on this.

For the second act our only certain evidence is the mosaic from Mytilene. This shows a girl standing in a doorway on the left, an old man hurrying towards it, followed by a youth. As this is the only fully drawn doorway in the whole series of mosaics, it must be a special doorway, and the suggestion that it is the shrine in the party wall is likely to be right. The *Dyskolos* and the original of the *Aulularia* both had a shrine between the two houses, but this is a special case, because a door in a party wall has become a door between and level with the doors in the front walls of the two houses. I do not think that Menander would shrink from this; it is only a different kind of improbability from the improbability in the *Epitrepontes* (563, 599) when Charisios, in one house, can overhear what Smikrines says to Pamphile in the other house, an improbability which he masks by bringing them both on to their doorsteps. If this is right, the girl is the apparition, and the two men are likely to be the two men at the moment most obviously concerned with her, young A and his father, who now discovers her on returning.

The one consequence that is certain is that father A goes on with preparations for the marriage of his son to the daughter of B. This is clear from P. Oxy. 2825, in which a cook is present and someone's marriage is 'on again'. The general situation is like that in the *Andria* and the *Perinthia*. The cook must have been fetched from the market place, and this scene cannot, therefore, be earlier than the third act, since the marketing, including the hiring of the cook, can have taken place only after the return of father A.

P. Oxy. 2825, fr. B, consists of eighteen lines of iambics followed by eighteen lines of trochaic tetrameters. Change of metre within an act suggests that someone new comes on stage: even in the *Dyskolos* (707) Myrrhine is brought on when Knemon changes from iambics to trochaic tetrameters. The speakers in the iambic scene are a slave, Syros, the cook, a youth who has a sister about to marry (6) and in the trochaic scene a *paidagogos* (11) and a youth who has a sister about to marry (17). As far away as we know, only the son of father B has a known sister, the girl whom young A is supposed to be going to marry. Young B is, then, the link character between the two scenes.

In the iambic scene Syros, who is evidently the slave of house A, tells young B that young A is going to marry; he has got over his melancholia. Then the cook comes out to borrow a pot (8). Syros refuses to help him and rushes in to house A. Possibly young B shouts to the slaves in house B (12). The cook goes back into house A, presumably at the end of the iambic scene. Whether Syros is simply telling the truth or whether he has some ulterior motive is unclear. As the loyal slave of young A, he cannot want the marriage, if he knows, as he surely does, that young A is in love with the apparition; but he may have his own reasons for wanting a report that the marriage is going ahead to reach house B. The 'melancholy' of young A refers back to act I: it must have been reported to house B as a reason for not going ahead with the marriage.

The tetrameter scene begins with the *paidagogos* coming out in answer to young B's call in col. i, 12. The text is difficult here. I think the *paidagogos* claims to be reporting Syros (perhaps he had met him in the *agora*, or it may be news from the act before). 'Then he dashed in again ... if the fit comes on him when the girl is shut up with him, he will eat her nose or her lips when he kisses her.' Young B's comments are first 'Was not he ashamed?' and then 'Alas, I have no charm'.[90] The *paidagogos*'s remarks relevant to him are 'You need someone to provide a way out ... this is perhaps all for the best; you will stop being in love if you see her in this state.' This must be an account of young A's passion for the apparition; it is no doubt grossly exaggerated, whether the embroidery comes from Syros or from the *paidagogos*. The new fact that is clear both from the youth's comments and from the *paidagogos*'s comments is that young B himself is in love with the apparition.

The game here is complicated, as in the slave intrigues of the *Andria*, *Heautontimoroumenos* and *Adelphi*. With a fragmentary text it is unclear how completely Syros is in control. He has certainly achieved, directly and indirectly, that young B is going in to talk to his sister, and expects her to be despondent about the marriage (ii, 17). The *paidagogos* has his own reasons for his report: he may or may not be concerned to stop the marriage; he certainly is concerned to stop young B's love affair with the apparition.

This has a further consequence. The tone here—'you need someone to provide a way out ... you will stop being in love'—is so like the tone of the slave dialogue in the Leningrad papyrus that the speakers must be the same. Compare, for instance, there 'If you were really ill you would have to look for a real cure. But in fact you are

<hr>

[90] The parallel for this is *invenustum*, Pamphilus' comment on himself when he hears that the marriage which he does not want has been arranged for him, *Andria* 245.

not. So find a bogus cure for a bogus disease.' The strict old *paidagogos* does not believe in young B's love for the apparition, and this was presented in the first act immediately after young A's statement of his genuine passion. Neither the *paidagogos* nor young B knows who the apparition is. For them she does not necessarily have the added piquancy of being an apparition; for them she is simply a poor free girl of doubtful parentage who lives in the house and works for wife B.

There remains fragment A of P. Oxy. 2825. The speakers are a man and a woman, husband and wife. They are discussing a past rape, which can only be the rape of wife A which produced the apparition; they must therefore be father B and wife B. The text is scrappy but ran something like this: *Husband*. 'Who was responsible for this? Who was the raper?' *Wife*. 'He was not seen. I do not know. I was a girl then, and there was a night festival and dances. Don't you understand? Won't you interrogate the victim? She will say in a brief word: "You, at the Adonia." When? I was not there. She wandered alone, poor dear, and met her doom.' *Husband*. 'Phoebus!' *Wife*. 'You will ask what happened before...' *Husband*. 'Phoebus Apollo, where do these words bring me?' *Wife*. 'The thing is clear and obvious, husband. You used to live away in Brauron once.'

This is probably the main recognition scene, and father B will need little more to convince him that he is the father of the apparition. This must be in the fourth act of the play. After it there must be an agreement between the two fathers that young A marries the apparition instead of the daughter of wife B. Father B switches his daughters in much the same way as Demipho gives Alcesimarchus his new-found daughter instead of his Lemnian daughter in the *Synaristosai/Cistellaria*. If Menander bothered to settle the jilted daughter, there is the apparition's step-brother, i.e.: the son of father A and wife A, mentioned in the Leningrad papyrus (5).

We know too little of the past history and of the play itself to do more than guess at how the recognition scene arose. The recognition scene shows that wife A knew who had raped her (or at least had a token which could identify him, if Menander made it more complicated). I assume that she gave the baby to wife B before she married father A and probably before wife B married husband B. I think that pressure was put on her from both sides: young A's passion continued to grow, and he threatened to break the silence that was imposed on him, and father A, having seen the apparition on his return, threatened to investigate. This forced her to go to wife B, who was by now on her side, convinced of the undesirability of young A

as a husband for her own daughter.[91] Either she identified father B
to wife B or they identified him together by means of tokens. In
some such way Menander led up to the recognition scene.

Plokion (before 306)

Adapted by Caecilius. A mosaic[92] from Mytilene illustrates the second
act; Moschion stands by; the elderly Laches strongly objects to his
wife Krobyle: he can hardly be driving her out. Krobyle is an heiress
and a tyrant, whether at this moment she is trying to marry off
Moschion to a girl of her choosing or has told Laches that he has to
sell the maidservant with whom she suspects that he has been
intriguing, as he complains in a soliloquy (333)[93] and also in a conversation with his neighbour (334; cf. 346). He accuses her of oppress-
ing not only him but also his son and daughter. Moschion does not
want the girl whom she has chosen, and protests against family as
a criterion (345; XV; cf. 612). But the marriage has been arranged
and Moschion's slave intrigues to prevent or delay it (XII, XIII, 347).[94]
Moschion raped the daughter of the neighbour, who is a widower
(III), at a night festival (VI, VII).[95] Now the neighbour's slave, Parmenon, from outside the door hears her cries as she gives birth and
then comments on her father's position (335–8: 343; IV, V, VIII, IX;
probably 342, 810[96] describe the girl working in her father's house).
Moschion must be identified. He may have left the necklace (plokion)
with her, but it is an unlikely ornament for a youth and it gives the
play its name, so that its function must have been complicated.[97]
Perhaps it was hers, and he broke it and went off with it; then his
slave somehow found out in the course of the play who the girl was.
The father of the girl consulted his friends in the agora and evidently
threatened Laches with legal proceedings (XVI, XVII). Laches per-

[91] P. Oxy. 2329 may belong between fr. B and fr. A. It would give: (1) the
end of a scene in which youth A is told to keep quiet by Syros, (2) youth B
enlists his mother's help in his desire to marry the Apparition and then calls
for Dromon (who will be the paidagogos) to keep watch for him. Then presumably wife B confers with wife A, and this leads to the recognition.

[92] L. Kahil, op. cit., pl. 3,1.

[93] Cf. Camberale, R.I.F.C., 95, 1967, 162. On 339 cf. Dedoussi, Charis Ver-
vouri, 290.

[94] Cf. Andria 313 f.

[95] Caecilius VII, 'Sleeplessness is a companion; it brings madness', VI, 'the
deed was done quickly in darkness', describe the rape, perhaps from a prologue
speech like Samia 43 ff.

[96] 810 K–T is identified as Plokion by the new Photios, Lustrum, 11, 1966,
140.

[97] Cf. the ring in the Daktylios. It is more likely that it implicated Moschion
than that it was one of the baby's tokens, cf. Perikeiromene 385.

suades Krobyle that the father regards Moschion's actions as a social
crime (XVIII). At the end at least one of the slaves is freed (XIX).

Pseudherakles (321–319)

The prologue speaks of two daughters brought up by the concubine
of their father (453). The presence of a nurse suggests that a child
was born in the course of the play (454). A rich or dissolute young
man presumably inhabits the house where a parasite and *hetairai* can
be seen (452). A tiresome and riddling cook arrives (451, 457). The
soldier is presumably a rival of the young man (455–6). He is tricked
out of the girl by someone, perhaps the parasite impersonating
Herakles (458).

Rhapizomene (before 306)

Listed in P. British Museum 2562. The girl who gets her jaw slapped
suggests a similar key scene to the *Empimpramene* and the *Perikeiromene*; and 359, 'a misfortune differs from injustice; one comes from
fortune, the other from choice', recalls the view taken of Polemon's
act in the *Perikeiromene* (45, 316). The presence of a nurse (365, probably also 370) suggests that a child is born, but its mother need not
necessarily be the girl who gets her jaw slapped. There seem indeed
to be two old men, one who praises his daughter and cannot see her
pregnancy (361, 367) and one who tries to escape notice, but the
truth comes to light (363; 366): this may be the father of the heroine,
who is recognised in the course of the play. There is also a cook who
uses archaic language (368; 364).

Samia (321–319)

The scene is two houses in Athens. A belongs to Demeas: in it are
also his adopted son Moschion, the *hetaira* Chrysis, the slave Parmenon, and the newly born child of Moschion and Plangon (who is
the daughter of Nikeratos), and the old nurse of Moschion. B belongs
to Nikeratos and houses his wife and his daughter, Plangon. When
the play opens, Demeas and Nikeratos are travelling abroad together.[98]

---

[98] *Samia* was first published in P. Bodmer 25 in 1969 and then by C. Austin
with *Aspis* (see above, n. 20). I have kept their numbering of lines (so also
Sandbach in O.C.T.) rather than adopt that of the Bude edition of J.-M. Jacques.
Add also P. Oxy. 2831, 2943. Cf. Dedoussi, *Entretiens Hardt*, 16, 1970, 157; Del
Corno, *Atene e Roma*, 15, 1970, 71 f.; *Acme*, 23, 1970, 99.

Act I, sc. 1. Moschion tells the story of his life to the audience. When
he had grown up, Demeas had fallen in love with Chrysis. (In the
twenty-two-line gap after l. 29 Moschion probably says that he persuaded Demeas to buy Chrysis and manumit her; that when Demeas
and Nikeratos went away he had gone off to the country to avoid
suspicion.) Then he goes on to his own love affair with Plangon,
whom he raped at an Adonis festival. He promised her mother that
he would marry her when his father returned. Meanwhile Chrysis
has taken over the child and will pass it off as her own and Demeas'
until the marriage is arranged. Some of this may have been told by
Chrysis herself. What we have is a twenty-eight-line gap after l. 57,
which conceals Moschion's departure to meet Parmenon and Chrysis
coming on stage. (1–60)

Sc. 2. At the end of her lost soliloquy Chrysis sees Moschion and
Parmenon coming. Parmenon has seen Demeas and Nikeratos arrive
in harbour, and urges Moschion to ask for the marriage as soon as
possible. Chrysis meanwhile will say that the child is her own.
Chrysis and Parmenon go in. (61–85)

Sc. 3. Moschion soliloquises on the difficulty of tackling Demeas.
He goes off to practise his speech. (87–94)

Sc. 4. Demeas and Nikeratos arrive, discussing the difference
between Byzantion and Athens. Before they go into their houses,
Demeas reminds Nikeratos that they have agreed on the marriage of
Moschion and Plangon and must set a day. (96–119)

Act II, sc. 1. Moschion returns, saying that he has been day-dreaming
about his wedding day. (120–8)

Sc. 2. Demeas comes out, furious about the child, proposing to turn
it and Chrysis out of the house. Moschion pleads with him. There is
again a gap of twenty-eight lines, in which the subject changes to the
marriage of Moschion and Plangon. Moschion joyfully accepts, but
gets out of the way so that Demeas can approach Nikeratos. (129–62;
P. Oxy. 2943)

Sc. 3. Demeas soliloquises that things are going unexpectedly well
and then (after another gap of twenty-seven lines) calls out Nikeratos
to make arrangements. Nikeratos evidently objects to being hurried:
he has not told his friends or his wife. Demeas sends Parmenon to
market and Nikeratos follows. Demeas goes in to make arrangements.
(163–205)

Act III, sc. 1. Demeas comes out, horrified because he has heard an
old woman say that the child is Moschion's and he has seen Chrysis
nursing it. (206–82)

Sc. 2. Parmenon comes back with the cook and takes him into the house. (283–95)

Sc. 3. Demeas summons him out again and interrogates him. He runs away. (296–324)

Sc. 4. Demeas alone considers the situation; it is Chrysis' fault, not Moschion's He will turn her out, although he loves her. (325–56)

Sc. 5. The cook comes out, looking for Parmenon. Demeas rushes in. (357–68)

Sc. 6. Demeas drives out Chrysis, the child, and the old woman (mute). The cook tries to intervene and goes in. (369–90; P. Oxy. 2831)

Sc. 7. Demeas tells Chrysis that she will come to a miserable end and goes in. (390–98)

Sc. 8. Nikeratos comes back from market with a sheep, finds Chrysis and the child, and takes them in to his wife. (399–420)

Act IV, *sc.* 1. Nikeratos comes out to talk to Demeas about Chrysis. (421–28)

Sc. 2. Moschion comes back, frustrated with waiting. Nikeratos tells him that Demeas has turned Chrysis out. (428–39)

Sc. 3. Demeas comes out, determined to go ahead with the marriage. Moschion tries to argue against the expulsion of Chrysis. The scene is rich in misunderstandings. Moschion does not realise that Demeas knows only half the truth (that Moschion is the father) and so makes things worse. Nikeratos realises that Moschion is the father and also believes that Chrysis is the mother. He goes in to turn Chrysis and the baby out of his house. (440–520)

Sc. 4. Moschion at last manages to tell Demeas that Plangon is the mother. Nikeratos bursts out; he has seen Plangon nursing the child. Moschion makes off. Nikeratos rushes in to look again. (520–47)

Sc. 5. Demeas says he ought to have realised how Nikeratos would behave. Nikeratos rushes out to say that he is going to kill his wife, and rushes in again. Demeas decides to tell him the truth. (547–67)

Sc. 6. Chrysis bursts out of the house with the child, pursued by Nikeratos. Demeas keeps him off and tells Chrysis to take refuge in his own house. Demeas manages to pacify Nikeratos, and finally both old men go into their houses to continue preparations for the marriage. (568–615)

Act V, *sc.* 1. Moschion returns, furious that Demeas had suspected him. He proposes to frighten Demeas by threatening to go off to the wars. (616–40)

Sc. 2. Parmenon returns and is sent in by Moschion to fetch cloak and sword. (641–63)

Sc. 3. Moschion waits, hoping that Demeas will come out to him. Parmenon returns, saying that marriage preparations are going ahead. Moschion sends him in again. (664–82)

Sc. 4. Moschion waits again. Parmenon comes out with cloak and sword. Then Demeas comes and Parmenon goes in again. Moschion is told to overlook his father's one mistake. (683–712)

Sc. 5. Nikeratos comes out to say that all is ready, and in his turn teases Moschion. Moschion gives in, and the play ends. (713–37)

Sikyonios (308–6)

The scene is two houses in or near Athens (Eleusis is within reach between acts, but this is the common convention of New Comedy; the 'messenger' came from the city to Eleusis (183) but may have returned when he gives his report: Kichesias lives in Skambonidai but may be in the city for the day). House A is occupied by Stratophanes, supposedly a Sikyonian soldier, his slave, Donax, a girl, Philoumene, and her slave, Dromon, a *hetaira*, Malthake, and is visited by a parasite, Theron. House B is occupied by Smikrines, his wife and their son Moschion.[99]

Act I, sc. 1. *Prologue speech*. Parts of about thirty lines are preserved. At the end or near the end (23) the audience are invited to observe the details for themselves. This is the same formula as Pan uses in the *Dyskolos* (45 f.). Here too it is probable that the prologue opens the play. So much in the play depends upon examination of credentials that Elenchos (examination) seems a likely speaker (cf. fr. 717 K–T).

The preserved portion tells us that a four-year-old girl (Philoumene, daughter of Kichesias) and a slave (Dromon) were abducted by pirates from Halai in Attica and sold as slaves to a Sikyonian (whose name may have been Hegemon) in Caria. But we must have been told a great deal more, and at least one column before l. 1 and one column between ll. 19 and 20 are needed. Lost Menandrian heroines with overseas adventures have complicated stories, as the *Andria* (796, 923) and the *Eunuch* (109, 130, 518) show, and here it has also to be explained that Stratophanes is in fact the son of Smikrines, handed over as a baby to the wife of Hegemon (281).

The following seems to me the most likely reconstruction of the events before the action begins. Hegemon had adopted Stratophanes before he went to Caria. When he returned to Sikyon with Philou-

99 Originally published by A. Blanchard and A. Bataille, *Recherches de papyrologie* 3, 1964, 103. I follow the line numbering of R. Kassel, *Kleine Texte* 185, Berlin, 1965, and now Sandbach, O.C.T. Cf. R. Coles and H. Lloyd-Jones, *Emerita*, 34, 1966, 131 ff.; H. Lloyd-Jones, G.R.B.S., 7, 1966, 131; Barigazzi, S.I.F.C., 37, 1965, 7; J. Quincey, *Phoenix*, 1966, 116.

mene and Dromon he ran into trouble, and much of his property was confiscated (fr. 4). Stratophanes, who was presumably rather older than Philoumene, went in his turn to Caria to recoup his fortunes; we are told that he had been poor (fr. 3, not from the prologue). Hegemon lost a lawsuit involving a lot of money and died: Stratophanes received the news in Caria (133). Stratophanes sent someone to his supposed mother to buy Philoumene and Dromon and bring them to Athens, where he would meet them, having set up house with the *hetaira* Malthake; when they arrived he sent his slave Pyrrhias to tell his supposed mother. (This combines what Theron says in 120–1 with fr. 1, where someone bids against others and buys a girl as a lady's maid but does not 'hand her over to this woman (Malthake?) but keeps her apart as a free woman'.) Finally, we must be told that the day before the action opened Moschion, the son of Smikrines, had met the girl and intends to marry her (307).

Sc. 2. At least one of the speakers is a woman (32–3) and seems to be complaining of the misery with which she has to live, and then someone (36–51) recommends a greedy man to learn a trade. It is likely that Malthake tells Theron to learn a trade, and he replies that the trade of a parasite is highly profitable. We know that Theron is a successful or at least boastful parasite (fr. 10) and that he wants Malthake (145), and possibly hopes to marry her (fr. 9). In this play, as in the *Epitrepontes*, there were two pairs of lovers, one estranged (Stratophanes will not take Philoumene although he loves her, 372) and the other thwarted (Malthake is there only to amuse Stratophanes, and finds him as unsatisfactory as Habrotonon finds Charisios).

After this comes a gap of some 500 lines before the text resumes in the last scene of the third act. All that is preserved is two separate fragments, each with bits of two adjoining columns. We can put down what we learn of this interval later in the play: (1) Moschion overheard Dromon talking to Stratophanes about the girl's claim to be a citizen (204). (2) Stratophanes knows Moschion's name (309). (3) Stratophanes knows that Moschion is working against him and trying to get control of the girl (255), and that the meeting at Eleusis is crucial (145 ff.). (4) Smikrines knows Moschion's plans (307), and presumably has been seen, since he must have left his house in the gap in order to return to it at the beginning of the fourth act (150). (5) Dromon and the girl have decided to go Eleusis, presumably to take asylum (190). (6) Moschion leaves after them (199). The following is a possible outline.

The first act may end with a scene with Stratophanes. We should see him and know his love for the girl and his despair. It is difficult to see what he can do or hope for. As Sikyonian, he cannot marry an Athenian; perhaps he hopes that the girl will fail to make good her claim, and then she will remain his slave.

Then in the second act Stratophanes and Dromon discuss the situation; Moschion enters from house B, recognises Dromon as the attendant of the girl whom he had seen the day before, and listens.[100] Stratophanes goes in and Moschion accosts Dromon. One of the two preserved pieces (VII, 72–109) may belong here. The text is very obscure, but it has been suggested[101] that in the first column Dromon rejects Moschion's proposal as disloyal to Stratophanes; in the second column (97) Moschion seems to be reporting Dromon's account of the girl's fear of her master and saying that nevertheless an effort must be made; if the girl is a citizen, he ought to be able to make common cause with Dromon. Then someone addresses Moschion as *meirakion* (youth). This cannot be his father; it could be Stratophanes, Theron or Dromon. Perhaps Stratophanes is the most likely; he has heard the new danger from Dromon and chases Moschion off. Conceivably a scene in which Stratophanes tells the story to Theron concludes the act.

The third act may start with Dromon telling Stratophanes that he and the girl must take asylum at Eleusis as a means of testing her claim. They then go off (unless this is the final scene of the second act). Moschion, I think, then comes on and states his plan: it ought to be easy to find a witness who can claim to have lost a child or given one away; particularly at festival time in Eleusis, when there is a distribution of meat, who will notice? Someone objects that it is not easy to carry out such a scheme single-handed, and Moschion answers that if he waits to hear all the objections it will be evening. The objector is probably Smikrines, who thus knows Moschion's plan and then goes off to the *agora*. This is the other preserved fragment (VIII, 52–71). Moschion then bangs on the door of house A, and is told, perhaps by Theron, that Dromon has gone with the girl; he hurries after.

Theron reports to Stratophanes, and this begins the scene which is preserved (110 ff.). We have only half-lines to start with. Theron is restraining Stratophanes from doing something that will make Moschion more eager. He has a plan which will enable Stratophanes to enjoy his property as his parents wished, and it seems to involve sale (113). I think that Theron is advising the sale of Dromon and the girl before her citizenship is established; then the loss will fall on the new purchaser and not on Stratophanes. But at this moment Pyrrhias

---

[100] The situation is not unlike Eunuch 302 or P. Grenfell II 8 b. If Coles's reading of Donax in 73 is right, this line must have been spoken by Dromon or Stratophanes.

[101] Barigazzi, *op. cit.*, 39.

arrives. He reports that the supposed mother of Stratophanes has died; before she died she wrote a letter saying that Stratophanes was not her son and enclosing recognition tokens, because she feared that his property would be adjudicated to the Boeotian who had successfully sued Hegemon. A glance at the letter (141) convinces Stratophanes that he is an Athenian, and he sweeps Theron and Pyrrhias off to Eleusis.

Act IV, sc. 1. Smikrines and another come on, discussing what has happened at Eleusis. Smikrines cannot believe that 'the weeping suppliant' had a just case or that a large assembly can make a true decision. The other calls him an oligarch and a thief who would stop only at house robbery in getting hold of other people's property. This whets the audience's appetite for the messenger speech. Instead of parting in anger, the man utters the tragic line (169): 'Old man, stop in the porch of your house', and Smikrines answers, 'I stop. What is the reason for your urgency?' This is the signal that the messenger speech, essentially a part of tragedy rather than comedy, is coming.

I have assumed that the man who enters with Smikrines is also the messenger.[102] One reason is economy. I do not believe that Menander introduced two unknown characters without naming them in twenty lines. Secondly, the characterisation of the speaker as a democrat opposed to the oligarchic Smikrines is carried over into the messenger speech; he is a terror at earning his juror's pay, he cries aloud about the common good, the kind of democrat who is the salvation of Athens (180 ff.). He is an Eleusinian and his name may be Blepes, and he went there to get a share of meat (cf. 59).

The speech tells that an Eleusinian assembly formed under Euthydemos to hear the girl's claim put forward by Dromon; Moschion tried to put in his oar and made a bad impression; Stratophanes arrived and suggested that she should be handed over to the priestess until her father was found; he asked that, if he could substantiate his own claim to be a citizen, he should be allowed to ask her father for her hand: Moschion again tried ineffectually to interfere. The speaker gives no names because he does not know them, but Smikrines would recognise the part that Moschion had played because he knew his plans.

Sc. 2. Eight fragmentary lines follow the speech before the text breaks off. Someone demands the arrest of slavers; someone answers, 'You are mad, boy (meirakion)'; the first speaker goes on, 'He suddenly popped up a citizen. That's rich.' The boy must be Moschion; he possibly recognises the messenger as a member of the

assembly and vents his anger at his defeat by Stratophanes on him.
(Line 305 shows that Moschion arrived at Smikrines' house before
Stratophanes.)

When the text resumes, Stratophanes is examining his recognition
tokens with Smikrines and Smikrines' wife. The gap must be a mul-
tiple of twenty-two lines, and sixty-six is consistent with the indica-
tions of the stichometric signs. The following outline seems likely.

Sc. 3. (The messenger has gone.) Smikrines confronts Moschion
with the failure of his plan and sends him, crestfallen, into the house.
Smikrines probably soliloquises.

Sc. 4. Stratophanes' letter has led him to Smikrines' house, which
is in fact next door to his own house, A. Theron and Pyrrhias (mute)
come with him. (Pyrrhias is later in house A (fr. 11), and Theron in
the next act knows that he will find Stratophanes in house B, 365.)
Theron goes off to find a father for Philoumene, and Stratophanes
discusses his letter with Smikrines.

Sc. 5. Smikrines summons his wife out to examine the recognition
tokens and at the end they all go into the house to tell Moschion.

Act V, sc. 1. Theron enters with a reluctant old man, whom he is
trying to bribe into saying that he is the father of the girl. In his
fury the old man gives his name and deme, Kichesias of Skambonidai.
As Theron goes on with his coaching it becomes clear that the old
man is in fact the father of the girl.

Sc. 2. Dromon enters (361),[103] saying, 'My mistress is safe,' and he
is going on, 'Now I must find her father,' when he recognises
the old man as Kichesias. Kichesias faints, and Theron rushes into
house B to fetch water and Stratophanes (a very neat way of freeing
an actor to play Stratophanes).

Sc. 3. Dromon tells Kichesias that his daughter is safe and still a
virgin. Stratophanes comes out and Dromon introduces him. They
will all go to the priestess to claim the girl. Kichesias and Dromon go
on ahead.

Sc. 4. Stratophanes calls Donax out of house A, and tells him to
arrange for the transfer of Malthake, her bags, the slaves, the donkeys
and the donkey drivers to house B; he will return when he has made
made arrangements with Kichesias. (He is clearing his own house so
that he can bring his bride back to it. He cannot, of course, in fact
return before the end of the play. 'Making arrangements with the
father of the girl' (396) covers claiming the girl from the priestess,
formal betrothal, marketing and beginning the marriage in Kichesias'
house.)

[103] Sandbach, *op. cit.*, 117, and now O.C.T.

Sc. 5. Moschion enters from house B. He is in misery because he cannot bear to be a third to Stratophanes and the girl; then something about a *hetaira*. Conceivably Moschion's thoughts have now turned to Malthake, and he is rebuked by Smikrines and possibly provided with a wife.

Two fragments remain. In the first, fr. 11, with Malthake, Theron and P(yrrhias), Malthake seems to be angry and to be cursing someone. The second (411 ff.), which gives the beginnings of the last thirteen lines of the play, is certainly compatible with the idea that Malthake, slightly mollified, goes off with Theron. Does the removal ordered by Stratophanes change into Theron's marriage procession?

Synaristosai (308-6)

Plautus adapted Menander's *Synaristosai* (*Women at breakfast*) and called it *Cistellaria*. In addition to the Menander fragments, two mosaics illustrate the opening scene from which the play took its name. One of them gives Menander's names for the characters: Plangon for Plautus' Selenium, Pythias for Plautus' Gymnasium, Philainis for Plautus' procuress.[104]

The scene is Sikyon; house A belongs to Demipho, a Lemnian with a second wife, Phanostrata, a slave, Lampadion, and a daughter by his first (Lemnian) wife, who is betrothed to Alcesimarchus. Alcesimarchus lives in house B with Selenium, who passes for the daughter of an old *hetaira*, Melaenis, and with a slave, Thyniscus.

Act I, sc. 1. The procuress and her daughter, Gymnasium, are taking breakfast with Selenium. Melaenis is withdrawing Selenium because Alcesimarchus is marrying Demipho's daughter. Gymnasium is asked to look after the house until Alcesimarchus (who is away) returns. Gymnasium goes into house B, Selenium goes back to Melaenis. The procuress, after a brief soliloquy, greatly enlarged by Plautus, goes home. (1-148; frs. 382, 385, 389)[105]

Sc. 2. Auxilium (in Menander Boetheia, 'assistance to the injured innocent') tells the complicated past history; when Phanostrata was a girl, Demipho had raped her on a visit from Lemnos; she gave the baby, Selenium, to her father's slave, Lampadio, to expose; he saw the procuress take the baby; she gave it to Melaenis, who brought it up

104 For the placing of the fragments in the *Cistellaria* see Suess, *Rh.Mus.*, 1935, 16 f.; 1938, 97 f. The mosaics, L. Kahil, *op. cit.*, pl. 5 (*Entretiens Hardt*, 16, 1970, pls. 2-3).

105 P. Heidelberg 200 is translated by *Cist.* 96-101. A. Thierfelder, *Studi Urbinati*, 35, 1961, 113, has recovered the first line: 'I have breakfasted, by Artemis, very pleasantly' (*Cist.* 11-5).

as her daughter. When Demipho returned and married Phanostrata, he sent Lampadio to search for her daughter. (149–201; fr. 387)[106]

In Menander another scene is likely before the entry of the chorus, which marks the end of the first act. Possibly Demipho and Lampadio set out from house A, he to the 'senate' (776) and Lampadio on his search.

For the next 300 lines Plautus' text is badly damaged, but the main lines are visible.

Act II, sc. 1. Alcesimarchus returns with his slave, finds Gymnasium and apparently threatens to go and carry off Selenium by force, but is finally persuaded to go and try to win over Melaenis. (203–304)

Sc. 2. Alcesimarchus' father arrives, presumably having pursued him from the country, mistakes Gymnasium for Selenium and sets up as his son's rival. (305–73)

Sc. 3. The procuress arrives to fetch Gymnasium. She drives off Alcesimarchus' father, and they go into Alcesimarchus' house to get her things. (374–81)

Sc. 4. Lampadio comes home, describing the women he has seen in his search. The procuress and Gymnasium come out of Alcesimarchus' house and go home. Lampadio recognises the procuress as the woman whom he had seen take the baby, and goes after them. (374–448)

Act III, sc. 1. Melaenis brings Selenium back (presumably she knows that the procuress was going to withdraw Gymnasium but does not know that Alcesimarchus has returned). When Alcesimarchus comes back, having missed her, she sends Selenium home. (449–60)

Sc. 2. Melaenis protests that Alcesimarchus' oaths are worthless; he is going to marry a rich Lemnian. He rushes into his house in fury. (460–527)

Sc. 3. While Melaenis wonders what to do, Lampadio comes back. She overhears Lampadio's report to Phanostrata: the procuress had told him that Gymnasium is her own daughter, but she had given away the exposed baby to a woman called Melaenis. Phanostrata goes in. Melaenis interrogates Lampadio, without giving herself away. Lampadio goes off to find the procuress. She goes home, resolved to restore Selenium to her true parents. (528–630)

Act IV, sc. 1. Melaenis returns with Selenium (mute in the original) and a maid Halisca (mute), to whom she gives the box with Selenium's recognition tokens, telling her to knock on Phanostrata's door (house A). Alcesimarchus, hearing them from his own house, fakes a suicide attempt. Selenium rushes to him and he carries her

---

[106] *Cist.* 155–6 may translate 763 K–T.

inside, pursued by Melaenis and Halisca, who has left the token box on Phanostrata's doorstep. (631–52)

Sc. 2. Lampadio returns (the procuress, warned by Melaenis, has refused to help him). He sees the token box and asks Phanostrata, when she comes out for his report, whether it belongs in the house. Phanostrata looks in the box and sees the tokens she had given the exposed baby. (653–70)

Sc. 3. Halisca comes out of Alcesimarchus' house to look for the box. They interrogate her, and she says that they belong to Melaenis' supposed daughter, whom Melaenis was bringing back to her mother. Phanostrata goes in with her to Alcesimarchus' house. Lampadio goes to look for Demipho. (671–773)

Act V. Plautus has reduced this act to a seven-line scene in which Lampadio tells Demipho the facts. This may well be how Menander's last act began. But Demipho must learn, probably from Phanostrata, the whole story of Selenium and Alcesimarchus; he has simply to betroth his new-found daughter to Alcesimarchus instead of his Lemnian daughter. But probably this cannot be done without Alcesimarchus' father, who may well come back to see what is happening to his son and what is happening about the marriage.

Thais

We hear only of the rich *hetaira*. In the prologue a lover describes her demands and perhaps has contrasted himself with someone who has fallen in love with a poor girl (185); 'she is utter disaster, yet I think in spite of what she has made me suffer I would gladly have her now' (186). It is a living death (188), and he is poorer than a thrush (190). His slave warns him off her bad company (187). According to Propertius (IV, v, 42), she can trick clever slaves and will accept anyone for money.

Theophoroumene (undated)

New light is thrown on this play by the Mytilene mosaic, which both identifies the speakers of the published papyrus and shows that the Dioskourides mosaic gives the next scene; the scene after that is given by a new papyrus in Florence. I cannot add much to E. W. Handley's discussion of these.[107]

---

[107] B.I.C.S., 16, 1969, 88, gives the latest text of the papyri as well as commentary and interpretation. The mosaics: L. Kahil, *op. cit.*, pl. 6 (*Entretiens Hardt*, 16, 1970, pl. 4). See also *J.H.S.*, 93, 1973 and Sandbach, O.C.T.

The Mytilene mosaic names two young men, Kleinias and Lysias, and a slave, Parmenon. Lysias certainly, Kleinias probably, and, I shall argue, Parmenon are the speakers of the published papyrus. The masks of the mosaics suggest that they may be brothers. It seems probable that their father occupies house A. The inn (*pandokeion*) mentioned in the papyrus is probably represented by the central door, which appears on the Dioskourides mosaic. House B may be occupied by Kraton (fr. 1), an old man, according to Plutarch, *Mor.* 739 F, who is evidently poor and unsuccessful.

The title means 'The girl possessed', and the new papyrus shows her when she is possessed or at any rate nearing possession. Like other titles composed of present participles, it refers to this single scene in the second act (the act number is given by the Mytilene mosaic), which is described as an 'experiment'. The title and the fact that she is in an inn tells us something about her. She is possessed by Kybele (*cf.* the new papyrus), and Alkiphron (IV, 19) implies that she made an 'inexpedient' prophecy. The connection between Kybele, possession, and prophecy is well attested (*cf.* Apuleius, *Met.* 8, 27; Lucian *Philops.* 38). The play must end happily, and so the inexpedience will have involved only temporary discomfort. As the experiment is designed to test her genuineness, it seems possible that before the second act she made her prophecy and it was not believed.

She is in an inn, and no Greek would expect to find a respectable woman in an inn. Some misfortune must have driven her to this: either she is the slave of the innkeeper, or someone else has sent her there to provide entertainment, or she is the kept girl of one of the diners. There are many possibilities, but they all suggest that she is to be recognised as the daughter of a citizen. Possibly Kraton is her father, and someone appears as a *deus ex machina* (fr. 5). This is our only clue to the end of the play.

One of the two young men must be in love with her, and the experiment must be a step, but an early step, towards his getting her. The slave Parmenon is involved. A fragment gives the phrase 'second course' (6), a standard formula for a slave intrigue which has gone wrong and has to start again. It shows that the play had a slave intrigue; how complicated this was we cannot tell because we do not know whether Kleinias and Lysias were in love with different girls or whether one was merely helping the other to get the 'possessed' girl. Only a very sketchy scenario can be offered:

Act I (1) A prologue speech is necessary if this is a recognition play; it may have come first or after a preliminary scene.

(2) A scene or scenes are necessary to set up the experiment. Kleinias (perhaps rather than Lysias) is in love with the girl. He has

seen her performance and heard her prophesy (that she is an Athenian citizen?). So first she must be proved genuine; Lysias may have disbelieved her (fr. 2). Then arise problems of getting her, possibly from a rival. They can test her by getting her musical instruments and a flute girl who knows the tune to which she must respond if she is genuine. The mechanics of this are unclear: I suspect that the young men (or perhaps Lysias, as younger and more lightly dressed) do the stealing and Parmenon acts as cover by volunteering for service at the wine party in the inn.

Act II, sc. 1. The young men come in with the cymbals and tambourine and the flute girl (mute). They discuss what has happened, and then Parmenon enters. This is the scene of the Mytilene mosaic. The old papyrus is badly damaged, but Handley is right in taking most of it as a report and associating frs. 3 and 4 with it. I think that the reporter is Parmenon, reporting partly in narrative and partly quoting direct speech. Fr. 3, 'Give them their first cup quickly and don't mix water with it,' is an instruction to Parmenon from one of the young men, who wants a rough-house to cover the thefts; Parmenon may include it in his report, or it may be the actual instruction from the planning scene in act I. Fr. 4, 'He was considerably drunk when he drained the cup', is report and probably describes the rival. This must come before the papyrus begins.

To understand the end of the report preserved in the papyrus there are two clues. First, Handley points the way by taking the beginning of l. 17 as 'I filled up'. This not only points to Parmenon as speaker but suggests that the 'dripping' things of l. 16 are not 'tears' but wine from an upset: something like 'on the drinkstand quickly dripping'—'I understand' (said by one of the young men, Lysias?)—'of drink'. Then the girl discovers and laments the loss of her gifts. Secondly (and this I owe to Mr John Feneron), the gifts are the cymbals and the tambourine (or perhaps rather her gift of prophecy, which depends on them). After the report of the girl's speech (17–18) the rival's words are reported in ll. 19–23. The beginning is not clear but 'What is the young man doing?' could very well refer to Lysias as the thief who has just been seen going out. Then the rival says that if she is really inspired she ought not to be outside but to be shut up where she can be consulted (I see a possible reference here to Kassandra in the Trojan Women, 341).

This is the end of the report. Kleinias says, 'This is nonsense. Here, at least, she is not pretending.' Lysias says that the experiment can now be made. The flute girl can play a tune which is relevant, and if the girl is genuine she will leap through the door (24–30). Parmenon must then go off, because the actor is needed for the girl.

Sc. 2. is given by the Dioskourides mosaic. The two young men dance and sing to tambourine, cymbals, and flute. The flute girl is a mute; the actual flute music is provided by the flautist who plays for the chorus to sing between the acts.

Sc. 3. is given by the new papyrus (*cf.* also fr. 8). The girl sings a hexameter hymn to Kybele, interspersed with instructions in iambics to the onlookers to respond with cries, to put incense on the fire, to play the flute and to play the cymbals. Then perhaps she goes on to prophesy.

For the rest of the play we know only that the intrigue was complicated (fr. 6) but the girl was recognised (fr. 5).

Thesauros (312–306)

Listed in P. British Museum 2562. Probably adapted by Luscius and partly summarised by Donatus on Terence, *Eun.* 9 ff.[108] The only certain scene that can be derived from it is the arbitration scene in which the old man who had bought the field claimed that the treasure in the tomb was his, buried there during an alarm, and the son of the man buried in the tomb claimed that it was his. The arbitration scene may well have been in the second act, preceded by the return of the old man and the slave of the young man from the tomb. Then the first act showed the young man, in spite of his poverty, sending his slave to take offerings to his father's tomb. The slave also discovered a letter in the tomb, which must have led the action forward like the letter brought to Stratophanes in the *Sikyonios*. The Greek fragments give very little: an old man in love (198, probably a musician as an object of love (200), and possibly a boastful soldier (201).

Thrasyleon

Adapted by Turpilius. Thrasyleon was the type of the 'wild' soldier. He has recently become rich (I). He asked a *leno* to show him his goods (V), and the *leno* seems to have tried to ingratiate himself with the slave or parasite of the young man who loved the girl (IX; *cf.* *Adelphi* 250). The young man had a disapproving *paidagogos* (II; *cf.* *Eunuch* 226; III), but an indulgent father (IV; 203) until it came to the question of marrying a poor girl (VIII; X). The intrigues of the young man (204–5; VI) were conducted by his parasite, who was despised by the soldier (207; *cf.* *Eunuch* 486). The girl perhaps tried to escape (206; VII, *cf.* *Misoumenos* 141, 216).

[108] *Cf.* C. Garton, A.J.P., 92, 1971, 17.

Titthe

Adapted by Caecilius. The nurse gives her name to the play, and probably spoke the prologue: 396 is a garrulous and over-polite address to the audience—'Dear men, did any of you ever borrow or lend a child?'—with the implication that she herself had. Taken with Caecilius I, 'she who has not borne has no milk', it implies further that she served as nurse in the house to which she gave the baby. Someone else describes this (IV): 'I have seen you bundled up on both sides, when you come to us.' It has been attractively suggested[109] that her name was Mania and that she spoke her first garrulous speech wearing fetters (873). A girl was raped at the mysteries (III);[110] if this was the supposititious child and she later married her assailant, she was perhaps found by the nurse rather than conceived by her. VI suggests a slave intrigue, and 395 may be a slave twitting a master. II contrasts town and country life; it is spoken to Syra, who is a country slave.

[109] T. Williams, *Hermes*, 91, 1963, 287.
[110] If this is the heroine as distinct from her mother, perhaps the *Skirophoria*, cf. ch. v, n. 1.

Appendix II

Papyri mostly unattributed or not included in published texts

A number of papyri have been used in this book which are not found in the texts of Menander so far published. They are listed below for easy reference, with an indication of their contents and some discussion where relevant. Some of them are discoveries made since the standard texts which can with certainty be attributed to them: they are referred to in their place in the analyses of the plays. The rest may or may not be Menander and may or may not be attributable to a particular play.

In answering both these questions the date of the papyrus itself may give some aid.[1] The papyri which can with some confidence be assigned to other poets of New Comedy are early: the Strobilos comedy, the 'Straton' cook fragment, the 'metrical' hypotheses,[2] are all of the third century B.C. Much later, in the first century A.D., is the long prologue which criticises the practice of other comic poets, P. Strasburg 53 (see below): this has no feel of Menander. As a rough rule, papyri dated before the beginning of the Christian era must be tested more thoroughly than later papyri before being accepted as Menander. I have marked these 'Early' and have noted where I have doubts.

Papyri of New Comedy dated in the Christian era are likely to be by Menander. It would be extremely useful to know something concrete about the survival of Menander.[3] What we have is selections of various dates made for different purposes. Sometimes later lists or papyri show that these selections omit plays which must in fact have

[1] Cf. Del Corno, *American Studies in Papyrology*, 7, 1970, 103.

[2] D. L. Page, *Greek Literary Papyri*, London, 1942 (abbreviated below as Page), Nos. 57, 64 (omitting 1 and 4), 72; Schroeder, *Novae Comoediae Fragmenta* (abbreviated below as Schroeder), No. 2, and appendix 1; *L.G.C.*, 145, 142 (with xiv). Note that P. Grenfell II 8 b is now dissociated from the Strobilos comedy, and is therefore included below. Sandbach, O.C.T., includes the Didot papyri, P. Ghoran II, P. Oxy. 10, the Strobilos fragments.

[3] Cf. Del Corno, *op. cit.*; A. Dain, *Maia*, 3, 1963, 288; C. Corbato, *Studi Menandrei*, Trieste, 1965, 9.

been in existence when they were made. What they include is therefore more reliable than what they exclude. I list them in approxi-
mately chronological order.

1 Late second century A.D. P. Oxy. 2462. Alphabetical lists of titles
  up to D. As the alphabetical arrangement extends only to the
  initial letter, it provides a check only for plays beginning with
  alpha, beta, gamma. *Anatithemene, Anechomenos, Aphrodisios,
  Glykera* have fallen out, and as far as I can see we have not later
  trace of them, except *Aphrodisios* (see 4 below).
2 Late second century A.D. A house in Ephesos has pictures of *Perikeiromene* and *Sikyonios*. This is probably the last trace of *Sikyonios*.[4]
3 Athenaeus in the third century quotes forty-six plays. Omissions
  for which we have contemporary or later evidence are *Achaioi,
  Aphrodisios, Apistos, Aspis, Georgos, Deisidaimon, Dis Exapaton,
  The sauros, Kybernetai, Leukadia, Messenia, Misoumenos, Nemesis,
  Plokion, Samia*. (It is perhaps worth noting of his other omissions
  that Donatus' quotations of *Andria* and *Eunuch* go back probably
  to earlier Terence commentaries and are not evidence for survival;
  the papyrus of the *Koneiazomenoi* is dated first or second century
  A.D.; on the *Sikyonios* see above.) The omissions in Athenaeus may
  not mean that the text of Menander which he used was defective
  but that he did not find anything to quote in these plays. But it
  probably is reasonable to assume that the plays surviving in the
  later third century did not amount to more than about sixty.
4 Third to fourth century. P. British Museum 2562. K–T, I, 150.
  Probably a bookseller's catalogue of sixteen plays. It includes
  Aphrodisios (omitted by 1 and 3 above) and *Nemesis* (omitted by 3).
5 Third to fourth century. Mosaics in Mytilene.[5] Perhaps based on
  an illustrated edition. Costumes and masks show that the produc-
  tions on which the scenes are based are not earlier than the late
  third century. They give *Plokion, Samia, Synaristosai, Epitrepontes,
  Theophoroumene, Encheiridion, Messenia, Kybernetai, Leukadia,
  Misoumenos, Phasma*. It is possible that further excavation may
  reveal more mosaics.
6 Third to four century. Mosaic at Oescus.[6] *Achaioi*, known otherwise only from 1 above and a single quotation.

Later quotations are from anthologies, grammarians, lexika, and our
only guide to what survived are the papyrus texts themselves.

[4] F. Eichler, *Anzeiger Wiener Akademie*, 105, 1968, 86, pl. 2; L. Kahil,
Antike Kunst, Beiheft 6, 1970, pl. 27; Webster, *Wiener Studien*, 1972, 456.
[5] L. Kahil, *op. cit.*; *Entretiens Hardt*, 16, 1970, 231 ff.
[6] *Cf.* appendix I, n. 2.

This chronology is of some use in indicating whether an attribution is likely or not. There is clearly no reason against attributing the *second century* papyri P. Oxy. 2329, 2658, P.S.I. 99, 1670 to *Phasma, Perikeiromene, Encheiridion, Theophoroumene* respectively. Similarly the *third century* P. Oxy. 862 can be *Heros*, and if P. Ant. 122 is *Dis Exapaton* it is covered by the firmly identified contemporary P. Oxy. P. Oxy. 1239 has been identified with the original of the *Aulularia*; if, as I believe, this is the *Apistos*, we have to admit that the last reliable trace of it is the late second century list of titles, 1 above; but that is near enough. P. Ant. 15 and P. Berlin 13892 have been attributed to the *Daktylios*, and the *Daktylios* is quoted by Athenaeus. The *fourth century* P. Ant. 55 is elusive: it should be noted that Athenaeus knows the *Misogynes* but not the *Proenkalon* (which is quoted only in an anthology). The *Fabula Incerta*, the first play of the fifth century Cairo papyrus, must have been famous (the earlier P. Oxy. 429 and 2533 probably belong); if the order in the Cairo papyrus is alphabetical, the initial letter was not later than eta: *Arrhephoros* seems a possibility, as it was known to Athenaeus and occurs in the second-century list of titles, 1 above.

P. Antinoopolis 15. See *Daktylios*.

P. Antinoopolis 55. Williams, *Rh.Mus.*, 105, 1962, 193. These fragments have considerable interest but are so small and badly preserved that the action cannot be reconstructed.

Fr. A, *verso*. Master and slave discover to their astonishment a legal summons on an altar, on which a fire has recently been lit (incense?). The master consults the slave, whose name, Dromon, appears in the second column.

If the altar is used to post a legal document, it must be a public altar, perhaps the altar of a deme shrine (*cf.*, however, Williams).

Fr. A, *recto*. The slave has suggested some course of action, of which the master washes his hands and goes. The young master, whom we have not yet seen, is in love, and the slave resolves to stay loyal to him.

Fr. B, *verso*. A dialogue in which it is reported that someone visited someone's daughter and she has borne a child. The adulterer has been seen, and later the name Moschion appears.

It is a natural assumption that Moschion is the young master of fragment A and that the father or other male representative of the girl is bringing a charge against him. In front of the report is a speaker's name, which is read doubtfully as Thras. This would be an abbreviation for Thrason or Thrasyleon, and certainly a soldier's name. It is an unlikely report for a soldier to make or hear, and I cannot help wondering whether the true reading may not be Thrat for Thraitta, a Thracian nurse.

Fr. B, recto. A dialogue between Moschion (or at any rate someone who is in love) and Dromon. Moschion is disturbed by something that has happened in the *agora* (his father has told him to marry?). Dromon diverts him to the more pressing problem of the tablet on the altar. It looks as if one of them says that he will visit the women while they are singing a hymn (*ololyge*) after depositing the summons on the altar. The reference to the *agora* suggests that this fragment belongs to a later act than fragment A.

Fr. C, verso. Someone says that he must find a reason and it should not be difficult. This sounds like an intrigue, possibly of the old master against the women.

Fr. C, recto. Apparently a report of a woman giving a watery drink to someone, possibly to prevent a malicious account of what was happening (cf. Lustrum 11, 1966, 141, No. 728b). The woman is described as 'the wise', but the editor is surely right in taking this as a name, Synete. The fragment could either refer to the arrival of the midwife for the birth or to a procuress like Philainis in the *Synaristosai*.

Fr. D, verso. Dromon is asked to help What goes before is difficult. Perhaps the father says that it would be useful to shatter Moschion's hopes and hand the cursed woman over to a brothel-keeper (cf. Hymnis). The word *mastigias* is generally used of a slave but is used of the brothel-keeper in Kolax 114.

Fr. D, recto. A slave says that he has promised to find some means of helping his young master, who is in love. This is Dromon remaining loyal to Moschion in spite of the appeal of his old master on the recto.

Fr. E, recto. Something about arranging affairs.

Fr. E, verso. Something about young men coming and (possibly) plundering. This has been referred to the entry of the chorus at the end of the first act, but could equally well be the fears of a brothel-keeper (cf. Kolax 120).

The smaller fragments give nothing useful. Fr. A comes from the bottom of a page; frs D, F, H come from the tops of pages, but I do not think any useful combinations can be made. I have assumed that verso precedes recto because this seems to give a sensible order in frs. A and D.

A young man in love with a girl, who has borne him a child; a slave, Dromon, who intrigues for him and resists his father, who wants the girl handed over to a brothel; someone on behalf of the girl proposes to go to law with Moschion or his father—this is all that can be seen; as stated above, the introduction of a soldier seems to me to rest on insufficient grounds. The *Misogynes* (Barnes) and the *Proenkalon* (Williams) have been suggested as titles: against the first is the absence of any clue that leads to the wife-hater of the title; it is unlikely that all the fragments belong to a sub-plot. The *Proenkalon* has two fragments: a father complains of the difficulties caused by daughters (350) and a slave says that it is safest to carry out orders (351). If this is the play, the title suggests that either Moschion or his father brought a counter-suit to anticipate the suit brought by the girl's representative. But the fragments come from Stobaeus' anthology and there is no other evidence of the play's survival.

P. Antinoopolis 122. The name Lydos occurs in vocative (*cf. Dis Exapaton*).

P. Berlin 9941. Page No. 67; Schroeder, No. 66. Slave complaining to his master that he is worked like a donkey. Early, and nothing suggests Menander.

P. Berlin 13892. See *Daktylios*.

P. Cairo 43227. See below, P. Oxy. 2533.

P. Cairo 65445. Page, No. 59a. Cook waits for slave and Simon. *Cf.* P. Oxy. 11, Vienna 29811. Perhaps *Paidion*.

P. Cairo, IFAO 89. See *Misoumenos*.

P. Cairo, IFAO 337. See *Dis Exapaton, Demiourgos*.

P. Didot A. Page, No. 34; Sandbach, p. 328. Early, but possibly Menander, *Adelphoi* A.

P. Didot B. Page, No. 53; Sandbach, p. 330. Prologue spoken by young man. Early, and probably not Menander.

P. Ghoran II. Schroeder, No. 4; Page, No. 65; LGC, XIV, 240; Sandbach, p. 331. Early, and probably not Menander. Slave, leaving house in fear of master meets Phaidimos, who accuses him. Master leaves house in fury at something that has happened to his daughter. Phaidimos accuses Nikeratos of marrying the girl, with whom he is in love. Chairestratos arrives and persuades Nikeratos to withdraw while he explains the situation. After the act end Phaidimos comes out again repentant.

P. Hamburg 120. See *Kekryphalos*. Early, but Menander.

P. Grenfell II, 8 b. Schroeder, No. 2, frs. a and e. Now disassociated from the Strobilus comedy (probably by Philemon). In fr. a someone stresses the need to find the girl for a young man in love. A slave says that he has found the house, but the young man has to contend with the rivalry of an Egyptian governor. In fr. e there is some play on the word 'fire'. See *Encheiridion*. Early, but may be Menander.

P. Harris II. Nothing useful.

P. Harvard, Houghton Gr. 24. M. Weinstein, *H.S.C.P.*, 75, 1971, 131. End of an act, with proverbial quotation. Skene perhaps used of an inn. Early.

P. Heidelberg 200. Dialogue in which one speaker is a woman. Something about a Lemnian girl, an old man next door, bringing up a daughter, and hindering marriage. The situation would fit the *Synaristosai*.

P. Hibeh 6. Schroeder, No. 1; Page, No. 63; L.G.C., 172; Bain Z.P.E., 8, 239. Much is obscure. A young man (perhaps Sostratos) has taken refuge in wartime with Demeas and wants to take away a girl and an old woman. Demeas has marketed and sends his slave to return a borrowed basket to his neighbour, Noumenios. Demeas gives the young man money and goes in to tell his wife to prepare provisions. Noumenios comes out, demanding that his wife abandon a child which an old woman has brought into the house. Later there seems to be a reference to a lawsuit. Early, and not obviously Menander. But Noumenios links to P. Oxy. 677 of the second century A.D.

P. Hibeh 12. Schroeder, No. 10. Servant sent by Antiphon to ask about a girl. Early.

P. Hibeh 180. Mette 184. Only single words remain. Early, the Menander quotation only hangs on three letters.

P. Hibeh 181. Mette 165. An appeal for help in getting hold of a girl, and an elaborate account of marketing by Daos. An addition by the second hand suggests that the young man who wants to get hold of the girl 'will bring the patron': she has therefore at the moment either metic or slave status. The word recurs in the beginning of the *Perinthia* (Ia): but this and the name Daos hardly justify attribution. Early, not obviously Menander.

P. Koeln 5031. See *Karchedonios*.

P. Lund 4. Körte, *Archiv* 13, 103. Someone bangs on a door and appears to be complaining. Something about hurrying away from a common breakfast. A man telling his wife that Daos will be branded in punishment.

P. Milan 8. Mette, 194. A man remarks that someone is coming out of
the door. A woman commiserates with the mother of the girl, who is
near giving birth. The man addresses the women in two lines of
iambics and then goes over into trochaic tetrameters, saying that an
excuse or argument must be found.

P. Oxy. 10. Schroeder, No. 8; Page, No. 68; Lloyd-Jones, C.R. 17, 1957,
9; Sandbach, p. 336. Good staccato monologue of slave who decides to
desert his young master who is in love, because he fears his old
master. All he desires is his freedom.

P. Oxy. 11. Schroeder, No. 5; Page, No. 62; L.G.C., 244. Daos argues
with his young master, who is abandoning a girl, although he has
already received part of the dowry, for a foreigner with an undesirable
companion. Daos, left alone, decides to stand by his young master:
this is not the job of a young and unpractised slave. Then Simon
comes in from his farm with a beast for sacrifice and orders the preparations for the marriage to go ahead. Cf. P. Cairo 65445, Vienna
29811. All three are early, but seem to fit with what we know of
Menander's *Paidion*.

P. Oxy. 429. Schroeder, No. 11. Beginnings of fourteen lines. Something about violent siezure, Laches, and the neighbours gathering.
Then another speaker uses the betrothal formula 'for the production
of children': he is not the father of the bride because the father is
mentioned in the next line, 'for whom the father (will decide the
dowry)'. It is conceivable that this fragment belongs to the same
play as P. Oxy. 2533 (? *Arrhephoros*).

P. Oxy. 430. Schroeder, No. 12. Eight lines of monologue addressed
to the spectators.

P. Oxy. 431. Schroeder, N. 13. Master threatens punishment and slave
expresses contrition.

P. Oxy. 677. Schroeder, No. 14; Page, No. 70. A slave says that he has
deserved manumission from his master, Noumenios. The rare name
connects this with P. Hibeh 6.

P. Oxy. 678. Schroeder, No. 19. Mention of three obols, and address
to a patron.

P. Oxy. 862. Schroeder, No. 15. Pheidias has heard something about a
child. A slave arrives and tells him more. He understands and hopes
to marry the girl. This may very well come from the *Heros* (cf. *J.H.S.*
93, 1973, forthcoming).

P. Oxy. 1239. Schroeder, No. 17; Mette, 192. See *Apistos*.

P. Oxy. 1824. Laches betroths his daughter Pam(phile), apparently without dowry to Meix(ias).

P. Oxy. 1825. Ends of lines on recto. Someone is prepared to make a trial; it will delay his marriage. Beginnings of lines on verso; apparently someone is going to suckle a child.

P. Oxy. 2329. Mette, 193; Lloyd-Jones, C.R. 16, 1966, 275. The unique *paragraphos* in l. 4 marks the end of a section (either scene or act end, or end of extract). In the first four lines someone, probably a young man, who is in great distress is told to keep quiet for a little, while the speaker goes and does something elsewhere. In the new scene a son, not necessarily the young man of the preceding scene, comes out of the house with his mother, to whom he has made a confession (that he is in love?). He has had some unexpected news about his sister, which may help him. But his father is acting against him; otherwise he would be marrying the daughter of Kle(oboule). The mother agrees to help, because, after she has gone, the son praises her kindness. Then he calls for Dromon, whom he needs to keep watch for him.

As the girl is called the daughter of her mother, the father must be either dead or unknown; she is therefore an undesirable choice made by the boy, not a suggestion by the mother.

The *Georgos* has been suggested (Barigazzi, Athenaeum, 44, 1956, 340) but the names rule this out. The *Phasma* is possible.

P. Oxy. 2533. Mette, 199. This has been recognised as coming shortly after P. Cairo 43227, known as the *Fabula Incerta* (see now Sandbach, p. 295). This was the first play of the Cairo papyrus. The plays were probably in free alphabetical order: *Heros* precedes *Epitrepontes* although it begins with eta. Popular plays beginning with letters from alpha to eta are therefore possible. Of these *Arrhephoros* is the most likely.

In the Cairo papyrus Chaireas tells Laches that Laches' son, Moschion, has been caught raping the daughter of the Areopagite Kleainetos, who had betrothed the girl to Chaireas. Laches asks for Chaireas' help and promises him his own daughter. Kleainetos then enters and sees them outside his door. Chaireas tells him that Laches agrees to the marriage, and then goes off (apparently into Laches' house to tell Moschion). The two old men are each surprised at the other's ready acceptance of the situation. Kleainetos explains that the girl had borne Moschion a child and that she had never been engaged to Chaireas. Laches then explodes in fury at what he regards as a conspiracy.

Laches had evidently been away a long time, like Demeas in the *Samia*, since he seems to have known nothing of the rape or the birth.

Chaireas was put up to persuade him, and Chaireas had his own objective, the daughter of Laches.

P. Oxy. 2533 comes from very near the end of the play. In the Cairo papyrus Chaireas had already gone in to see Moschion. Presumably Laches and Kleainetos went into their respective houses at the end of the scene (the end of the fourth act?). In P. Oxy. 2533 Chaireas and Moschion have come to see Kleainetos. Chaireas says that he has not to give up the girl he has long loved (Laches' daughter). Kleainetos agrees with him and betroths his own daughter to Moschion, who accepts the arrangements for the dowry.

It is possible that P. Oxy. 429 immediately precedes 2533. Chaireas tells Kleainetos the story that he had used to persuade Laches into allowing the marriage of Moschion and Kleainetos' daughter. Kleainetos tells Chaireas that Laches, who had not taken the deception in good part, will nevertheless allow Chaireas to marry his daughter.

P. Oxy. 2534. See *Adelphoi* B and *Heautontimoroumenos*.

P. Oxy. 2654. See *Karchedonios*.

P. Oxy. 2655. See *Kolax*.

P. Oxy. 2658. See *Perikeiromene*.

P. Oxy. 2825. See *Phasma*.

P. Oxy. 2826. Young man in distress about someone whom he considered his wife. Syros enters to sympathise. As Syros says that he has not come out to observe the stars but to sympathise, it is presumably a night scene and a prologue.

P. Oxy. 2827. Too small to use.

P. Oxy. 2828. Gives the name Philotis.

P. Oxy. 2829. See *Epitrepontes*.

P. Oxy. 2830. See *Perikeiromene*.

P. Oxy. 2831. See *Samia*.

P. Oxy. 2943. See *Samia*.

P. Rylands 16. Schroeder 18. Ends of twenty lines. Syros is one of the speakers. 'having seen them (feminine) . . . safely' might belong to the context of *Heautontimoroumenos* 263 ff.

P. Ryands 484. Ends of lines. Return from market with Syros.

P. Rylands 498. Too little to use.

P.S.I. 99. See *Encheiridion*.

P.S.I. 723. Too little to use.

P.S.I. 847. Bartoletti, *S.I.F.C.* 34, 1962, 21; Handley, *B.I.C.S.*, 16, 1969, 95. Beginnings of lines above and below a badly preserved picture of a seated person. One speaker seems to be denying knowledge of identity and origin. The other asks, 'How then are you walking about?' Bartoletti saw the possible connection with the *Theophorou-mene*—the girl coming out of her trance. The only indication of the sex of either speaker is the leg of the figure in the picture, which appears to be that of a seated male. Perhaps, therefore, *Hiereia*.

P.S.I. 1176; Page, No. 61; *L.G.C.*, 143 (Philemon); Mette, *Lustrum*, 10, 1965, 148 (*Koneiazomenai*); Corbato, *Maia*, 1970, 340 (*Plokion*).

At the beginning Moschion is persuaded to go into his father's house, and leaves his slave to deal with a difficult situation. The slave's troubled soliloquy lasts until the appearance of Moschion's father, Laches, with someone else; then he goes in, saying that he will find a suitable opportunity to join them (a phrase which implies a slave intrigue).

Laches' companion complains that Laches has used him badly, having sent him from 'there' to tell Moschion about marriage and give his daughter. The two men had evidently been abroad together, and the companion had come home early to arrange the marriage, which Moschion had refused. The father's return is presumably the difficult situation which the slave has announced to Moschion in the preceding scene.

The arguments for giving this fragment to Philemon are no longer compelling. The long image of seafaring in the slave's monologue now has its parallel in the *Samia* (206, *cf.* also fr. 656), and self-apostrophe is a well attested form in Menander. It is not yet clear from what play it comes. The *Fabula Incerta* can be ruled out: the companion cannot be Kleainetos, since Moschion would have had no objections, nor can it be Chaireas' father, since Laches in the *Fabula Incerta* had to be bluffed into giving his daughter to Chaireas, and to have a third father would be uneconomical. Similar objections can be made to *Plokion*. *Demiourgos* is a possibility because of the agreement of 10 ff. with Turpilius VIII.

P. Strasburg 53; Schroeder, No. 7; Page, No. 60. Prologue, not by Menander.

P. Vienna 29811. Körte, *Archiv* 14, No. 965. Beginnings of trimeters at the end of an act and of trochaic tetrameters at the beginning of the new act. Körte takes as the report of a slave, Daos, to his master

(Simon?), ending with the assertion that no one has raped the girl, i.e. the intrigue was a false report of rape. The old man says that he will discuss the matter with his acquaintances. (It should be noted that 'has raped' is pure restoration; and it is not clear whether we should understand 'no one of us' or 'the girl in our family'.) *Cf.* P. Cairo 65445 and P. Oxy. 11. Perhaps *Paidion.*

P. Vienna 30486. Körte, *Archiv*, 14, No. 970. Conversation of an older and a younger man. The older man says that he is keeping watch (or guard) on the girl.

Index locorum

General index